...cs

...ACT

...itizen of Geneva', an ...u, a skilled craftsman ...awareness to his son. Rousseau's mother died soon after his birth. Virtually self-taught, and having voluntarily exiled himself from his native city at the age of 16, he led an unsettled life in France until his mid-thirties, when he began to make a name for himself in Paris, first as a musician. A friend of some of the leading younger thinkers of the time, notably Denis Diderot, later the chief editor of the huge and epoch-making *Encyclopédie*, Rousseau first achieved fame as a writer by his denunciation of the state of modern, as compared with ancient, society (the 'First Discourse'). His Second Discourse, on social inequality, broadened the scope of the attack, but also presented man as a being with potential for goodness. From this point Rousseau's thought diversified into several areas, connected by his intense preoccupation with the moral aspect of social life; his wide-ranging novel in letter form, *Julie* (1761), scrutinizes private and domestic relations, while in *Émile* he wrote unforgettably on the upbringing of a future citizen. The *Social Contract*, published in 1762, the same year as *Émile*, deepens and extends political ideas put forward in embryonic form in the Second Discourse and, more fully, in the *Discourse on Political Economy*, originally an article published in 1755 in the *Enclyclopédie*. Rousseau's profundity, originality, and intellectual daring, as well as his policy of declaring his own anonymity, brought him serious trouble: legal measures were taken against both the *Social Contract* and *Émile*, which included a long and very audacious section on religion. For some years Rousseau again became a wanderer, in Switzerland and England, then, under an assumed name, in France. The personal works he wrote in later years, notably the extraordinary *Confessions*, remarkably candid but also picturesque and informative, have been just as significant as his ideas for readers of later generations. The precise extent of his undoubted influence on the French Revolution remains a matter of debate, but one revealing sign is that in 1794 his ashes were transferred to the Panthéon in Paris.

CHRISTOPHER BETTS is a Senior Lecturer at the University of Warwick, where he has been in the Department of French Studies since its inception in 1965. He has published books and articles on eighteenth-century French literature and thought and has translated Montesquieu's *Lettres persanes*.

OXFORD WORLD'S CLASSICS

*For almost 100 years Oxford World's Classics have brought
readers closer to the world's great literature. Now with over 700
titles—from the 4,000-year-old myths of Mesopotamia to the
twentieth century's greatest novels—the series makes available
lesser-known as well as celebrated writing.*

*The pocket-sized hardbacks of the early years contained
introductions by Virginia Woolf, T. S. Eliot, Graham Greene,
and other literary figures which enriched the experience of reading.
Today the series is recognized for its fine scholarship and
reliability in texts that span world literature, drama and poetry,
religion, philosophy and politics. Each edition includes perceptive
commentary and essential background information to meet the
changing needs of readers.*

OXFORD WORLD'S CLASSICS

JEAN-JACQUES ROUSSEAU

Discourse on Political Economy

AND

The Social Contract

Translated with an Introduction and Notes by
CHRISTOPHER BETTS

OXFORD
UNIVERSITY PRESS

OXFORD

UNIVERSITY PRESS

Great Clarendon Street, Oxford OX2 6DP

Oxford University Press is a department of the University of Oxford.
It furthers the University's objective of excellence in research, scholarship,
and education by publishing worldwide in

Oxford New York

Athens Auckland Bangkok Bogotá Buenos Aires Calcutta
Cape Town Chennai Dar es Salaam Delhi Florence Hong Kong Istanbul
Karachi Kuala Lumpur Madrid Melbourne Mexico City Mumbai
Nairobi Paris São Paulo Singapore Taipei Tokyo Toronto Warsaw

with associated companies in Berlin Ibadan

Oxford is a registered trade mark of Oxford University Press
in the UK and in certain other countries

Published in the United States
by Oxford University Press Inc., New York

First published as a World's Classics paperback 1994
Reissued as an Oxford World's Classics paperback 1999

British Library Cataloguing in Publication Data

Data available

Library of Congress Cataloging in Publication Data

Rousseau, Jean-Jacques, 1712–1778.
[Discours sur l'oeconomie politique. English]
Discourse on political economy and The social contract/Jean-
Jacques Rousseau; translated with introduction and notes by
Christopher Betts.
p. cm.—(Oxford world's classics)
Translation of: Discours sur l'oeconomie politique: Du contrat social.
Includes bibliographical references.
1. Political science. 2. Social contract. I. Rousseau, Jean-
Jacques, 1712–1778. Du contrat social. English. 1994.
II. Title. III. Title: Social contract. IV. Title: Discourse on
political economy. V. Series.
JC179.R86 1994 320'.01—dc20 93–48985

ISBN 0–19–283597–1

3 5 7 9 10 8 6 4

Printed in Great Britain by
Cox & Wyman Ltd.
Reading, Berkshire

ACKNOWLEDGEMENTS

I should like to thank Professor Donald Charlton for the first suggestion, and for making me think hard about some problems in Rousseau; the advisers and staff of Oxford University Press, for their scrupulous and expert assistance, without which this translation would have been considerably more imperfect than it is; and my wife Ann for advice, information, and unfailing support.

C.J.B.

October 1993

CONTENTS

viii. The People   79
  ix. The Same Continued   81
   x. The Same Continued   84
  xi. The Various Systems of Legislation   86
 xii. The Categories of Law   89

BOOK III

   i. Government in General   91
  ii. The Constituent Principle of the Various Forms of
       Government   96
 iii. The Classification of Governments   99
  iv. Democracy   100
   v. Aristocracy   102
  vi. Monarchy   104
 vii. Mixed Forms of Government   110
viii. That Not All Forms of Government Are Suitable
       for Every Country   111
  ix. The Signs of Good Government   116
   x. The Abuse of Government and Its Tendency to
       Degenerate   118
  xi. The Death of the Body Politic   121
 xii. How Sovereign Authority Is Maintained   122
xiii. The Same Continued   123
 xiv. The Same Continued   125
  xv. Deputies or Representatives   126
 xvi. That the Institution of a Government Is Not a
       Contract   129
xvii. The Institution of a Government   130
xviii. A Means of Preventing Government from
       Usurping Power   132

BOOK IV

   i. That the General Will Is Indestructible   134
  ii. Voting   136
 iii. Elections   139
  iv. The Roman *Comitia*   141
   v. The Tribunate   151
  vi. The Office of Dictator   153

CONTENTS

INTRODUCTION

IN 1755, the publication of Rousseau's *Discourse on Inequality* brought him considerable success, but also created obligations. The *Discourse*, in tracing the moral decay of man in society, drew a large-scale contrast between the state of nature, in which man had at least the potential for good, and the social state, which as Rousseau described it had led to misery and tyranny. The contrast between nature and society made it possible to denounce many political and social evils, but left fundamental questions unanswered; the author owed it to himself and to his public to develop his ideas further. One question was how the individual's potential for good could be preserved in the social milieu of the mid-eighteenth century, and to this the answer came with *Émile, or Education* (1762); another was whether coexistence in society necessarily made all the citizens hostile to each other, seeking their own interests at the expense of everyone else. The historical approach of the *Discourse*, together with the discreet omission of direct political references, left it unclear whether the evils depicted by Rousseau were those only of his own time and place, or were inevitable in all societies at every period. The *Social Contract*, expanding some hints in an enigmatic paragraph of the *Discourse*, denies this inevitability and offers a more optimistic evaluation. However, the optimism is fragile; Rousseau shows that politically organized society, 'the state' as he usually calls it, can be beneficial and just, but also that the threats to a well-ordered state are persistent and ubiquitous.

During the years that it took for his thought to mature, he contributed his article *Political Economy* to Diderot and d'Alembert's *Encyclopédie* and discussed the social and moral aspects of culture in the long *Letter to d'Alembert on Theatre* (1758). He also wrote one of the century's most popular and influential novels, *Julie*, but abandoned an ambitious project he had started, a work on political institutions generally. He says at the beginning of the *Social Contract*, which appeared in 1762, the same year as *Émile*, that it is all that remains of this larger work. The paragraph in the *Discourse on Inequality* (towards the end of Part II) had sketched the main theory in outline: 'The people having, as regards their social relations, concentrated all their wills into one, the several articles in respect of which this will is expressed become so many fundamental laws . . . and one of the articles regulates the choice and power of the magistrates [officers of state] appointed to watch over the execution of the rest'. Rousseau introduces the passage with a guarded remark that he is here adopting the 'common opinion' that society is based on a contract, or binding agreement; he thus acknowledges that he was working within a particular conceptual tradition, the contract theory of the state. This dated back to ancient times, and had been of fundamental importance in European thought since the sixteenth century.

As regards Rousseau's contribution to the tradition, two preliminary observations should be made: that for most educated Europeans the standard view, even as late as 1762, was probably not the contract theory, despite its influence, but the belief that kings had a divine right to rule, a right that was seen as the origin and basis of social organization; and secondly, that among those who preferred the contract theory, the usual view again favoured monarchy, interpreting the contract as some kind of agreement between ruler and subjects (a 'contract of submission') by which the subjects consent to be ruled. Rousseau made a great change. It lies in the words 'having concentrated all their wills into one'. The notion thus expressed was later, in the article *Political Economy*, to become the 'volonté générale', or general will. It is this concept, rather than his view of the contract, which is Rousseau's lasting contribution to political theory. Its appearance in the *Contract* is a clear sign that monarchist theories of the state were beginning to give way to democratic ideas, 'the people' having (in Rousseau's formulation of the contract) an active rather than a passive role. In an even wider context, the concept of the general will is of importance to anyone reflecting on the relationship of the individual to the social group or groups of which he is a member, since it seeks to define the nature of the bond by which the group is created.

The *Political Economy* article, though published like the second Discourse in 1755, seems likely (the point is debatable) to have been written after it, the *Discourse* dating back to an essay competition announced in 1753. Rousseau wrote the article when he and Diderot were close friends; they quarrelled a few years later. Diderot commissioned the article, and he and Rousseau seem to have cooperated in working out their political ideas, since Diderot wrote, for the same volume, an article on Natural Law (*Droit naturel*) to which Rousseau's article refers, and on which he must have reflected deeply. A chapter discarded from the *Contract*, given here in the Appendix, refutes some of its arguments. 'La volonté générale', however, is a phrase used also by Diderot, and Rousseau's reference to him in the *Encyclopédie* concerns the general will; it appears in a passage which compares society, 'the body politic', to a human body. This is part of an argument that a social group, while it consists of separate individuals, possesses a single will, which like the will of a particular person 'tends always to the conservation and well-being of the whole'. What part Diderot played in the genesis of the idea now always connected with Rousseau is unclear, but the passage in the *Political Economy* article testifies to an important stage in its development.

In various other respects also Rousseau's article, commonly known as his *Discourse on Political Economy*, is transitional between the *Discourse on Inequality* and the *Social Contract*. It retains the high moral tone and some of the indignant rhetoric of the earlier discourse, for instance in the third section when contrasting the situations of rich and poor, and displays already the later work's anxiety about the maintenance of the social bond, constantly at risk because of the selfishness and partiality of particular elements of society, whether individuals or groups. Less methodical and abstract than the *Contract*, and superficially more modern in that there are fewer illustrations taken from the ancient world, it tackles one major subject barely mentioned in the *Contract*, that of taxation, and has much to say on patriotism, which the *Contract* does not discuss explicitly; the link between patriotism and the maintenance of social feeling, however, will be clear. The feel of the two works is different, too. Perhaps in adapting himself to the authoritative style expected from an encyclopaedia, Rousseau tends in his article to treat society from the administrative angle, a manner that seems not to have suited him, because he did not return to it. He was prepared to play the loftier role of legislator, as in his *A Projected Constitution for Corsica* (written in about 1764–5) or his *Considerations on the Government of Poland* (1771–2), but not that of public official. In the *Social Contract*, the voice is that of the theorist, but one who is more on the side of the individual than of government. The essential vision is that of the member of society, the figure Rousseau usually calls the citizen, a man (it has to be accepted that, whether out of obedience to convention or deliberate choice, Rousseau's terminology is consistently masculine) who is not isolated, as he conceivably would be in the 'state of nature', but one among many others of the same kind forming a society.

The precise date at which Rousseau began working towards his treatise is not known. In the *Confessions*, Book X, he explains that it was on moving house late in 1757 that he abandoned most of the larger project on political institutions in general. Of the *Contract*, a partial first version has survived in what is called 'the Geneva manuscript'. It contains roughly the same material, differently arranged, as the first two books of the published work, breaking off soon after the beginning of the third; there is also a draft of the last main chapter, on civil religion.

The manuscript also shows that Rousseau hesitated over his title. Apparently not fully satisfied with the word *Contract*, he at one time preferred 'On civil society'. In the text, he often uses synonyms such as *pact*, notably in the title of the sixth chapter of Book I, a basic chapter which follows some preliminary arguments rebutting earlier theories of society. The essential idea is that of a voluntary agreement among a group. Initially, the agreement is seen as the answer to the problem of ensuring joint protection for a number of people living in unsafe conditions; later it becomes something more like a consensus on the value of living in society. Even in the formulation of the problem in I. vi, the concept of the general will is hinted at, and the definition of the pact, when it comes, in effect defines the general will also. Beginning in terms of self-interest—each future associate seeks to remain free, while receiving benefits from the cooperation of all the others—the argument leads towards the mutual surrender of individualism; after agreement is reached the association transforms itself into a corporate entity with a single will.

It is in the transformation of the many into the one, a change which is not only conceptual but essentially practical or even emotional, that the radical force of Rousseau's logic lies, and it remains the source of the fascination which his theory exerts, both for supporters and enemies. In the previous contractual tradition, to which in the recent past Thomas Hobbes and John Locke had belonged (to mention only English thinkers), the central notion had usually fallen into one of two categories: it was either the contract of submission, by which an already existing social group agrees under certain conditions to submit to a ruler (the version which favoured monarchical opinions), or else the simple contract of association, by which a number of people organize themselves into a group or society, but without necessarily sacrificing their autonomy or rights. The second type, of which the classic example is perhaps the convenant made by the Pilgrim Fathers on landing in Massachusetts in 1620, is on the face of it the type expounded by Rousseau. However, although he denies, in III. xvi, that the operation of establishing a government is a contract, he also insists in I. vi that the associates commit themselves to obeying the general will. As Rousseau formulates the contract, then, it enacts a double operation: it is both the creation of a unified social entity consisting of a number of individuals, and their acceptance of that entity's authority over them.

One reason for the thoroughgoing nature of Rousseau's formulation, besides his habit of taking ideas to their limit, was no doubt his own complex personality; the only parent he knew was his somewhat wayward father. From adolescence onwards he was in many respects a social outsider. He seems to have yearned for the sense, which he never had, of belonging to a group. A factor of quite a different order is his adaptation of another tradition in political theory besides contractualism, the quasi-legal terminology of the Natural Law school, the most important of whose members as regards Rousseau are Hugo Grotius or de Groot, whom Rousseau often criticizes sharply, and Samuel Pufendorf, who also had a theory of the contract. In Natural Law thought a sophisticated manner of conceptualizing the activities of legally constituted groups had developed. Its abstract vocabulary, utilizing such terms as 'moral person', 'rational entity', or 'moral entity' to denote such groups, was a solution to the problem of how to discuss the activities of groups when they act as an individual person might, for instance in making and keeping agreements. At all levels of society, from the local association to the nation as a whole, group decisions are taken which are considered as actions of the whole group behaving as one, even if, as is usual, the decision is not unanimous but some sort of compromise or majority view. Phrases like 'moral entity' implicitly recognize the element of convention in the situation by treating the group in question as a single thing. Conceptually, this is a necessary move, but one that tends in the same direction as the idea of the contract of association: towards the view that a society is a unity, rather than a haphazard mass of particular people. The same tendency can be seen in the metaphors to which Rousseau (and of course innumerable others, not least Diderot) resorts when he calls society the 'body politic' or considers it as an organism or a machine.

In respect of the history of political theory, then, Rousseau was positively influenced by the basic concepts and methods of his predecessors, even when, as with Hobbes, whose political ideas were no less radical than his own, he fiercely opposed their conclusions. As regards history in general, his home town of Geneva exerted the strongest influence. Viewed with a certain degree of idealism (as evinced in the fervent remark that ends the treatise's introductory paragraph), it must nonetheless have provided Rousseau with a model of social unity. Historians inform us that the real Geneva was an oligarchy run by a closely-knit nexus of patrician families, but its constitution at least suggested that all the citizens (a word not synonymous with inhabitants) participated in the process of government. The inspiration given to Rousseau by the republics of the ancient world, especially Sparta and pre-imperial Rome, was perhaps no less powerful, even though, or perhaps because, it reached him through the medium of literary treatment, in such writers as Plutarch and Livy. The Greek and Roman republics very often provide the examples he needed to make his theory more plausible to his readers, almost all of whom, of course, had some knowledge of classical antiquity, and had been taught since childhood about the legislative achievements of such figures as Lycurgus or the heroic patriotism of the younger Cato. Ancient tyrants too, the likes of Caligula, were also grist to Rousseau's democratic mill. He was debarred from mentioning most modern figures by eighteenth-century norms of censorship (though he later suffered from them even so).

Once Rousseau has defined what he means by the contract in the chapter 'The Social Pact', it remains for him to elucidate obscurities, explain how it might work in reality and put forward remedies for its drawbacks. Of the host of accessory problems that arise, many cluster around the abstractness of the basic concept. It is at the abstract level, many would say, that Rousseau's theory works best; some of his fiercest critics have been those most aware of the irreducible realities of political life. Thus it is a simple logical step for him to argue that the object of a society's general will is the good of that society, and there are some cases, such as war, in which the good is obvious: it is victory, or at least the avoidance of defeat. But when in a real situation the question is asked: 'How is victory to be ensured?', the general will is unlikely to provide the answer; as Rousseau himself insists, it cannot pronounce on particular cases. (Even so, he sometimes writes as if he thought that civic enthusiasm alone, which ought to accompany any exercise of the general will, is enough to make an army victorious.) So too with other objectives such as national prosperity or social justice.

The consequence is that particular decisions, which means virtually all practical political decisions, have to be taken by a body set up for the purpose, namely a form of government. Rousseau does not advocate 'instant democracy', nor the use of referendums, nor even majority vote, which might seem to be ways of actualizing the general will; as he points out in one of his most concise and effective chapters, II. iii, the people is often mistaken over what, in reality, will be good for it. As his argument develops, it becomes clear that—again with complete logic—the general will can concern itself only with general matters, on which its decisions become law; but it seems that there will be few laws of this kind. The provision of constitutional law will be handed over to an expert, a figure whom Rousseau calls 'the legislator', in clear imitation of semi-legendary figures such as Lycurgus. Modern commentators tend to be unenthusiastic about the chapters on the legislator, but it should be remembered that at the time constitutions were not uncommonly drawn up for new colonies (John Locke provided one for South Carolina), and in the revolutionary era which began not long after the publication of the *Contract* the business of devising constitutions became necessary in a way that Rousseau can hardly have envisaged.

As for laws in the ordinary sense, decisions of governments about internal affairs, they are not Rousseau's concern. The general will is that the state should have the best government (Book III discusses the merits of the different types), and it is the legislator who will decide which form of government is the best for a particular nation. He will bear in mind numerous considerations, such as climate and history, which had been the particular province of Rousseau's great predecessor Montesquieu, whose influence pervades the chapters on the legis-lator and on forms of government. Once in place it is the government, monarchical, aristocratic, or democratic, that will pass particular laws. What does concern Rousseau is the source of political authority, and here he is firm: it lies not with the government, of whatever kind, but with the people as a whole, expressing the general will, and therefore sovereign. He had made the same point in the *Political Economy* article, and it is in this respect, far more than in his reserved comments on democracy as a form of government, that his thought can be said to anticipate modern democratic attitudes. To write of the sovereignty of the people was a bold stroke when monarchical government still prevailed; it is another aspect of Rousseau's radicalism, following necessarily as it does from the concept of the general will. At the same time its importance is less practical than theoretical or ideological, since as we have seen he does not favour democracy as the executive counterpart to the people's authority.

If it is a government that handles executive decisions, and if the constitution (including the form of the government) is the business of the legislator, the establishment and functioning of the state have been assured; but not its continuance as a society faithful to the pact on which it is founded. According to Rousseau, men come together and remain in a society ruled by the general will because it is in their interest to do so. Their personal benefit, not only freedom from harm and access to the means of maintaining life, but also the availability of many other advantages inherent in association with others, coincides with the interests of every other associate, and so forms the general will, the desire for the good of all. But individuals living in society do not cease to be individuals; they therefore retain their own personal will and self-interest. Further, they are free to be part of other associations, smaller than the complete society of which they are members. At their level, these associations also necessarily possess their own general wills, which Rousseau calls 'partial' wills. They, and the 'particular' wills of single individuals, tend to run counter to the general will of the entire society, threatening its cohesion, and at worst even causing it to disintegrate. Powerful men can pursue their own purposes at the expense of the general good; so too can governments, which naturally want to retain power. Religious bodies also have the kind of unity which favours devotion to their own cause rather than that of the society in which they exist.

Numerous passages in the *Contract*, varied in nature, are based on Rousseau's desire to combat this threat. Often he simply warns against it. At the end of Book II, he seeks to counter it by appealing to moral standards as a means of preserving the civic spirit. In the legislative domain, he suggests in III. xii–xiv, but without complete conviction, that general assemblies of the people may preserve their sovereign authority (and goes on in the next chapter to attack representative government, contrary to modern assumptions, on the grounds that it diminishes sovereignty and obliterates the general will). Previously, in the *Political Economy*, explaining the distinction between the general and partial wills, he had urged members of a government not to allow their personal interest to override the public interest; in this prevalent tendency lies the greatest and most constant danger of the abuse of government, in Rousseau's eyes, which if unchecked will bring complete tyranny.

Most ordinary citizens will be inclined to agree with passages such as these. Agreement is less likely to be forthcoming for two arguments, perhaps the most notorious stumbling-blocks in all Rousseau's works, in which his quest for civic unity and the proper exercise of the general will leads to conclusions which seem paradoxical at best, and have made him vulnerable to the accusation that he fosters tyranny himself. In the chapter (I. vii) which follows the definition of the social contract, Rousseau affirms that anyone who refuses to obey the general will must be compelled to do so, since otherwise the contract remains void. He adds, in a phrase made famous by its air of self-contradiction, that such a person would be 'forced to be free'. The meaning is that compulsion would be required, but that the result of it would be freedom from the insecurity of life outside society, together with the freedom to act within the limits imposed by social life. The paradoxical phrase has aroused much indignation, not always entirely sincere—Rousseau, as a believer in the authority of the people, has often been attacked by those whose real targets were more modern political adversaries—and has seemed to many critics to be an attempt, in a system which claims to preserve freedom, to disguise an objectionable degree of constraint by a mere trick of expression. At bottom, however, the idea is a variant on two commonplaces of political thought: that living in a social group necessarily involves some loss of freedom, and that every such group, if it is to subsist, must have some means of ensuring that its members obey its rules.

The other difficult passage occurs in the work's last chapter (neglecting the postscript), the long discussion, controversial in many respects, of 'civil religion', a religion intended to divinize the state. Rousseau decided only at a very late stage of composition to include the chapter. Its basic idea, that religion should be regarded as a state institution, is ancient, and was no doubt familiar to him from writers such as Plutarch, as well as from more recent writers of Utopias, who often invented religions for their ideal states. Rousseau's version is another of his many attempts to guard against elements within the state having 'partial wills' which are divisive. Among them, in his view, is Christianity, since it claims a form of authority distinct from that of the sovereign. The part of the chapter that rejects Christianity is audacious enough on its own, but before listing the articles of his 'purely social profession of faith' (which is similar to, but not precisely identical with, the religious beliefs expounded at length in *Émile*), Rousseau also insists that anyone refusing to believe in them can be banished, while anyone who accepts them but then 'conducts himself as if he did not believe them' is liable to be punished by death. So vaguely defined a crime too closely resembles the charges of conduct contrary to the good of the state and their like, to which tyrannical regimes resort when removing otherwise guiltless opponents, for it not to seem a source of danger rather than a social safeguard. In his anxiety to maintain the social bond—the last article of the civil religion is 'the sanctity of the social contract and the laws'—Rousseau has gone beyond the normal limits of provision for the punishment of antisocial behaviour, showing all too vividly how good intentions can produce ferocious results. A less extreme position is taken up in the chapter on capital punishment (II. v), which nonetheless allows for its retention.

The lesson that has often been inferred from these passages is that Rousseau's political theory should not be trusted, because it involves unacceptable views, more likely to cause oppression than to bring social justice. Whether the need to ensure civic unity requires such drastic sanctions as that proposed in the final chapter does seem doubtful, but it is also doubtful (to my mind) that the sanction is a necessary part of Rousseau's system.

When his thought is not driven by the fear that social unity will be disrupted, Rousseau is often more moderate than his basic principles might suggest. Under the contract, each individual gives himself 'and all his rights' to the community. This might seem to entail the communistic view that private property should be abandoned in favour of state ownership, a view that was not unknown in Utopian writing at the time. However, what we find in the relevant chapter (I. ix) is that the right to private property is firmly maintained. In this Rousseau may have been influenced, as is often argued, by John Locke's second *Treatise on Civil Government*, since in the English thinker's version of the contract theory the guarantee of property rights was an essential element; but Rousseau was not one to be influenced against his own judgement. The *Political Economy* article is more emphatic than the later work about the right to property, although it also recommends state ownership of large amounts of territory. This idea, which seems to stem from Roman custom, was dropped in the *Contract*, where (although some of the argument is vague) Rousseau seems to say that an individual's alienation or transferral of his property to the community results in his possession being firmer, since it is legitimized, guaranteed by public authority, rather than being based on a natural right, the right of the first occupant.

On property, then, though perhaps at the risk of some inconsistency, Rousseau does not push his argument towards Utopian ideals. Another example of comparative moderation is found in his treatment of the choice of government. Judging by the principles of the contract—the general will and the sovereignty of the people taken in conjunction—one might expect Rousseau to support popular rule, but, when he discusses the different forms of government, the kind he seems to favour most is what he calls elective aristocracy: 'the best and most natural order of things is that the wisest should govern the multitude' (III. v). Even so, he again warns of the risk that governmental self-interest may become dominant. Moreover—another consideration that militates against any dogmatic view of the best government—while sovereign authority resides with the people, authority and rule are two different things; fitness to rule is not an absolute, like sovereignty, but a relative matter. Hence the form of government which is suited to one state is unlikely to suit another. In weighing up the various factors involved, Rousseau reveals that he is tempted to believe in a true democracy such as that of the Greek city-states, but admits that it would not be feasible in a modern state (and also that the ancient Greeks depended on slave labour). The end of the discussion, in III. xv, is an acknowledgement that any form of government will be imperfect, Rousseau commenting that the rights of the people can be preserved only in a very small state.

It would seem, therefore, that the logic of the theory is rigorously pursued at the level of fundamentals, while matters specific to any one society must be decided with due regard to its particularities. Unlike the Utopian theorists, such as Veiras or Morelly, with whom he is sometimes bracketed, Rousseau is not concerned to produce a detailed blueprint for the rationally perfect society, a systematic scheme which is supposed to be adopted by the human race generally. In whatever direction the argument goes, whether he is surveying the factual constraints on legislation in Book II or debating the merits of different types of government in Book III, there comes a point at which Rousseau implicitly accepts that abstract general reasoning cannot take him any further. After this point the discussion turns to the practical, and becomes a consideration of the various matters that need to be borne in mind by the well-intentioned thinker faced with the problems of any one real state. In Book III, while examining methods of strengthening the state's constitution, he admits that there is no remedy for the inevitable ageing of 'the body politic'. This is another tacit admission that political perfectionism is not sustainable.

Despite these concessions to the realities of social life, and despite the occasional excesses of theory, Rousseau's ideals never desert him; throughout the discussion, there is a clearly perceptible effort to preserve the purity of the general will and the contract, 'laws as they can be', or right, against the dangers of human self-interest, 'men as they are', in the words of Book I's introductory note. It is this sense of effort towards the fulfilment of an ideal, but an ideal that is always under threat from within the society it is supposed to direct, that gives Rousseau's argument its enduring ability to provoke and inspire reflection.

A NOTE ON THE TEXT
AND TRANSLATION

THERE are two texts of the *Contract* which have authority: that of the first edition, published by Marc-Michel Rey in 1762; and the text in the first volume of the posthumous edition of Rousseau's works, brought out by his friend Du Peyrou in 1782. The differences between them are small. I have followed the 1762 text, as given by Robert Derathé in the Pléiade edition and by Ronald Grimsley in his edition (see Bibliography), mentioning significant 1782 variants in the Explanatory Notes. For the text of the manuscript chapter in the Appendix I follow the same two modern editions. For the *Political Economy* the position is the same: two texts, that of the original article, under the heading 'Economie ou œconomie (Morale et Politique)', in Volume V (1755) of Diderot and d'Alembert's *Encyclopédie*, and that in Du Peyrou's 1782 edition, entitled 'Discours sur l'économie politique', which has only a few differences from the 1755 text. There is also a manuscript version. I have followed the 1755 text in the Pléiade edition.

When it seems desirable I mention specific problems of translation in the Explanatory Notes. The general problem in translating Rousseau, in my experience, is to preserve the combination in his writing of close reasoning and emotional commitment. In the belief that the famous 'clarté' of the French language, especially in the eighteenth century, is not a mere myth, I have sought clarity above all, or in other words to transmit Rousseau's ideas faithfully. When there has been a conflict between faithfulness and any purely stylistic quality, the former has taken precedence, and in some particularly well-known passages I have tended towards literalness. However, Rousseau's political writings contain many passages which, while remaining clear, appeal primarily to emotion, often in the form of civic pride and virtue, and in such cases I have allowed myself slightly more latitude.

SELECT BIBLIOGRAPHY

THE standard critical edition of Rousseau is the *Œuvres complètes*, edited by Bernard Gagnebin, Marcel Raymond, and others, 4 vols. published (Bibliothèque de la Pléiade), Gallimard, Paris, 1959–69. The *Contrat social* and other political writings, edited by Robert Derathé and others, are in Volume III (1964). Editions with English annotation include one by Ronald Grimsley (Oxford, 1972) and two by C. M. Vaughan: the first in Volume I of his edition of Rousseau's *Political Writings*, 2 vols. (Cambridge, 1915), the second separate (Manchester, 1918). The Pléiade volume and Vaughan's 1915 edition also contain the text of the *Political Economy* and the Geneva manuscript.

A full bibliography of Rousseau's political thought would fill many pages. The following selection of books concerning the subject (including a few that are critical of Rousseau) consists mainly of studies in English or available in English translation, but has some of the most important French works.

BERMAN, MARSHALL, *The Politics of Authenticity: Radical Individualism and the Emergence of Modern Society* (New York, 1973).

CASSIRER, ERNST, *The Question of Jean-Jacques Rousseau*, trans. and ed. Peter Gay (Indiana, 1963).

CHARVET, JOHN, *The Social Problem in the Philosophy of Rousseau* (Cambridge, 1974).

COBBAN, ALFRED, *Rousseau and the Modern State* (London, 1934; 2nd edn. 1964).

COLEMAN, PATRICK, *Rousseau's Political Imagination* (Geneva, 1984).

CROCKER, LESTER G., *Rousseau's Social Contract: An Interpretive Essay* (Cleveland, 1968).

DENT, NICHOLAS J. H., *Rousseau: An Introduction to his Psychological, Social and Political Theory* (Oxford, 1988).

DERATHÉ, ROBERT, *Rousseau et la science politique de son temps* (Paris, 1950).

DURKHEIM, EMILE, 'Rousseau's Social Contract' (1918), trans. R. Manheim, in *Montesquieu and Rousseau, Forerunners of Sociology* (Michigan, 1960).

EINAUDI, MARIO, *The Early Rousseau* (Ithaca, NY, 1967).

ELLENBURG, STEPHEN, *Rousseau's Political Philosophy. An Interpretation from Within* (Ithaca, NY, 1976).

FRALIN, RICHARD, *Rousseau and Representation: A Study of the Development of his Concept of Political Institutions* (New York, 1978).

GILDIN, HILAIL, *Rousseau's* Social Contract: *The Design of the Argument* (Chicago, 1983).

GOLDSCHMIDT, VICTOR, *Anthropologie et politique. Les principes du système de Rousseau* (Paris, 1974).

HALL, JOHN C., *Rousseau: An Introduction to his Political Philosophy* (London, 1973).

LAUNAY, MICHEL, *Jean-Jacques Rousseau écrivain politique* (1712–1762) (Geneva and Paris, 1971; 2nd edn. 1989).

MCDONALD, JOAN, *Rousseau and the French Revolution* 1762–1791 (London, 1965).

MASTERS, ROGER D., *The Political Philosophy of Rousseau* (Princeton, NJ, 1968).

MELZER, ARTHUR M., *The Natural Goodness of Man: On the System of Rousseau's Thought* (Chicago, 1990).

PERKINS, MERLE L., *Jean-Jacques Rousseau on the Individual and Society* (Kentucky, 1974).

PLAMENATZ, JOHN, *Man and Society*, 2 vols. (London, 1963) (Vol. i).

RILEY, PATRICK, *The General Will Before Rousseau: The Transformation of the Divine into the Civic* (Princeton, NJ, 1986).

SHKLAR, JUDITH N., *Men and Citizens. A Study of Rousseau's Social Theory* (Cambridge, 1969).

STAROBINSKI, JEAN, *Jean-Jacques Rousseau: La transparence et l'obstacle* (Paris, 1957; revised edn. 1971), trans. A. Goldhammer: *Jean-Jacques Rousseau, Transparency and Obstruction* (Chicago, 1988).

TALMON, J. L., *The Origins of Totalitarian Democracy* (Boston, 1952).

VIROLI, MAURIZIO, *La Théorie de la société bien ordonnée chez Jean-Jacques Rousseau* (Berlin, 1988), trans. D. Hanson: *Jean-Jacques Rousseau and the 'Well-Ordered Society'* (Cambridge, 1988).

A CHRONOLOGY OF
JEAN-JACQUES ROUSSEAU

1712   Birth in Geneva, 28 June, of Jean-Jacques, second son of Isaac Rousseau, a clockmaker, and his wife Suzanne Bernard; she dies on 7 July. He is brought up mainly by his father.

1728   Having been apprenticed to an engraver since 1725, he leaves Geneva; he is briefly a convert to Catholicism in Turin and so forfeits Genevan citizenship.

1729   At Annecy, he is taken in by Mme de Warens, through whom he had been converted; he earns his living through various musical, secretarial, and teaching jobs.

1735–8   Liaison with Mme de Warens at her house Les Charmettes.

1742   Largely self-taught, he goes to Paris intending to make a career as a musician and composer.

1743–4   Post at French Embassy in Venice under Comte de Montaigu; his first direct contact with political life.

1745   Return to Paris; his opera *Les Muses galantes* is performed; he meets Thérèse Levasseur who is to be his permanent companion and the mother of his five children, all left at the Paris orphanage; he is friendly with Diderot and the philosopher Condillac; secretarial and musical work, including articles on music for Diderot and d'Alembert's *Encyclopédie*.

1748   Publication of Montesquieu's great work on political theory and other subjects, *The Spirit of Laws* (*De l'Esprit des lois*), which is to be an important influence on Rousseau's thought in the Contract.

1750   Rousseau gains prize with essay for Dijon Academy competition, *Whether the Restoration of the Arts and Sciences has assisted in the purification of morals* (*Si le rétablissement des sciences et des arts a contribué à épurer les moeurs*), his 'First Discourse'.

1752   Success of his opera *The Village Soothsayer* (*Le Devin du village*).

1754   The 'Second Discourse', also for the Academy of Dijon: *On the origin and foundations of inequality* (*Sur l'origine et les fondements de l'inégalité*), dedicated to the city of Geneva; Rousseau makes public return to Geneva and Calvinism.

1755   Publication of the *Second Discourse*, and of Volume V of the *Encyclopédie*, containing Rousseau's article on *Political Economy* (*Economie politique*). He studies the political writings of the Abbé de Saint-Pierre and begins an all-embracing political work later abandoned.

1757–58 Nebulous love affair with Sophie d'Houdetot; quarrel involving her but mainly with Diderot and other *philosophe* friends.

1758   Publication of *Letter to d'Alembert on Theatre* (*Lettre à d'Alembert sur les spectacles*), which attacks a plan for a theatre at Geneva, desired by Voltaire among others; preparation of *Social Contract* and other works.

1761   Publication of *Julie, or the New Héloïse* (*Julie ou la Nouvelle Héloïse*), one of the century's best-selling novels; in July, writes to publisher Rey to say that his treatise on politics is ready.

1762   April: publication of *The Social Contract* (*Du Contrat social*) by Rey in Amsterdam; May: publication of *Emile, or Education* (*Emile, ou De l'éducation*) by Duchesne, in Holland and secretly in France. Both books are condemned by the authorities in Paris and Geneva. Rousseau leaves France to take refuge in Yverdon, in Bernese territory, and then (when expelled by the Berne government), in Neuchâtel, governed by the King of Prussia.

1763   Publication of the *Letter to Christophe de Beaumont* (the Archbishop of Paris), answering the Archbishop's criticisms of the religious ideas in *Emile*. Rousseau gives up Genevan citizenship. J.-R. Tronchin attacks the *Social Contract* in his *Letters from the Country* (*Lettres de la campagne*).

1764   Rousseau replies to Tronchin in the *Letters from the Mountains* (*Letters de la montagne*), also criticizing Genevan institutions. His cause is taken up by the 'Représentants' party in Geneva. He undertakes *A Projected Constitution for Corsica* (*Projet d'une constitution pour la Corse*); decides to write his *Confessions*.

1765   After difficulties with the Swiss religious authorities and a stone-throwing incident (the 'lapidation de Môtiers'), he returns to Bernese territory, only to be expelled again; he goes to Berlin and Paris, where he is much visited. Voltaire publishes (probably—perhaps earlier) his *Idées républicaines*, in large part a critique of the *Contract*.

1766   Rousseau leaves for England at the invitation of David
        Hume and lives for a while at Wootton in Staffordshire.

1767   After quarrelling with Hume he returns to France incognito
        to live for three years in the south-east.

1770   He returns to Paris and copies music for a living.

1771   He writes the *Considerations on the Government of Poland* (*Con-
        sidérations sur le gouvernement de la Pologne*) at the invitation of
        a Polish nobleman, Wielhorski; gives readings of the *Confes-
        sions*.

1778   Having written mainly personal works (*Dialogues; The Rêveries
        of the Solitary Walker*) in his last years, he dies on 3 July at
        Ermenonville, north of Paris, where he is buried on a lake
        island.

POLITICAL ECONOMY

('Discourse on Political Economy')

Rousseau's article in Volume V (1755)
of Diderot and d'Alembert's *Encyclopédie*

Economy, or *Œconomy*. (Ethics; Politics.) The word comes from the Greek *oikos*, 'house', and *nomos*, 'law', and originally meant only the wise and lawful government of a household for the common good of the whole family. The meaning of the term has since been extended to cover the government of the greater family, which is the state. To distinguish between the two senses, the name of *political* or *general economy* is used in the second case; and in the other, *private* or *domestic economy*. Only the second is the subject here; on domestic economy, see the article 'Paterfamilias'.*

Even if, between state and family, the relationship were as close as several authors claim, it would not therefore follow that the rules of conduct which are suited to the one society would be appropriate for the other. They differ too greatly in size for them to be administered in the same way, and there will always be an enormous difference between domestic government, where the father is able to observe everything himself, and civil government, where the ruler can scarcely observe anything except through the eyes of others. In order for matters to be equal in this respect, it would be necessary for the father's talents and strength, and all his faculties, to increase in proportion to the size of his family, or for the soul of a powerful emperor and the soul of an ordinary citizen to be in the same ratio as his empire is to the estate of a private person.*

But what resemblance could there be between governing the state and governing a family when the two are so differently based? A father being physically stronger than his children, his power over them, during the time that they need his help, is considered with reason to have been instituted by nature. In the greater family, in which all members are naturally equal, political authority is in respect of its institution purely arbitrary and can be founded only on conventions,* while the officers of the state can have command over others only by virtue of the laws.* A father has his duties dictated to him by natural sentiments, and in a tone that seldom allows him to disobey.

Rulers have no similar orders, and their obligations towards the people extend in reality only to what they have promised and what the people have the right to insist on. Another even more important difference is that, since children possess nothing except those things given them by their father, it is obvious that all the rights of property either belong to him or emanate from him; quite the contrary occurs in the greater family, its general administration being established only in order to provide security for private property, which is anterior to it.* The principal aim, in the work of the household as a whole, is to preserve and increase the father's patrimony, so that he may one day divide it between his children without making them poorer; whereas the wealth of the treasury is only a means, often much misunderstood, of maintaining peace and prosperity among private citizens. In a word, the small family is destined to disappear one day, and dissolve into several other families like it; but while the great family is made for a state of permanence, the smaller has to enlarge itself in order to multiply; and not only is it sufficient for the other to conserve itself, but it would be easy to prove that any enlargement does more harm than good.

For a number of reasons inherent in the situation, it is the father who should command within the family. First: as between father and mother, authority should not be equal; it is necessary that the family government should be single, and that when there is a difference of opinion one side should be preponderant and decide. Second: however slight we may consider the woman's specific incommodities to be, they always cause her to be temporarily inactive, which is a sufficient reason to exclude her from the position of authority; for when the balance is perfectly equal, a straw is enough to tip it. Moreover, the husband ought to have surveillance of his wife's conduct, because it is important for him to be certain that the children whom he is forced to nourish and recognize as his are not the children of other men. The wife, having nothing of the kind to fear, does not have the same right over the husband. Third: the children should obey the father first by necessity and then out of gratitude; having had their needs met by him for half their lives they should devote the other half to providing for his. Fourth: as regards servants, they owe him service in return for his maintaining them, under the condition that they may break the bargain when it ceases to suit them. About slavery I have nothing to say, because it is contrary to nature and no right can authorize it.*

Nothing like this is found in political society. The ruler, far from having a natural interest in the happiness of private people, not infrequently seeks happiness for himself while making them wretched. If positions of authority are hereditary, a child will often be in command of men; if they are elective, the innumerable disadvantages of elections make themselves felt. In both cases, all the benefits of paternal authority disappear. If you have a single ruler, you are at the mercy of a master who has no reason to love you; if several, you have to endure both their tyranny and their own quarrels. In a word, abuses arise inevitably, and with fateful consequences, in any society where laws and the public interest have no natural strength, and are constantly under attack from the self-interest and the passions of the society's members and ruler.

Although the functions of the paterfamilias and the head of state should be directed towards the same end, the ways that they take are so different, and their duties and rights so distinct, that we cannot treat them similarly without conceiving a false idea of the fundamental laws of society, and falling into errors that are fatal for the human race. For while the voice of nature is the best source of counsel that a good father can have in the proper fulfilment of his duties, for the officer of state it is merely a false guide, tending constantly to lead him away from duty, and sooner or later, unless he is held back by the most sublime virtue, impels him both to his own ruin and that of the state. The only precaution that is needed by the paterfamilias is to preserve himself from depravation, and to ensure that in him the natural inclinations remain uncorrupted; but in the officer of state it is they that corrupt. In order to do good the father has only to consult his heart, but the other becomes a traitor the moment he consults his; he should even suspect his own reason, and the only rule he should follow is public reason, which is the law. Hence nature has made quantities of good fathers, but it is doubtful whether, since the world began, human wisdom has produced ten men capable of governing their fellows.*

From all I have just said it follows that it is right to have distinguished *public economy* from *private economy*, and that, there being nothing in common between the state and the family except the obligation that their chiefs have to make each happy, the same rules of conduct cannot apply to both. These few lines will be enough, I believe, to destroy the detestable theory which Sir Robert Filmer has tried to uphold in his work entitled *Patriarcha*,* refuted in the books of two famous men who have done it too much honour by writing against it.* The error in question* is in any case very ancient, since Aristotle himself judged it necessary to attack it, with arguments which can be read in the first book of his *Politics*.

I ask my readers to distinguish clearly also the public economy of which I shall be speaking, and which I call *government*, from the supreme authority, which I call *sovereignty*;* the distinction is that the latter has the right to legislate, and in certain cases imposes obligations on the nation as a body, while the former has the power only to execute, and can impose obligations solely on private individuals. (See the articles *Politics* and *Sovereignty*.)

Let me use for a moment a common comparison, imprecise in many respects, but appropriate for the better understanding of my meaning.

The body politic, considered as a single entity, may be regarded as a living body organized similarly to that of a man. The sovereign power corresponds to the head; laws and custom are the brain, which controls the nerves, and is the seat of the understanding, the will, and the senses, while the organs of sense are the judges and public officers; commerce, industry, and agriculture are the mouth and stomach, making nourishment available to all; public finance is the blood which economic wisdom, performing the function of the heart, guides throughout the body, distributing life and subsistence; the citizens are the limbs and body that make the whole machine move, live, and work, and which cannot be injured in any part without a sensation of pain being transmitted to the brain, provided that the animal is in a healthy state.

The life of both man and state is the self of the whole entity, the mutual sensibility and internal correlation of all the parts. Should their intercommunication cease, their formal unity be dissolved, and their adjacent elements no longer belong to each other except in being juxtaposed, then the man dies, or the state disintegrates.

The political body, therefore, is also a moral being* which has a will; and this general will, which tends always to the conservation and well-being of the whole and of each part of it, and which is the source of laws, is, for all members of the state and in relation to it and them, the rule of what is just or unjust; a truth which (I mention in passing) shows how little sense there is in the way so many writers have treated as theft the Spartan children's compulsory acquisition of their frugal meals by stealth,* as if anything ordained by law could not be lawful. (See, in the article 'Right', the source of this great and luminous principle, which the present article does no more than develop.)*

It is important to note that this rule of justice, which is reliable as regards every citizen, may be misleading for foreigners. The reason is obvious: it is that the will of the state, although general in relation to its members, ceases to be so in relation to other states and their members, becoming instead, for them, a particular and individual will, the justness of which is governed by natural law. This too comes under the principle I have established, since in this case the great city of the world becomes a political body, its general will is still the natural law, and its individual members are the various states and peoples.

These distinctions, when applied to each political society and its members, provide the surest and most universal rules for judging whether a government is good or bad, and in general for judging the morality of all human actions.

Every political society is composed of other smaller societies, of different kinds, each of which has its own self-interest and code of conduct.* However, although everyone is aware of these societies, because they have an official outward form, they are not the only ones really existing in a state: all the groups of individuals united by a common interest compose others, permanent or temporary, whose power is no less real for being less perceptible, and whose interrelationships, when properly observed, give true knowledge of social behaviour. It is all these groupings, formal and informal, that in so many ways affect the manifestations of the public will by the influence of their own. The will of these particular societies always has a double relationship; for the members of the group it is a general will, and for the greater society it is a particular will. Often it can be rightful in the first respect and damaging in the other: a man can be a devout priest, or a courageous soldier, or a zealous lawyer, but a bad citizen. A collective decision can be advantageous within the smaller society and pernicious in the larger. It is true that, since particular societies are always subordinate to the societies that contain them, we should always obey the latter rather than the former; the duties of the citizen take precedence over those of the senator, and the duties of the man over those of the citizen. But unhappily the strength of personal interest is always in inverse ratio to the strength of duty, and increases in proportion as the particular society is the more cohesive and loyalty to it less sacred; which is an irrefutable proof that the most general will is also the most just, and that the voice of the people is truly the voice of God.

It does not therefore follow that public resolutions are always equitable; where foreign affairs are concerned, they may not be, for the reason that I have given.* Thus it is not impossible that a well-governed republic should go to war unjustly. It is possible also that in a democracy the governing council may decide in favour of bad decrees and declare the innocent guilty; but such a thing never happens unless the people has been misled by particular interests, which it has been led to sub-stitute for its own interest by the influence and persuasiveness of a few clever men.* In this case the collective decision is one thing and the general will another. Hence Athenian democracy must not be seen as an objection to my argument,* because Athens was in reality not a democracy, but an extremely tyrannical aristocracy, controlled by philosophers and orators. If you examine carefully what happens during any public deliberation, you will see that the general will is always for the common good; but often through secret divisions and tacit alliances the natural disposition of the assembly is eluded in favour of particular purposes. Then the social body is in fact divided into others, the members of which acquire a general will that is good and just in respect of the new body, but unjust and bad in respect of the whole, their membership of which they abandon.

It will be clear how easy it is, with the assistance of these principles, to explain the apparent contradictions that are to be observed in the behaviour of so many men who, full of scruples and honour in certain respects, are deceitful and fraudulent in others, trampling the holiest of duties underfoot while remaining faithful unto death in undertakings that can often be contrary to the law. Thus the most corrupt of men always keep faith to some kind of public commitment; and thus (as the author of the article 'Right'* has observed) even brigands, who in society as a whole are virtue's enemies, have in their lairs a simulacrum of virtue to which they are faithful.

In making the general will the first principle of the public economy and the fundamental rule of government, I have not thought it necessary to examine seriously whether officers of state belong to the people or the people to the officers, or whether in public affairs it is the good of the state or the good of its chiefs that should be considered. For a long time now one answer to this question has been given in practice, and a different one by reason; and in general terms it would be a great folly to hope that those who are in fact the masters might prefer some other interest to their own. It would therefore be appropriate to add a further distinction, between the popular and the tyrannical forms of public economy. The first kind is that of every state in which a unity of will and interest reigns between the people and its chiefs; and the second kind necessarily exists everywhere where the government and the people have different interests, and contrary wills as a result. The policies of the second kind are inscribed at length in the archives of history and in Machiavelli's satires;* those of the first are to be found only in the writings of the philosophers who dare to proclaim the rights of humanity.

I. The first and most important maxim of a lawful or popular government,* that is to say a government which has as its object the good of the people, is therefore, as I have said, to follow the general will in everything; but in order to be followed, it must be known, and above all it must be clearly distinguished from the particular will, beginning with that of the individual self. To distinguish these two things is always very difficult, and only the most sublime virtue is capable of giving the necessary enlightenment. Since, in order to will, it is necessary to be free, there is another difficulty scarcely less great: that of ensuring both public freedom and governmental authority. Seek out the motives by which men, in the greater society united by need, have been led to unite themselves more closely in civil societies: the only one you will find is to guarantee each member's property, life, and liberty by putting them under the protection of all. But how can men be forced to defend the freedom of one of their number without the freedom of the rest being infringed? And how can provision be made for public needs without affecting the private property of those who are forced to contribute? Whatever sophisms are used to disguise all this, there is no doubt that if my will can be constrained I am no longer free, and that I am no longer the master of my own property if somebody else can touch it. This problem, which must have seemed insuperable, has been solved, like the first, by the most sublime of all human institutions, or rather by heavenly inspiration, showing men how to imitate on earth the immutable decrees of the Divinity. By what unimaginable art was a means found of subjugating men in order to make them free?* to employ in the service of the state the possessions, the bodily strength and even the lives of its members, without constraining them or consulting them? to enchain their wills with their own consent? to make consent prevail over refusal, and force them to punish themselves when they act in a way that they did not will? How can it come about that they obey without anyone commanding, and serve without having a master, all the freer in fact because, under the appearance of subjection, none loses any share of his freedom except what may damage the freedom of another? These miracles are worked by the law. It is to law alone that men owe justice and liberty. This is the salutary means of expressing the will of all, which restores in right the natural equality between men. It is the celestial voice which dictates to every citizen the precepts of public reason, teaching him to act according to the maxims of his own judgement and not to be in contradiction with himself. This is also the only voice that should be heard when the nation's chiefs command; for so soon as one man, independently of the laws, attempts to make another submit to his private will, he at once quits the civil state and, in relation to the other, puts himself into the pure state of nature, where obedience is never ordained except out of necessity.

The most urgent interest of the ruler, and the most indispensable of his duties, is therefore to ensure compliance with the laws which he administers, and on which his entire authority is based. And if he must see that others keep them, so much the stronger are his reasons for keeping them himself, benefiting as he does from all their prestige. For the example he gives has such power that, even if the people saw fit to allow him to ignore the law's constraints, he should be careful not to take advantage of so dangerous a privilege, which others would soon try to usurp in their turn, and often to his detriment. At bottom, since all social commitments are by nature mutual, it is not possible to put oneself above the law without abandoning the advantages it brings, and nobody owes anything to a man who claims that he owes nothing to others. For the same reason, in a well-ordered government, no exemption from the law will ever be granted on any grounds at all. Even those citizens who have earned their country's gratitude should be rewarded by honours, never by privileges; for the republic is on the brink of ruin as soon as anyone can entertain the thought that it is a fine thing not to obey the laws. If the nobility or the military, or any other social order in the state, were to adopt such a maxim, everything would be completely lost.

The power of the laws depends even more on their own wisdom than on the severity of their ministers, and the will of the public gains its greatest weight from the reason which dictated it. This is why, in Plato's opinion,* it is of the highest importance to take the precaution, in the introduction to an edict, of having a preamble which gives the arguments demonstrating its justice and utility. For the first law of all is that laws must be respected; rigorous punishments are a futile expedient that was invented by small minds, in the aim of using terror as a replacement for the respect which they are unable to earn. It has constantly been observed that the countries which have the most terrible penalties are the countries which resort to them the most frequently. So that cruelty in punishment merely indicates that the number of infringements is high, and when equally severe penalties are applied to every case, offenders are forced to commit crimes in order to escape being punished for their misdeeds.

But although the government does not control the law, it is no small thing to be its guarantor, and to possess innumerable ways of making men cherish it. It is in this that the art of ruling consists. With force at one's disposal, no skill is needed to make all men afraid, and little even to win their hearts; for peoples have long ago learnt by experience to give a ruler much credit for all the harm he does not do, and to worship him when he is not an object of hatred. A fool who is obeyed is as capable as anyone of punishing crime, but the true statesman knows how to prevent it; he earns respect by imposing his authority on men's wills rather than their actions. If he could ensure the good behaviour of all, he himself would have nothing more to do, and the highest achievement of his labours would be to be able to remain at leisure. It is at least certain that the greatest talent that rulers can have is to make their power less odious by disguising it, and to lead the state so peacefully that no leader seems to be needed.

I conclude then that, just as the first duty of a legislator* is to make the laws conform to the general will, the first rule of public economy is that the administration should conform to the laws. The legislator will even have done enough to prevent the state from being badly governed if he has made proper provision for everything that is made necessary by geographical situation, climate, the nature of the soil, custom, the surroundings, and all the specific relationships in which the people for whom he is drawing up a constitution are involved. This will not prevent an infinite number of details of political order and economy being left to the wisdom of the government, but it always has two infallible rules of good administration in such circumstances: one is the spirit of the law which must guide decisions in cases which it has been impossible to foresee; the other is the general will, the source and complement of all laws, which must always be consulted when they are lacking. How, it will be said, can we know the general will in cases on which it has not pronounced? Must the whole nation be called to assembly at every unforeseen event? It is so much the less necessary to do so in that the assembly's decisions are not certain to express the general will; in that such a method is impracticable for a large nation; and in that it is seldom necessary when the government's intentions are good: for rulers are well aware that the general will is always on the side of decisions which are the most favourable for the public interest, that is to say, the most equitable; so that the only thing necessary, to be sure of following the general will, is to be just. When the general will is too manifestly thwarted, it makes itself felt despite being restrained by terror of the public authorities. The examples to follow in such cases are the nearest I can find.* In China, the ruler's constant principle is to assume that his officials are wrong in any dispute between them and the people. Suppose bread costs too much in some province: the administrator is sent to prison; suppose a riot breaks out in another: the governor is dismissed. Each mandarin is responsible, on pain of death, for everything that goes wrong in his district.* This is not to say that each affair is not looked into later, in a formal enquiry; but long experience has caused its verdict to be anticipated thus. Seldom is it necessary to put right an injustice that has been done in this way; the emperor, convinced that no public outcry arises without cause, never fails to discern, behind the seditious clamour that he punishes, the justified grievances that he redresses.

Much will have been achieved if order and peace have been made to prevail in every part of the republic; much too if the state is undisturbed and the law respected; but if no more than that has been accomplished, it will all be more in appearance than reality, and the government will have difficulty in making itself obeyed if ensuring obedience is its only objective. It is good to know how to use men taking them as they are, but it is much better still to make them what it is needful that they should be; the most complete authority is the kind that penetrates the inner man, and influences his will as much as his actions.* There can be no doubt that, in the long run, nations are what their governments make of them: warriors, citizens, men, when it wants them to be; a rabble or mob, as it pleases. Every ruler who despises his subjects dishonours himself, since he shows that he has failed to make them worthy of respect. Train them therefore to be men, if it is men that you wish to command; if you want the laws to be obeyed, make sure that they are loved, and that men, in order to do as they ought, need only reflect that there is something which they ought to do. Herein lay the great skill of ancient governments, in those far-off times when philosophers gave the nations their laws, using their authority only to render them wise and happy. This is the origin of so many sumptuary laws, so many rulings on behaviour, so many maxims of public policy the acceptance or rejection of which was the subject of the greatest care. Even tyrants did not forget this important aspect of administration, and were seen to pay as much attention to the corruption of their slaves as the administrators of justice paid to improving the conduct of their fellow-citizens. But our modern governments, who believe that they have done all that can be done when they have extracted money, cannot even imagine that it is possible or necessary to go any further.

II. The second essential rule of public economy is no less important than the first: do you want the general will to be carried out?—ensure that every particular will is in accordance with it; and since virtue is nothing other than this conformity of particular wills to the general, make virtue reign, to put the same thing in one word.

If politicians were less blinded by ambition, they would see how impossible it is that any institution, of whatever kind, can function according to the spirit in which it was established, unless it is directed by the law of duty; they would realize that political authority has its main source of power in the citizens' hearts, and that in the maintenance of government nothing can replace public morality. For one thing, it is only men of integrity who can administer the law; for another, it is at bottom only people with standards who know how to obey them. If a man succeeds in defying remorse it will not be long before he defies punishment, which is a less severe and continuous form of discipline, and one from which there is at least the hope of escape; whatever precautious are taken, men who postpone their misdeeds only until they can do them with impunity will scarcely lack means of evading the law or escaping without penalty. And when every particular interest unites against the general interest, which ceases to be the interest of anyone, public vice has greater power to disable the law than the laws have to put down vice; and finally the corruption of the people and its leaders extends to the government, however wise it may be. The worst abuse of all is to obey the laws only in appearance, so as to infringe them safely in reality. Soon the best laws become the most destructive: it would be a hundred times better if they did not exist; that would at least be a resource that would remain when every resource has gone. In such circumstances edict is piled on edict, regulation on regulation, but in vain; it all serves only to bring in new abuses, without curing the old ones. The more laws you add, the more they fall into disrepute, and all those whom you appoint as supervisors simply become new offenders, who either share with the present ones or take their plunder separately. Soon it is brigandage that gains the prize for virtue; the most degraded men are those who win the greatest acclaim; the greater their position the more despicable they are; their infamy is made manifest by their distinctions, and the honours they receive dishonour them. If they buy protection from women or favour from the nation's leaders, it is so that they in their turn can put justice, duty, and the state on sale; and the people, who cannot see that its vices are the original cause of its misfortune, cries out in discontent and lamentation: 'All our woes are due only to those whom we pay to protect us from them.'

Then it is that, in place of the voice of duty, which no longer speaks in men's hearts, their leaders are forced to substitute the cry of terror, or the lure of apparent advantage, by which they deceive their creatures. It is then that they have to resort to all the small and contemptible ruses which they call 'the maxims of statecraft' or 'the secrets of cabinet'. The government's last remaining energies are applied by its members in disgracing and replacing each other, while its business is neglected, or carried out only to the extent that is required by personal interest, and in the manner it chooses. In a word, the skill of these great political leaders lies entirely in fascinating the gaze of those whom they need to such a degree that each man believes himself to be working in his own interest when he is working for theirs; I say 'theirs' on the assumption that the true interest of leaders is really to extinguish a people in order to keep it in subjection, or to ruin their own property in order to ensure their ownership.

But when the citizens love their duty, and the trustees of public authority apply themselves sincerely to the task of encouraging this love through example and their own efforts, every difficulty vanishes, and administration becomes so easy as to render unnecessary those dark arts whose skill lies entirely in lack of scruple. Those minds so wide in scope, so dangerous and so much admired, all those great ministers whose glory is inseparable from the people's distress, will no longer be regretted; public integrity replaces the genius of political leaders; the more virtue extends its rule, the less is talent needed. Even the ambitious benefit more under duty than under usurpation; the people is convinced that its chiefs' only purpose is its happiness, and its deference dispenses them from the need to impose their power. Time after time history teaches that the authority the people grants to those whom it loves, and who love it, is a hundred times more absolute than all the tyranny of usurpers. This does not mean that the government should be afraid to use its power, only that it should use it in a legitimate manner. A thousand examples can be found in history of ambitious but cowardly rulers who fell because of their softness or pride; and none of rulers who came to grief simply through being equitable. But negligence should not be mistaken for moderation, nor weakness for mercy. To be just requires severity: to tolerate wickedness, when one has the right and the power to repress it, is to be wicked oneself.

It is not enough to say to the citizens: 'Be good'. They must be taught; and teaching by example, which in this domain is the first lesson, is not the only method that should be em-

ployed. The most effective is the love of country; for as I have
said already, every man is virtuous when his particular will
conforms in all things to the general will, and we are glad to
want those things that are wanted by the people we love.

It seems as though our feelings of humanity evaporate and
weaken as they extend across the earth, as though we cannot
be as sensitive to calamities in Tartary or Japan as to those that
are suffered by a European people. Concern and compassion
have in some way to be limited and compressed, in order that
they should be active. And as these inclinations of ours can be
useful only to those with whom we have to live, it is good that
the feeling of humanity should so be concentrated among
fellow-citizens that in them it takes on renewed strength,
because of their habitual meetings and the common interest
that unites them. Certainly, the greatest marvels of virtue have
been done out of patriotism: a vigorous and pleasurable feeling
which joins the power of self-love to virtue in all its beauty,
giving it energy without disfiguring it, and so creating the most
heroic of all passions. This feeling was the cause of all those
immortal deeds which dazzle our feeble eyes by their lustre,
and produced all the great men whose ancient virtues, now that
patriotism has been turned to scorn, are thought to be mythical. We should not be surprised. The ecstasies of lovers appear
so much nonsense to anyone who has not felt them, and the
love of country, which is a hundred times keener and more
delicious than the love of a sweetheart, can likewise be understood only when it is felt; but in every heart that is fired by it,
in all the deeds it inspires, we can easily perceive that sublime
and impetuous ardour which does not adorn even the purest
virtue from which it is absent. In this respect Cato* can be
compared with Socrates himself: the one was more the citizen,
the other more the philosopher. Socrates, once Athens was on
the brink of ruin, had no country other than the whole world,
but Cato carried his with him in the depths of his heart; he
lived for it alone and could not survive its passing. The virtue
of Socrates is that of the wisest of men, but Cato, between
Caesar and Pompey, has the look of a god among mortals. One
of them teaches a few individuals, combats the Sophists* and
dies for truth; the other defends the state, freedom, and law

against the conquerors of the world, and finally quits the earth when he can see that there is no longer a country for him to serve. A pupil of Socrates who was worthy of him would be the most virtuous of his contemporaries; a worthy rival of Cato would be the greatest. The former would be happy through virtue, the latter would seek his own happiness in that of every man's. From the one we should learn, but by the other we should be led, and this in itself decides which of them is to be preferred, for, while no one has ever produced a nation of wise men, it is not impossible to make a nation happy.

Do we want nations to be virtuous?—let us begin then by making the people love their country; but how can they love it, if their native land means no more to them than it does to foreigners, and if what it does for them is only what cannot be refused to anyone? It would be much worse still if they could not even enjoy security as citizens, and if their property, their lives or their freedom were at the mercy of powerful men, without being able or allowed to risk having recourse to the law. Then, subjected to the duties of the civil state, but without enjoying even the rights of the state of nature, and unable also to use their own strength in order to defend themselves, they would be in the worst condition that free men can be in, and for them the sense of the words 'my country' could only be hateful or ridiculous. It cannot be believed that the arm can be injured or cut off without the head feeling pain; and it is no more believable that the general will can consent to any member of the state being injured or destroyed by any other, whoever he may be, than that the eyes of a man having the use of reason can be put out by his hands. So closely is the safety of individuals linked to public confederation that, were it not for the allowances that must be made for human frailty, the social convention would rightly be dissolved if, within the state, a single citizen were to perish when he could have been saved; if a single convict were to be kept in prison wrongly; and if a single lawsuit were obviously to be lost against justice; since, when the fundamental conventions* are infringed, there is no longer any visible right or interest which could make the people maintain the social union, unless they were kept within it by force alone, which causes the dissolution of the civil state.

For does not the body of the nation make an undertaking to provide for the conservation of the least of its members with as much care as for all the others? and is the welfare of one citizen any lesser part of the common cause than the welfare of the whole state? If it were to be said that it is well for one to die for the sake of all, I should admire the saying in the mouth of a virtuous and worthy patriot who voluntarily goes to his death out of duty, for the good of his country; but if the meaning is that a government is permitted to sacrifice an innocent person for the good of the mass, I hold this maxim to be one of the most execrable that tyranny has ever invented—the falsest that could be devised, the most dangerous if it is accepted, and the most directly contrary to the fundamental laws of society. That a single man should die for all is so far from the truth that, rather, all have committed their property and lives to the defence of each single man, in order that personal weakness should always be protected by the public strength, and every member by the whole state. As a supposition, let one individual after another be excluded from the people, and then urge those who favour this maxim to explain more fully what they mean by 'the body of the state'; you will see that in the end they will reduce it to a small number of men, who are not the people but the officers of the people, and who, having sworn by a special oath to perish themselves for the people's good, claim to have proved thereby that it is for the people to perish for their good.

If examples are needed of the protection that the state owes to its members, and of the respect it owes to their persons, they will be found only among the most celebrated and courageous nations of the earth; the worth of a man is scarcely understood except among free peoples. The perplexity felt by the whole republic of Sparta, when it was faced with the question of punishing a guilty citizen, is well known. In Macedon, a man's life was a matter of such importance that the king, the great Alexander, at the height of his power, would not have dared to have put to death in cold blood any Macedonian who had committed a crime, until the accused man had defended himself in court in front of his fellow citizens and been pronounced guilty by them. But it was the Romans who, more

than any other nation on earth, distinguished themselves by
their government's consideration for private persons, and the
scrupulous care it took to respect the inviolable rights of every
member of the state. Nothing was more sacred than the life of
an ordinary citizen. In order for one to be found guilty nothing
less than the whole assembly of the people was required;
neither the Senate nor the consuls, in all their majesty, had the
right to do so,* and among the mightiest people in the world
the crime and punishment of one of its citizens brought public
desolation. Whatever crime he had committed, so harsh did it
seem to shed his blood that, by the Porcian law,* the death
penalty was replaced by a sentence of exile, which was passed
on anyone who, once having lost his beloved country, still
desired to live. Everything, in Rome or in the army, reflected
the love that fellow-citizens bore for one another and their
respect for the word *Roman*, which raised the courage and
awoke the virtue of anyone who had the honour of bearing it.
At the celebration of a triumph, a cap belonging to a citizen
who had been delivered from slavery, and the civic crown given
for saving another citizen's life, were the most welcome sights;
and it is interesting that only the civic crown, and that given to
the general for whom the triumph was held, were made of grass
and leaves; all the others were merely of gold. That is what
virtue meant in Rome, and how she became the mistress of the
world. Ambitious politicians!—a shepherd can govern his dogs
and his sheep; and he is the lowest of men. If it is great to
command, it is only when those who obey us can hold us in
honour; respect your fellow citizens and you will earn respect
yourselves; respect freedom and your power will increase every
day; do not exceed your rights, and soon they will be limitless.

Let their country therefore be a common mother to all the
citizens; let the advantages which they enjoy there make them
cherish it; let the government allow them a share in public
administration sufficient to make them feel that they are in
their home country, and let the laws, in their eyes, be nothing
less than the guarantee of liberty for all. These rights, valuable
as they are, belong to all men; but without seeming to attack
them directly, hostility to them on the part of rulers can easily
nullify their effects. When powerful men abuse it, the law

becomes an offensive weapon for them and a shield against the weak, and the pretext of public security is always the most dangerous scourge of the people. The most necessary and perhaps the most difficult task in government is to show strict integrity in rendering justice to all, and above all to protect the poor against the tyranny of the rich. The worst has already happened when there are poor people to defend and rich people to restrain. The full force of the law is felt only by those in between; laws are equally powerless against the rich man's wealth and the poor man's destitution, the former evading them and the latter escaping from them: one breaks the net, the other passes through it.

One of the most important things for a government to do, therefore, is to prevent extreme inequality in wealth, not by depriving the rich of their possessions, but by denying everyone the means of accumulating them; and not by building poor-houses but by ensuring that the citizens do not become poor. When the population is unevenly distributed across the country, some places being crowded with men while others are deserted; when preference is given to the pleasing arts and the products of pure ingenuity, instead of to trades that are useful but laborious; when agriculture is sacrificed to commerce; when tax-collectors become necessary because of the bad administration of state funds; when, finally, venality grows to such an excess that esteem is measured in gold coins and the virtues themselves are sold for money: these are the most tangible causes* of opulence and poverty, of the substitution of private interest for public, of mutual hatred between citizens, of the indifference they feel for the common cause, of the corruption of the people, and the weakening of all the resources of government. These therefore are ills which are hard to cure once they have appeared, but which a wise administration should prevent, so as to maintain proper standards of beha-viour, together with respect for law, love of country, and a strong general will.

But all these precautions will be insufficient unless we begin still further back. I end this part of my article on public economy with the subject with which I should have started. Love of country cannot subsist without freedom; nor freedom without virtue; nor virtue without citizens. If you can create citizens you have gained everything, but otherwise all you will have is wretched slaves, beginning with the leaders of the state. But the making of citizens is not the work of a single day, and in order to have citizens when they are men it is necessary to educate them when they are children. If I were to be told that anyone having men to govern should not look beyond the limits of nature for qualities of perfection of which they are incapable; that he should not try to extirpate their passions; that the accomplishment of such a plan would no more be desirable than it would be possible: I would willingly agree with all of this in that a man without passions would certainly be a very bad citizen; but it must also be agreed that, although men cannot be taught to love nothing, it is not impossible to teach them to love one thing rather than another, and to love something of true beauty rather than something ugly. If, for instance, they are trained early enough to consider their individual selves only in relation to the body of the state, and to see their own existence, so to speak, only as a part of its existence, they may finally come to identify themselves to some extent with the greater whole, to feel that they are members of their home country, to have towards it those supreme feelings that every man living in isolation has only towards himself, to raise their souls constantly to this higher level, and so transform the dangerous inclination towards self-love, the source of all our vices, into a sublime virtue.* That such a change of direction is possible can not only be demonstrated by philosophy, but is gloriously exemplified countless times in history. If examples are rare among us, it is because no one cares that we should have citizens; even less is any thought given to starting their education early enough. It is too late to change our natural inclinations when their course has already been fixed, and habit has been added to self-love; it is too late to take us out of ourselves once the 'human self' that is concentrated in our hearts has acquired that contemptible energy which absorbs every virtue and, for little souls, is their life. How can patriotism take root amidst all the other passions that smother it? and in a heart already divided between greed, a mistress, and vanity, what share is left for one's fellow citizens?

It is from the first moment of life that we must learn how to be worthy to live; and since we participate from birth in the rights of citizens, it is at the instant of our birth that the exercise of our duties should begin. If there are laws for adult life, there should be laws for childhood, which teach obedience to the others; and just as the reason of each man is not left to be the sole judge of his duties, so too the education of children should not be left to their fathers' capacities and prejudices, especially since it is even more important to the state than to their fathers; for in the natural course of things the father's death often deprives him of the ultimate benefits of having educated his child, but his country will sooner or later feel the effects of what he has done: the state remains while the family is dissolved. If the public authorities, by replacing fathers and fulfilling their important functions, acquire their rights in carrying out their duties, they have the less grounds for complaint since, in this respect, all that happens, properly speaking, is that they are described differently, and that under the name of citizens they hold the same authority, in common, over their children as they had separately under the name of fathers; they will be as well obeyed when they speak in the name of the law as they were when speaking in the name of nature. Public education,* following rules prescribed by the government, and controlled by officers established by the sovereign, is therefore one of the fundamental principles of the popular or legitimate form of government. If children are brought up in common on terms of complete equality, if they are imbued with the laws of the state and the maxims of the general will, and instructed to respect them above everything, if they are surrounded with examples and objects that unceasingly speak to them of the tender mother who provides for them, of the incalculable gifts they receive from her and the gratitude they owe her in return—we cannot doubt that they will learn in this way to cherish each other like brothers, to want nothing except what is wanted by society, to replace the sterile and empty chattering of the sophists by the actions of men and citizens, and one day to become the defenders and fathers of their country, whose children they have been for so long.

I will say nothing on the subject of the officials appointed to preside over this form of education, which is certainly the state's most important affair. It will be realized that if such a mark of public trust were bestowed casually, if this public function, assigned to men who have worthily performed all the others, were not to be the reward for their labours, an honourable and satisfying repose in their old age, the greatest of all honours, then the whole enterprise would be useless and education produce no results; for whenever a lesson is not supported by authority, and precept by example, teaching is fruitless; virtue itself loses its credit in the mouth of a man who does not practise it. But if courage is preached by famous warriors stooping under the burden of their victory wreaths; if justice is taught by judges full of probity, grown old in their robes in the courts of law, such teachers will shape successors for themselves, and from age to age transmit to later generations the leaders' experience and ability, the citizens' courage and virtue, and the ambition shared by all, that of living and dying for their country.

I know of only three peoples among whom public education was practised in former days: the Cretans, the Lacedaemonians, and the ancient Persians.* In all it had the greatest success, and for the last two it performed marvels. When the world became divided into nations that are too large to be well governed, this method was no longer practicable; and other reasons that the reader will easily understand* have prevented it from being tried by any modern nation. It is most remarkable that the Romans were able to do without it,* but for five hundred years Rome was a continual miracle, which the world cannot hope to see again. The virtue of the Romans, engendered by their hatred of tyranny and the crimes committed by tyrants, together with their innate love of their country, meant that their houses all became so many schools for citizens; and the limitless power of fathers over children made private discipline so strict that the father was more greatly feared than the judge, acting in a domestic law-court as the censor* of behaviour and the law's avenger.

It is thus that a careful and well-intentioned government, constantly occupied in preserving or restoring its people's habits of morality and love of their country, takes measures far in advance to avert the evils that sooner or later result from the citizens' indifference to the fate of the republic, and to keep within strict limits that personal interest which isolates individuals to such an extent that the state, becoming weaker as they grow stronger, can expect nothing from their good will. Whenever the people love their country, respect the laws, and live simply, there is little that remains to do in order to make them happy; and in public administration, where chance plays a smaller part than with the fortunes of private people, wisdom is so close to happiness that the two things cannot be separated.

III. It is not enough to have citizens and protect them. Their subsistence must also be considered, and the satisfaction of public needs, which is an obvious inference from the general will, is the third essential duty of government. This duty, it should be realized, does not consist in filling up the granaries of private citizens and dispensing their owners from work, but in ensuring that prosperity is sufficiently accessible that, in order to acquire it, work is always necessary, and never superfluous. The same duty also extends to all the operations that concern the management of the public purse and the expenses of public administration. Thus having discussed general economy with regard to the government of persons, it remains for us to consider it with regard to the administration of property.*

This aspect of the subject furnishes as many difficulties to resolve and contradictions to remove as before. It is certain that the right of property is the most sacred of all citizens' rights, and in some respects more important than freedom itself, whether because it is more closely connected with the preservation of life; or because, a man's property being easier to appropriate and harder to defend than his person, the thing that is the more readily taken should be the more respected; or finally because property is the true foundation of civil society* and the true pledge of the citizens' fidelity in fulfilling their obligations: for if possessions did not answer for a person's acts, nothing would be simpler than to evade one's duties and flout the law. Another consideration is this: there is equally no doubt that the maintenance of the state and government demands a financial outlay; and since whoever wills the end cannot refuse the means, it follows that the members of society should contribute some of their possessions to its maintenance. Moreover it is difficult to protect private property in one respect without attacking it in another, and all the regulations about the order of inheritance, wills, and contracts are necessarily bound to restrict citizens, in some way, as regards the disposal of their own property, and will consequently restrict their right to it.

But besides what I have said already about the concordance that exists between the law's authority and the freedom of the citizen, there is an important observation to be made in relation to the disposal of property, which avoids many difficulties. It is that, as Pufendorf has shown,* the nature of the right of property is such that it cannot extend beyond the lifetime of the owner, and that from the moment of a man's death his possessions no longer belong to him. To lay down conditions under which he may dispose of them, therefore, is at bottom not to diminish his rights in appearance, but rather to extend them in reality.

In general, although the institution of the laws controlling the power of individuals to dispose of their own belongings is a matter for the sovereign alone, the spirit of these laws, which the government should follow in applying them, is that in passing from father to son or from one person to another, possessions should as far as possible not go out of the family and be alienated. There is an obvious reason for this in favour of the children; for them the right of property would be entirely useless if their father left them nothing, and having often contributed, moreover, through their labour, to their father's acquisition of his property, they have a share in his rights on their own account. Another reason, less tangible but not less important, is that nothing is more fatally damaging to the republic and its moral standards than continual changes of fortune and circumstances among the citizens. Such changes are the proof and the source of innumerable ills, overturning and confusing everything; they cause people brought up for one occupation to be faced with another, so that neither those who rise in society, nor those who fall, are able to acquire the principles and knowledge suitable to their new positions, much less carry out their new duties.

Let us turn to the subject of public finance. If the people governed themselves, with no intermediaries between the citizens and the state administration, all they would need to do is to club together in order to pay as required, in proportion to the public need and private means; and since each would always be able to keep watch over the collection and utilization of public money, no fraud or abuse would be able to creep into its management. The state would never be overburdened with debt, nor the people weighed down by taxation, or, at least, they would be consoled for high taxes by confidence about the way in which they were used. But things cannot be run in this way; however small the boundaries of the state, the civil society within it is always too large for it to be governed by all its members. Public funds must necessarily pass through the hands of its leaders, who, besides the interest of the state, all have their own private interests, which are not the last to be considered. The people for their part, less aware of public needs than of the avarice and unbridled expenditure of their chiefs, protest at seeing themselves forced to go without necessities in order to provide luxuries for others; and once they have been embittered beyond a certain point by such manoeuvres, the most scrupulous administration will be unable to regain their trust. In these circumstances, if contributions are voluntary, they will produce nothing; if they are made compulsory, they are illegitimate; and in this cruel dilemma, whether to allow the state to perish or to attack the sacred right of property, lies the difficulty of preserving a wise and just economy.

The first thing, after instituting the laws, that the founder of a republic must do is to create sufficient funds for the upkeep of the legal and other officers and for all public expenses. If the fund is in money it is called the *aerarium* or treasury,* and if in land, the public demesne,* which latter is much to be preferred to the former, for reasons that are easily understood. Whoever has examined the matter in sufficient depth can scarcely fail to take the same view as Bodin,* who regards a public demesne as the most upright and reliable method of providing for the needs of the state; and it is worth noticing that in the distribution of land made by Romulus,* his main concern was to devote one-third to this purpose. I admit that it is not impossible that the product of a badly administered demesne could be reduced to nothing, but it is not of the essence of a public demesne that it should be badly administered.

Before any use is made of it, this fund must be assigned, or accepted by the assembly of the people or the country's estates-general,* which should thereupon determine how it is to be used. After this ceremony, which makes the fund inalienable, it changes in nature, so to speak, and the revenues it produces become sacred, so sacred, in fact, that it is not only the most infamous kind of theft, but a crime of high treason to misappropriate the slightest amount for a purpose contrary to what was intended. It was a great dishonour for Rome that the integrity of Cato, as quaestor,* should have been a cause for comment, and that an emperor, when rewarding a talented singer with a few crowns, should have needed to add that the money came from his family's funds and not from those of the state. There are few enough Galbas;* but where shall we find another Cato? Once vice is no longer dishonourable, what ruler will be scrupulous enough to leave untouched the public revenues that have been left to his discretion, or to avoid being led soon to deceive even himself, as he pretends to be unable to distinguish between the glory of the state and his own vain and scandalous wastefulness, or between the means of increasing the state's power and the extension of his own authority? In this delicate area of administration especially, the only effective instrument is virtue, and the only means of restraining the avarice of government officials is their own integrity. The financial managers' registers, with all their accounts, do not so much reveal their misdemeanours as cover them up; prudence is never as quick to think up new precautions as fraudulence is in evading them. Abandon your account-books and your papers, therefore, and entrust your finances to faithful hands; it is the only way to ensure that they are faithfully managed.

Once the public fund is set up, the chief officers of the state are its administrators by right, since its administration is a part of government, and a part that is always essential, though not always equally essential. Its influence increases in proportion as the influence of the other resources of government diminishes; a government may be said to have descended to the furthest degree of corruption when its only motive is money. And since all governments constantly tend towards laxity, this one consideration shows why no state can subsist unless its revenues are continually on the increase.

The first realization that such an increase is necessary is also the first sign of internal disorder in the state, and a wise administrator, while reflecting on ways of raising money to provide for the present need, does not neglect to investigate its remoter causes; as a sailor who sees water rising inside his vessel does not forget, while working the pumps, to search out the leak and stop it.

From this rule is derived the most important maxim in financial administration, which is to devote much greater care to anticipating needs than to increasing revenue. Whatever the degree of diligence, a remedy that only follows the disease, and more slowly, always leaves the state sick: while thought is being given to putting right one defect, another makes itself felt, and the measures that are adopted produce new deficiencies themselves; the result is that, eventually, the nation is taxed too highly, the people are oppressed and the government loses all its vigour, spending much money to little effect. I believe that it is because this great maxim had been firmly established in antiquity that governments then achieved such miracles, doing more by their parsimony than ours with all our treasure; which is perhaps the origin of the usual sense of the word *economy*, since it is commonly understood to mean the wise management of what one has, rather than the means of acquiring what one does not have.

Apart from the public demesne, which brings income to the state in proportion to the probity of those who control it, people would be astonished, if they were sufficiently well acquainted with the full powers of the general administration, especially when it is confined to legitimate methods, at the resources that are available to rulers to anticipate every public need without touching private property. Since they are the masters of all the state's trade, there is nothing easier for them than to direct it in a manner that provides for everything, often without appearing to be concerned in it. The distribution of goods, money and merchandise in just proportion, with regard to time and place, is the real secret of finance and the source of wealth, provided that the administrators are able to take a long enough view of things, and to suffer an apparent present loss on occasion, in order to make a huge real profit in the distant future. When one sees a government paying duty, instead of receiving it, on the export of corn in years of abundance, and on its importation in years of shortage, it is necessary to have such facts in front of one's eyes in order to believe them, and they would be regarded as fantasy if they had occurred in antiquity. Let us suppose that, in order to prevent shortages in bad years, it was proposed to establish public storehouses; would not the upkeep of so useful an establishment, in most countries, be the pretext for new taxes? In Geneva wise government has established and maintains such storehouses, providing assistance to the public in bad years and, in every year, the main source of income for the state. *Alit et ditat* is the fine inscription that can be read on the face of the building.* In explaining here the economic system of a good government I have often looked to the government of the Genevan republic, happy to find that my own country gives an example of the wisdom and contentment that I would be glad to see in every country.

If we were to examine the way in which the needs of the state increase, we should find that it often happens in the same way as with private citizens: less out of real necessity than by the growth of useless desires; and that, in many cases, additional expenses are incurred only in order to have a pretext for raising revenue. Thus the state would sometimes benefit by omitting to acquire wealth, and its apparent wealth is at bottom more of a burden than poverty would be. It is true that governments hope to keep their peoples in greater dependence by giving them with one hand what they have taken from them with the other, which was the policy adopted by Joseph with the Egyptians;* but this empty sophism is all the more disastrous for the state because the money taken does not return to the hands from which it was taken. With maxims like this, all one does is to enrich men who are idle with money taken from those who are useful.

A liking for conquest* is one of the most obvious and dangerous causes of this increase in need. It is a liking often engendered by ambition of a kind different from what it apparently reveals, and is not always what it seems to be; its true motive is less the overt desire for national aggrandizement, and more the hidden desire to increase the internal authority of the rulers, by adding to the number of troops and diverting the citizens' attention by the thought of war.

One thing at least is beyond doubt, that no one is so oppressed or wretched as a conquering nation, and that its very success increases its wretchedness. Even if we did not learn it from history, reason is enough to prove that the greater the size of a state, the more heavy and onerous in proportion its expenses become; for every province has to contribute its share to the cost of the general administration, and each has in addition to spend the same amount for itself as if it were independent. Furthermore, fortunes are always made in one place and spent in another, which soon destroys the balance between production and consumption, impoverishing much of the country in order to enrich a single town.

There is another cause of the increase in public needs, which is connected with the preceding one. A time may come when the citizens no longer regard themselves as being involved in the common cause and cease to be defenders of their country, and when the officers of state prefer to be in command of mercenaries rather than free men, if only to use the former, as and when necessary, in order to subjugate the latter.* This was the condition of Rome towards the end of the Republic and under the emperors; for all the Romans' early victories, like Alexander's, had been won by the courage of the citizens, who for the sake of their country were capable of giving their blood, if needed, but never sold it. Only at the siege of Veii* was payment for the infantry introduced. Marius, in the war against Jugurtha,* was the first to dishonour the legions by bringing in freedmen, vagrants and other mercenaries. Having become the enemies of the people whom they had undertaken to make happy, the tyrants raised regular troops, outwardly for the purpose of keeping foreign nations in check, and in fact to oppress the inhabitants. In order to create troops, it was necessary to take labourers from the land: the reduction in their numbers caused the quality of goods to fall, while their maintenance brought in taxes, which increased prices. This initial failure made the people discontented; in order to repress them it was necessary to have more troops and, therefore, more poverty; the greater the despair, the greater the necessity to increase it yet further, in order to avert its consequences. The mercenaries, on the other hand, whose character may be evaluated by the price for which they sold themselves and who took pride in their own degradation, despised both the laws which protected them and their brothers whose bread they ate, believing themselves more honoured to be henchmen of an emperor than defenders of Rome; having promised blind obedience their function was to hold a knife to their fellow-citizens' throats, ready to slaughter all of them as soon as the signal came. It would not be difficult to show that this was one of the main causes of the fall of the Roman Empire.

The invention of artillery and fortification has in our day forced the sovereigns of Europe to reintroduce regular troops in order to guard their fortresses; but although their motives are more legitimate than before, it is to be feared that the result will be equally disastrous. It will be no less necessary to deplete the countryside in order to create armies and garrisons; in order to maintain them it will be no less necessary to oppress the people. For some time now these dangerous creations have been spreading so rapidly in every area that it is impossible not to anticipate the imminent depopulation of Europe, and, sooner or later, the ruin of the nations which inhabit it.

However that may be, it is bound to be apparent that such institutions inevitably reverse the true economic system, which is to take the state's principal income from the public demesne; they leave it no other resources but the unpopular expedient of public contributions and taxes, which it remains to discuss.

Here we must remember that the foundation of the social pact is property, and that its first condition is that everyone should be guaranteed the peaceful enjoyment of what he owns.

It is true that, by the same treaty, everyone undertakes, at least tacitly, to contribute to public needs; but this undertaking cannot damage the fundamental law, and supposing that the contributors accept that the need is obvious, it will be clear that their contributions, in order to be legitimate, must be voluntary, not through individual acts of will, as if it were necessary to have the consent of each citizen, who would provide only as much as he pleased, directly contrary to the spirit of the joint agreement, but through the general will by majority vote, following a proportional tariff which would prevent the imposition being in any way arbitrary.

The truth that taxes cannot be legitimately imposed without the consent of the people or its representatives has been generally recognized* by every philosopher or jurist, not excepting Bodin himself, who has gained any reputation in questions of public law. If some have laid down principles that are contrary in appearance, it is easy to see the particular reasons they have had for doing so, and in any case they make so many conditions and limitations that basically the situation is exactly the same; for whether the people can refuse, or whether the sovereign ought not to insist, are matters of indifference as regards right; and if it is only a question of force, to examine what is legitimate or not is entirely useless.

Contributions that are levied on the population are of two kinds: real, when they are due on things;* and personal when they are paid by head. Both kinds are called *imposts* or *subsidies*; when the people fixes a sum to pay, the tax is known as a subsidy; when it grants all the revenue from a kind of tax it is an impost. We read in *The Spirit of Laws** that taxation by head is more appropriate to servitude and that real taxes are more suitable to freedom. This would be undeniable if the amounts paid by each person were equal, for nothing would be more disproportionate than such a tax, and the spirit of freedom consists above all in the exact observance of proportion. But if the tax per head is exactly in proportion to the individual's resources, as could be the case with the tax known in France as the *capitation*, which thus becomes both real and personal, then it is the most equitable tax, and consequently the tax best suited to free men. Proportionality here seems at first very easy

to maintain, because it relates to the position that each man
has in society, and the indications on which it is based are
always public; but apart from the fact that avarice, influence,
and fraud find ways of evading even manifest truth, it is
unusual, when the calculations are made, for attention to be
paid to all the factors that should be taken into account. First
to be considered is the quantitative relationship, according to
which, other things being equal, a man having ten times the
wealth of another man should pay ten times as much in tax.
Secondly there is the relationship of consumption, that is to say
the distinction between necessities and luxuries. A man who
owns only the bare necessities should pay nothing at all,
whereas the tax paid by a man whose possessions are superfluous to his needs may, if required, amount to the whole of the
sum by which his necessities are exceeded. This man will say
that, in relation to his rank, something that would be a luxury
for a man of lower rank is a necessity for him, but it is a lie:
for a great nobleman has two legs like a cattle-drover, and like
him has only one stomach. Moreover the so-called necessities
are so unnecessary to his station in life that, if he were capable
of giving them up for a praiseworthy motive, he would be all
the more respected. The people would kneel in adoration to a
minister who went on foot to meetings of the council of state,
if the reason was that he had sold his carriages when the state
was in urgent need. In a word the law does not make
ostentation a duty for anyone, and social decorum is never an
argument against right.

A third factor that is never included in the calculations, and
which ought to come first, is the relationship between the
benefits that each person receives from his membership of
organized society, which powerfully protects the rich man's
immense possessions, while scarcely permitting the poor man
the enjoyment of the cottage which he has built with his own
hands. Are not all the advantages of society for the rich and
powerful?* are not all the lucrative posts filled by them alone?
is not every favour and every exemption reserved for them? is
not public authority entirely on their side? If a man with
influence robs his creditors, or commits some other swindle, is
he not always sure to have impunity? The beatings he deals

out, the acts of violence he does, even the murders or assassinations of which he is guilty—are they not affairs which are kept quiet, and after six months is anything more heard of them? But if this same man is robbed, the whole police force is at work immediately, and woe betide any innocent person who is the object of his suspicions. Suppose he visits a dangerous area: an escort is at once arranged; an axle breaks on his coach: everyone flies to his assistance; there is too much noise outside his house: he says a word and all is quiet; he is inconvenienced by a crowd: he makes a sign and everyone stands aside; a carter is in the way: his men get ready to beat him up; and fifty decent people going about their business on foot will be knocked down sooner than an idle rogue delayed in his coach-and-pair. All this consideration costs him not a penny; it is the right of a rich man, not the cost of being rich. How different is the picture for the poor man!—the more he is owed by humanity, the more society refuses him. Every door is closed to him, even when he has the right to have them opened; if he sometimes obtains justice, it is harder for him to do so than for another to obtain a pardon; if the *corvée* has to be done, or a militia raised,* it is he who has the preference; besides his own share of the work, he always has to do the share of his richer neighbour, who has enough influence to be exempted; if the slightest accident happens to him, everyone abandons him; if his miserable little cart overturns no one helps him, and he is lucky indeed, I think, if he can avoid being mistreated in passing by some young duke's impudent servants. In a word, any voluntary assistance slips away from him when he needs it, precisely because he lacks the means to pay for it; and I would think him to be a ruined man if he has the misfortune to possess an honest soul, an attractive daughter, and a powerful neighbour.

Another consideration, of equal importance, is that a poor man's losses are much harder to make good than a rich man's, and that the difficulty of making money always increases in proportion to need. Nothing comes from nothing: the saying is no less true in business than in physics; money is the seed of money, and the first gold crown is sometimes harder to acquire than the second million. Not only this, but everything the poor man pays is lost to him for ever, and remains with the rich man or goes back to him; and since the product of taxation passes sooner or later solely to those who have a share in government or to those who are close to them, it is obviously in their interest, even if they pay their share, that taxes should be raised.

Let me briefly sum up the social pact between the two classes.* 'You need me, because I am rich and you are poor; let us therefore make an agreement: I will allow you to have the honour of working for me, on condition that you give me the little that you still have in return for the trouble I take to give you my orders.'

If we carefully consider all these things in combination, we shall find that in order to distribute the tax burden equitably, and in a truly proportionate manner, it should not be levied on taxpayers simply in the ratio of their possessions, but in a compound ratio, based on the differences in their rank and in the amounts they possess superfluous to their needs. It is a highly important and difficult operation performed daily by multitudes of respectable clerks with a knowledge of arithmetic, but which the Platos and Montesquieus of this world would not have dared to undertake without trembling and praying to Heaven for enlightenment and integrity.

Another disadvantage of personal taxation is that the payer is too much aware of it, and that too much harshness is employed in its collection, which does not prevent it being subject to frequent non-payment, since it is easier for a person than for possessions to avoid being registered and pursued.

Of all the other imposts, the charge on land or real tax has always been considered as the most convenient in countries where more regard is paid to the amount produced, and the reliability of collection, than to reducing the burden on the people. Some have even dared to assert that the peasant had to be taxed in order to shake him out of his lazy ways, and that he would do nothing if he had nothing to pay. But among every nation in the world experience disproves this absurd maxim: it is in Holland and England, where the farmer pays very little, and in China where he pays nothing, that the land is best cultivated. By contrast, wherever the labourer is taxed in proportion to the produce from his field he leaves it fallow, or takes from it exactly what he needs in order to live. For if a man loses the product of his work, doing nothing is a gain; and to impose a fine on work is a strange way of preventing idleness.

The taxation of land or corn, especially when it is done to excess, has two drawbacks so terrible that in time they are bound to depopulate and ruin any country in which it is established.

The first is due to the lack of circulation of money, for commerce and industry attract into the capital all the money from the countryside, while taxation destroys the proportion that might still exist between the labourer's needs and the price of his corn, so that money flows in constantly and never returns; the richer the city, the poorer the country. The product of the real taxes goes out of the hands of the ruler or financier into those of the tradesman or merchant; and the farmer, who receives only the smallest fraction of it, finally exhausts himself by always paying out the same amount and always getting less back. How is a man supposed to live if he has veins but no arteries, or if his arteries carry his blood only a few inches away from his heart? Chardin says that in Persia the king's dues on goods are paid in kind; this custom, which according to the testimony of Herodotus* was formerly prac-tised in that country as far back as the time as Darius, may be able to avert the harm that I have just described. However, unless in Persia the king's agents, administrators, clerks, and storemen are different from everywhere else, I find it difficult not to believe that the king fails to receive even the smallest part of all these goods, that the corn rots in all the granaries, and that most of the storehouses get burnt down.

The second drawback is due to what seems to be a benefit, but one that allows the damage to grow worse before it is noticed. It is that corn is a product which is not made more expensive by tax in the countries where it is grown, and which, despite its absolute necessity, diminishes in quantity without increasing in price;* the result being that many die of hunger even though corn remains cheap, and the farmer alone remains liable for the tax, which he has not been able to take from the proceeds of his sales. It should be carefully noted that the tax

on things cannot be discussed in the same terms as dues by
which the prices of all kinds of merchandise are increased,
and which are consequently paid by the customer rather than
the merchant. For such dues, however high, are nonetheless
voluntary, and are paid by the merchant only in proportion to
the goods that he buys; and since he buys only in proportion
to his sales, he adjusts the price to the individual customer. But
the farmer who, whether he makes any sales or not, is obliged
to pay tax at a fixed rate on the land he cultivates, is not in a
position to wait for the price of his goods to be fixed at the level
that suits him, and even if he were not to sell them in order to
maintain himself, he would be forced to sell them in order to pay
the tax, so that sometimes it is the enormous tax that keeps the
price of the goods at a low level.

Note also that the resources of commerce and industry do
not make the tax on land any more tolerable because of the
abundance of money, but instead make it more onerous. I shall
not insist on something quite obvious: that, while the greater
or lesser quantity of money in a state can bring it more or less
credit externally, it does not change the real prosperity of the
citizens in any way, and makes them neither more or less
wealthy. But I shall make two important observations: one is
that, unless the state has an excess of goods, and the abundance
of money comes from sales abroad, the towns in which trading
takes place are the only places in which its abundance has any
effect, while all it does for the peasant is to make him relatively
poorer; the other is that, with the growth in the supply of
money, the price of everything goes up, so that taxes necessarily go up in the same proportion, and the labourer finds himself
paying higher taxes without having greater resources.

It must be apparent that the tax on land is in reality a charge
on what the land produces. Yet everyone agrees that there is
nothing so dangerous as a charge on corn that is paid by the
buyer: why is it not recognized that the harm is a hundred
times worse when the tax is paid by the farmer himself? Is
it not an attack on the very source of the state's subsistence?
Is it not the most direct attempt possible to depopulate the
country, and consequently, in the end, to ruin it? for the worst
shortage from which a nation can suffer is a shortage of men.

In the imposition of taxes, it is only the true statesman who has the capacity to raise his sights higher than the financial objective, and to transform burdensome charges into useful instruments of policy, making the people ask themselves whether such impositions are not intended for the good of the nation, rather than to increase tax revenue.

Dues on the importation of foreign merchandise, desired by the inhabitants but not needed by the country, or on the export of merchandise produced in the country, but not to excess, and which foreigners cannot do without, or taxes on over-profitable goods produced by skills of the non-utilitarian kind, or tolls paid by townships on purely ornamental objects, and in general taxes on every item of luxury, all achieve this double objective. It is impositions such as these, which relieve poverty and place the burden on wealth, that are required in order to prevent the continual increase in inequality of personal fortune, the attendance on the rich of multitudes of unnecessary workers and servants, the growth in the numbers of the idle in towns, and the desertion of the countryside.

It is important to keep the taxes due on goods proportionate to their price, so that greedy individuals will not be too much tempted into fraud by the amount of profit to be made. In order not to make smuggling easy, moreover, goods that are the hardest to conceal should be taxed in preference to others. Finally it is appropriate that tax should be paid by the person using the object taxed rather than by the person selling it, who would have greater temptations, and more ways of eluding the taxes, because of the large number he has to pay. This method has always been usual in China, which of all the countries in the world is the one where taxes are the highest and the most regularly paid: the tradesman pays nothing; only the purchaser pays the dues, and no discontent or sedition results, because the products that are necessary to life, such as rice and corn, are completely free of tax; the people are not downtrodden and the tax is paid only by the well off. In any case, all these precautions should be dictated less by the fear of smuggling than by the care that a government should take to guard people from the allure of unlawful profit, which, after turning them into bad citizens, will soon make them dishonest.

High taxes should be put on livery, coaches and carriages, mirrors, candelabras and furnishings, cloth and gilding, on the courtyards and gardens of private residences, on entertainment of all kinds, on unnecessary professions such as dancing, singing, and play-acting; in a word, on the whole mass of objects of luxury, amusement, and idleness visible everywhere, which are the less capable of being hidden because their only function is to be on show, and which would be useless if they were not seen. There need be no fear that revenue from them is unreliable because it is based only on things that are not completely necessary; we have very little knowledge of men if we believe that, once they have yielded to the temptations of luxury, they can ever give it up. They would a hundred times sooner give up their necessities, and would even prefer to die of hunger rather than shame. The additional expense will merely be a further reason to bear it, the vanity of proving one's wealth being encouraged both by the object's price and by the payment of tax on it. As long as there are rich men they will want to distinguish themselves from the poor, and the state could not find an easier or more certain source of revenue than one based on this desire.

For the same reason, industry would not suffer in any way from economic arrangements which would enrich public finances and revive agriculture, while giving relief to the labourer, and would gradually bring all personal fortunes nearer to that middling condition which ensures the true strength of a state. It might happen, I admit, that these taxes would contribute to the more rapid passing of some fashions, but never without their replacement by others, from which the worker will profit without any loss in tax revenue. In a word, on the supposition that the spirit of government were constantly to impose tax on surplus wealth, only one of two things can happen: either the rich will renounce their luxury expenditure and spend money only on utilities, which will be of increased benefit to the state, and in this case the imposition of tax will have the effect of the best sumptuary laws: the state's expenses will be bound to diminish in line with the expenses of individuals, so that the treasury could not receive less income without having much less to pay out; or otherwise, if the prodigality of the rich were not to decrease, the treasury will be able to draw on tax revenue for the funds it seeks in order to meet the real needs of the state. In the first case, the treasury grows rich because of all the expenses that it does not have to face; in the second, it also grows rich, from the unnecessary expenditure indulged in by individuals.

Let me add to all this a distinction which is important as regards political right, and which governments, in their jealous desire to do everything themselves, should consider with close attention. I have said* that since both personal taxation and taxes on objects of absolute necessity make a direct attack on the right of property, and consequently on the true foundation of political society, they always tend to produce dangerous results unless they are imposed with the express consent of the people or their representatives. It is not the same with dues paid on objects the use of which is optional, for in this case the individual is not absolutely forced to pay, and his tax contribution can be regarded as voluntary. Thus the separate consent of each individual is a substitute for general consent, and even, in some degree, presupposes it: for why should the people be opposed to any charge which bears only on those persons who are prepared to pay it? To me it seems beyond doubt that anything that is neither banned by law nor contrary to morals, and which the government can prohibit, can also be allowed by the government on payment of a tax. For example, if the government can prohibit the use of carriages, it has even stronger reasons to impose a tax on them, which is a wise and valuable method of showing disapproval for their use without preventing it. The tax can then be considered as a kind of fine, the revenue from it acting as compensation for an abuse which the tax punishes.

Someone may perhaps object that since those whom Bodin calls *imposers*,* that is to say those who impose or invent taxes, come from the wealthy class, they will take care not to spare others at their own expense, and will not burden themselves in order to relieve the poor. But we must reject such ideas. If, in each nation, those to whom the sovereign entrusts the government of the people were its enemies because of their position, what they should do to make the people happy would not be worth examining.

THE SOCIAL CONTRACT
OR
THE PRINCIPLES OF
POLITICAL RIGHT

by

JEAN-JACQUES ROUSSEAU
Citizen of Geneva

. . . foederis aequas
Dicamus leges. *
Aeneid, XI.

PREFATORY NOTE

This short treatise is taken from a more extended work, now long abandoned, which I once undertook without realizing my limitations. Of the various pieces that it was possible to extract from what I had done, this is the most considerable, and seemed to me the least unworthy of being offered to the public. The rest no longer exists.

BOOK I

I INTEND to examine whether, in the ordering of society, there can be any reliable and legitimate rule of administration, taking men as they are, and laws as they can be. I shall try, throughout my enquiry, to combine what is allowed by right* with what is prescribed by self-interest, in order that justice and utility should not be separated.

I begin my discussion without proving the importance of my subject. People will ask me whether I write on politics because I am a ruler or a legislator. I answer that I am not; and that is the reason why I write on politics. If I were a ruler or legislator, I should not waste my time saying what ought to be done; I should do it, or hold my peace.

I was born a citizen of a free state and a member of its sovereign body,* and however weak may be the influence of my voice in public affairs, my right to vote on them suffices to impose on me the duty of studying them. How happy I am, each time that I reflect on governments, always to find new reasons, in my researches, to cherish the government of my country!

Chapter i

The Subject of the First Book

MAN was born free,* and everywhere he is in chains. There are some who may believe themselves masters of others, and are no less enslaved than they. How has this change come about? I do not know. How can it be made legitimate? That is a question which I believe I can resolve.

If I were to consider force alone, and the effects that it produces, I should say: for so long as a nation is constrained to obey, and does so, it does well; as soon as it is able to throw off its servitude, and does so, it does better; for since it regains freedom by the same right that was exercised when its freedom was seized, either the nation was justified in taking freedom back, or else those who took it away were unjustified in doing so. Whereas the social order is a sacred right, and provides a foundation for all other rights. Yet it is a right that does not come from nature; therefore it is based on agreed conventions. Our business is to find out what those conventions are. Before we come to that, I must make good the assertion that I have just put forward.

Chapter ii

The First Societies

THE most ancient of all societies, and the only one that is natural, is the family. Even in this case, the bond between children and father persists only so long as they have need of him for their conservation. As soon as this need ceases, the natural bond is dissolved. The children are released from the obedience they owe to their father, the father is released from the duty of care to the children, and all become equally independent. If they continue to remain living together, it is not by nature but voluntarily, and the family itself is maintained only through convention.*

This shared freedom is a result of man's nature. His first law is his own conservation, his first cares are owed to himself; as soon as he reaches the age of reason, he alone is the judge of how best to look after himself, and thus he becomes his own master.

If we wish, then, the family may be regarded as the first model of political society: the leader corresponds to the father, the people to the children, and all being born free and equal, none alienates his freedom except for reasons of utility. The sole difference is that, in the family, the father is paid for the care he takes of his children by the love he bears them, while in the state this love is replaced by the pleasure of being in command, the chief having no love for his people.

Grotius denies that all human power is instituted for the benefit of the governed.* He cites slavery as an example; his commonest mode of reasoning is to base a right on a fact.[1] A more logical method could be employed, but not one that is more favourable to tyrants.

It is therefore doubtful, following Grotius, whether the human race belongs to a hundred or so men, or whether these hundred men belong to the human race, and he seems inclined, throughout his book, towards the former opinion. This is Hobbes's view also.* Behold then the human race divided into herds of cattle, each with its chief, who preserves it in order to devour it.

'As a shepherd is of a nature superior to that of his flock, so too the shepherds of men, their chiefs, are of a nature superior to their peoples'—this argument, according to Philo, was used by the Emperor Caligula;* who would conclude (correctly enough, given his analogy) either that kings were gods or that the people were animals.

The reasoning employed by this Caligula amounts to the same as that of Hobbes and Grotius. Aristotle* too had said, earlier than any of them, that men are not naturally equal, but that some are born for slavery and some for mastery.

Aristotle was right, but he took the effect for the cause. Any man who is born in slavery is born for slavery; there is nothing surer. Slaves in their chains lose everything, even the desire to be rid of them; they love their servitude, like the companions of Odysseus, who loved their brutishness.[2] If there are slaves by nature, it is because slaves have been made against nature. The first slaves were made by force, and they remained so through cowardice.

I have said nothing of King Adam or of the Emperor Noah, the father of three great monarchs who shared the universe among themselves, like the children of Saturn, with whom they have been identified.* I hope that my restraint in this respect will be appreciated; for, being descended directly from one or

---

[1] 'Learned researches on political law are often no more than the history of former abuses, and it is misguided diligence to take the trouble of studying them too deeply'—from the manuscript *Treatise on France's interests as regards her neighbours*, by the M. d'A.* This is exactly what Grotius did.

[2] See a short treatise by Plutarch,* entitled *That animals employ reason.*

other of these princes, and maybe from the senior branch of the family, who knows but that, if my entitlement were verified, I might not find that I am the legitimate king of the human race? However that may be, it cannot be denied that Adam was sovereign over the world, like Crusoe on his island, for so long as he was the sole inhabitant; and the advantage of this form of rule was that the monarch, firm on his throne, had neither rebellions, nor wars, nor conspirators to fear.

Chapter iii

The Right of the Strongest

THE stronger party is never strong enough to remain the master for ever, unless he transforms his strength into right, and obedience into duty. This is the source of the 'right of the strongest', a right which people treat with apparent irony* and which in reality is an established principle. But can anyone ever explain the phrase? Force is a physical power; I do not see how any morality can be based on its effects. To yield to force is an act of necessity, not of consent; at best it is an act of prudence. In what sense can it be a duty?

Let us suppose for a moment that this alleged right is valid. I say that the result would be completely senseless. For as soon as right is founded on force, the effect will alter with its cause; any force that is stronger than the first must have right on its side in its turn. As soon as anyone is able to disobey with impunity he may do so legitimately, and since the strongest is always right the only question is how to ensure that one is the strongest. But what kind of a right is it that is extinguished when that strength is lost? If we must obey because of force we have no need to obey out of duty, and if we are no longer forced to obey we no longer have any obligation to do so. It can be seen therefore that the word 'right' adds nothing to force; it has no meaning at all here.

'Obey the powers that be'.* If this means: 'Yield to force', it is a sound precept, but superfluous; I can guarantee that it will never be violated. All power is from God, I admit; but all disease is from God also. Does that mean we are forbidden to call the doctor? If a highwayman ambushes me on a road by a wood, I must give him my money by force, but if I can keep it away from him am I obliged in conscience to give it up? After all, the pistol that he holds is also a power.

Let us agree then that might is not right, and that we are obliged to obey only legitimate powers. Thus we return to my original question.

Chapter iv

Slavery

SINCE no man has a natural authority over his fellow, and since strength does not confer any right, it follows that the basis remaining for all legitimate authority among men must be agreed convention.*

If, says Grotius, an individual is able to transfer* his liberty, and become the slave of a master, why should an entire nation not transfer its liberty and become subject to a king?* Here we have several equivocal words that need elucidation, but let us keep to the term *transfer*. To transfer is to give or to sell. Now a man who becomes the slave of another does not give himself: he sells himself, in exchange, at the very least, for his subsistence. But in exchange for what does a nation sell itself? A king, far from providing subsistence to his subjects, takes it all from them, and as Rabelais says, a king doesn't live cheaply. So will his subjects give him their persons on condition that he will take their property also? I cannot see what they still have to keep.

It will be objected that a despot ensures civil peace for his subjects. Very well; but what do they gain thereby, if the wars that his ambition brings down on them, his insatiable greed, and the troubles inflicted by his administrators, plague them more sorely than their dissensions would? What do they gain thereby, if civil peace itself is a source of misery? Prisoners live peacefully in their dungeons; is that enough for them to feel comfortable there? The Greek captives in the cave of the

Cyclops* lived there peacefully, while awaiting their turn to be devoured.

To say that a man gives himself for nothing is an absurd and incomprehensible statement; such an action is illegitimate and void, simply because anyone who does it is not in his right mind. To say the same about an entire people is to imagine a nation of madmen, and madness does not make rights.

Even if each person could transfer himself, he could not transfer his children; they are born men, and free; their freedom belongs to them, and nobody except them has the right to dispose of it. Until they reach the age of reason, their father can stipulate, in their name, the conditions for their con-servation and well-being, but he cannot make a gift of them, irrevocably and without condition; such a gift is contrary to the purposes of nature and exceeds the rights of fatherhood. In order, then, for an arbitrary government to be legitimate, it would be necessary for the people, at every new generation, to have the power to accept it or reject it; but in that case the government would no longer be arbitrary.

To renounce our freedom is to renounce our character as men, the rights, and even the duties, of humanity. No compensa-tion is possible for anyone who renounces everything. It is incompatible with the nature of man; to remove the will's freedom is to remove all morality from our actions. Finally, a convention is vain and contradictory if it stipulates absolute authority on one side and limitless obedience on the other. Is it not obvious that we have no obligations towards a person from whom we can demand anything, and that this condition, requiring nothing in return or exchange, is enough to render the covenant null? For what right can my slave have against me, since everything he has belongs to me? His rights being mine, a right of mine against myself is a word without a meaning.

Grotius and the others take war to be another origin of the so-called right of slavery.* The conqueror having the right, according to them, to kill the conquered, the latter may redeem his life at the expense of his freedom; an agreement that is the more legitimate because it is to the advantage of both parties.

But it is clear that this so-called right to kill the conquered does not derive in any way from the state of war. For the simple reason that men who are living in their original condition of independence are not in a sufficiently continuous relationship with each other for a state either of peace or war to exist, they are not naturally enemies.* It is the relationship of things, not of men, that constitutes a state of war, and since the state of war cannot be engendered merely by personal relationships but only by relationships between things,* a private war between man and man cannot exist—either in the state of nature, in which there is no permanent possession of property, or in the social state, in which everything is controlled by laws.

Single combat, duels, and chance encounters are actions which do not produce a state of affairs; and with respect to private wars, which were authorized by the Establishments of Louis IX of France and abrogated by the Peace of God,* they were an abuse due to feudal government, an absurd system if ever there was one, contrary both to the principles of natural law and all good polity.*

War is not, therefore, a relationship between man and man, but between state and state, in which individuals become enemies only by accident, not as men, nor even as citizens,[1] but as soldiers; not even as members of their own nation, but as its defenders. Furthermore each state can be enemy only to other states, and not to men, given that between things diverse in nature no true relationship can be established.

---

[1] The Romans, who understood and observed the laws of war better than any other nation on earth, carried their scruples on this point so far that citizens were not allowed to serve as volunteers unless they committed themselves to fighting against the enemy, and an enemy specifically named. When the legion in which the younger Cato had fought his first campaign was disbanded, the elder Cato wrote to Popilius to say that if he wished his son to continue to serve with him he would have to take the military oath again, because, once the first oath had been cancelled, he could no longer bear arms against the enemy. And Cato also wrote to his son telling him to take care not to go into battle without taking the new oath. I know that the siege of Clusium and other particular incidents could be used against my argument, but for my part I am citing laws and customs. Of all peoples the Romans transgressed their laws least often, and their laws were the finest of all.*

The principle involved conforms, moreover, to maxims accepted in every age, and to the constant practice of every politically organized nation. Declarations of war are notices given less to national powers than to their subjects.* A foreign king, or private individual, or people, who pillages, kills or detains a ruler's subjects, without declaring war on the ruler, is not an enemy, but a brigand. Even in war proper, a just ruler will indeed take possession, when he is in enemy territory, of anything belonging to the public, but will respect the person and property of individuals; he is respecting the rights on which his own are founded. The purpose of war being to destroy the enemy state, its defenders may rightfully be killed so long as they are carrying arms; but as soon as they lay them down and surrender, ceasing to be enemies or agents of the enemy, they become simply men again, and there is no longer any right over their lives. On occasion it is possible to kill the state without killing any of its members; war confers no rights that are not necessary to its purpose. These are not Grotius's principles; they are not based on the authority of poets, but derive from the nature of things, and are based on reason.*

As regards the right of conquest, its only foundation is the right of the strongest. If war does not give the victor the right to massacre the vanquished people, this right that he does not possess cannot create the right to enslave them. One has the right to kill an enemy only when it is impossible to make a slave of him: therefore the right to enslave him does not come from the right to kill him; therefore it is an iniquitous exchange to make him pay with his freedom for his life, over which one has no right. Is it not plain that there is a vicious circle in basing the right of life and death on the right to enslave, and the right to enslave on the right of life and death?

Even if we were to admit this terrible right of massacre, I say that men enslaved in war, or a conquered people, have no obligation at all to their masters, beyond obeying them to the extent that they are forced to do so. The conqueror has not spared the slave's life when he has taken the equivalent of life: instead of killing him without profit he has killed him usefully. So far from any authority having been added to the power that the one has over the other, the state of war continues between them, and their relation is the consequence of it. The enforcement of a right of war does not create the assumption that a peace treaty has been made. An agreement has indeed been reached, but this covenant is far from destroying the state of war, and makes the assumption that it still continues.

From whatever angle the question is considered, then, the right of slavery is void, not only because it is illegitimate, but because of its absurdity and meaninglessness. The words *slavery* and *right* contradict each other; they are mutually exclusive. Whether made by one man addressing another, or by a man addressing a nation, this statement will always be equally senseless: 'I make a covenant between us which is entirely at your expense and entirely for my good, which I will observe as long as I please, and which you will observe as long as I please.'

Chapter v

That It Is Always Necessary to Go Back to an Original Convention

EVEN if I were to grant the truth of everything that I have refuted up to now, the instigators of despotism would be no further forward. There will always be a great difference between subjugating a multitude of men and ruling a society. If a series of men, in succession, are made to submit to one other man, all I can see in them is a master with his slaves, however many of them there may be; I cannot see a people and its leader. It could be said to be an aggregation, but it is not an association; there is no public good, no body politic. The one man, even if he were to have subjugated half the world, is still only an individual; his self-interest, separate from that of the rest, is still only a private interest. If this same man comes to his end, his empire after him is scattered and dissolved, as an oak breaks up and falls into a heap of ashes after being consumed by fire.

A people, says Grotius, can give itself to a king.* A people is a people, therefore, according to Grotius, before it gives itself to a king. The gift itself is a civil act, and assumes some public deliberation. Hence it would be as well, before we examine the act by which a people elects a king, to examine the act by which a people is a people. For this act is necessarily anterior to the other, and is the true foundation of society.

For if there were no prior covenant, where would the obligation be (if the election were not unanimous) for the minority to submit to the choice of the majority, and how could it be right for the votes of a hundred who wanted a master to be binding on ten who did not? The law of the majority vote itself establishes a covenant, and assumes that on one occasion at least there has been unanimity.*

Chapter vi

The Social Pact

I make the assumption that there is a point in the development of mankind* at which the obstacles to men's self-preservation in the state of nature are too great to be overcome by the strength that any one individual can exert in order to maintain himself in this state. The original state can then subsist no longer, and the human race would perish if it did not change its mode of existence.

Now as men cannot generate new strength, but only unify and control the forces already existing, the sole means that they still have of preserving themselves is to create, by combination, a totality of forces sufficient to overcome the obstacles resisting them, to direct their operation by a single impulse, and make them act in unison.

The totality of forces can be formed only by the collaboration of a number of persons; but each man's strength and freedom being the main instruments of his preservation, how can he commit them to others without harming himself, and without neglecting the duty of care to himself? The difficulty as it relates to my subject may be defined in the following terms:

'Find a form of association which will defend and protect, with the whole of its joint strength, the person and property of

each associate, and under which each of them, uniting himself to all, will obey himself alone, and remain as free as before.' This is the fundamental problem to which the social contract gives the answer.

The clauses of this contract are so closely determined by the nature of the act in question that the slightest modification would make them empty and ineffectual; whence it is that, although they may perhaps never have been formally pronounced, they are the same everywhere, and everywhere tacitly recognized and accepted, until, should the social pact be violated, each associate thereupon recovers his original rights and takes back his natural freedom, while losing the freedom of convention for which he gave it up.

Properly understood, the clauses can all be reduced to one alone, namely, the complete transfer of each associate, with all his rights, to the whole community. For in the first place, each giving himself completely, the condition is the same for all; and the condition being the same for all, none has any interest in making it burdensome to the others.

Further, the transfer being carried out unreservedly, the union between the associates is as perfect as it can be, and none of them has any further requirements to add. For if individuals retained some rights, there being no common superior to give judgement between them and the public, each would make his own judgement on certain points, and would soon aspire to do so on all of them: the state of nature would remain in force, and the association would become, necessarily, either tyrannical or meaningless.

Finally, each in giving himself to all gives himself to none, and since there are no associates over whom he does not acquire the same rights as he cedes, he gains the equivalent of all that he loses, and greater strength for the conservation of what he possesses.

If therefore we set aside everything that is not essential to the social pact, we shall find that it may be reduced to the following terms. *Each of us puts his person and all his power in common under the supreme direction of the general will; and we as a body receive each member as an indivisible part of the whole.**

Immediately, this act of association produces, in place of the individual persons of every contracting party, a moral and collective body, which is composed of as many members as there are votes in the assembly, and which, by the same act, is endowed with its unity, its common self, its life, and its will. The public person that is formed in this way by the union of all the others once bore the name *city*,[1] and now bears that of *republic* or *body politic*; its members call it *the state* when it is passive, *the sovereign* when it is active, and a *power* when comparing it to its like. As regards the associates, they collectively take the name of *people*, and are individually called *citizens* as being participants in sovereign authority, and *subjects* as being bound by the laws of the state. But these terms are often confused, and one is taken for another; it is enough to know how to distinguish between them on the occasions when they are applied with complete precision.

Chapter vii

The Sovereign

IT will be seen from the formulation above that the act of association involves a reciprocal commitment between public and private persons; each individual enters on a contract with

---

[1] The true sense of this word has almost disappeared in modern writers. Most of them take a town to be a city and a town-dweller to be a citizen. They are unaware that it is houses that make a town, but citizens who make the City.* The same error once cost the Carthaginians dear. In my reading I have not seen the title of *cives* given to the subjects of any ruler, not even to the Macedonians in ancient times, nor to the English nowadays, although they are nearer to being free than any others. The French alone call themselves *citizens* as a matter of course, because they have no true idea of what it means, as can be seen from their dictionaries; otherwise, they would be guilty of treason in usurping it. Among them, the name expresses a virtue, not a right. Bodin, meaning to discuss our citizens and burgesses, made a sad blunder in taking the one for the other.* M. d'Alembert did not make the same mistake in his article *Geneva*, where he correctly distinguished the four orders (or even five, if you count those who are simply foreigners) to which those living in our city belong, only two of them constituting the Republic. No other French author, to my knowledge, has understood the true sense of the word *citizen*.

himself, so to speak, and becomes bound in a double capacity, namely, towards other individuals inasmuch as he is a member of the sovereign, and towards the sovereign inasmuch as he is a member of the state.* But the maxim used in civil law, that none is held to an undertaking made with himself, cannot be applied here, for to have an obligation towards oneself is quite different from having an obligation towards a whole of which one is a member.

We must note also that public decisions can put each subject under an obligation towards the sovereign, because he may be considered in his two different capacities, but, for the opposite reason, they cannot put the sovereign under any obligation towards itself; and in consequence, it is contrary to the nature of the body politic that the sovereign should impose on itself a law that it cannot infringe. Since it can be considered only in one capacity, it is in the situation of an individual contracting with himself; whence it will be seen that there is no kind of fundamental law, and cannot be any, not even the social contract, which is binding on the people as a body.* This does not mean that, in any matter not affecting the contract, the people cannot have a binding obligation towards others; for in respect of foreign nations it becomes a single being, an individual.

But since the body politic or the sovereign derives its being solely from the sanctity of the contract,* it cannot oblige itself to do anything that derogates from this original deed; for instance, to alienate some portion of itself or to submit to some other sovereign. To violate the act through which it exists would be to destroy itself, and that which is nothing can give rise to nothing.

As soon as the multitude is united thus in one body, it is impossible to injure one of its members without attacking the body, and still less to injure the body without its members being affected. Hence duty and self-interest oblige both contracting parties equally to give each other mutual assistance, and the same individuals must seek, in their double capacity, to take advantage of all the benefits which depend on it.

The sovereign, then, consisting solely of the individual persons which form it, has and can have no self-interest that is contrary to theirs; as a result, it does not need to give any form of guarantee to its subjects,* because it is impossible that the body should want to harm all its members; and as we shall see later,* it cannot harm any one individually. Simply by virtue of its existence, the sovereign is always what it should be.

But the position is different for the sovereign in relation to the subjects, because, despite the common interests of the two, nothing guarantees their commitment to it unless it can find a means of ensuring their fidelity.

For each individual can have, as a man, a personal will that is contrary or dissimilar to the general will that he has as a citizen. His personal interest can speak to him quite differently from the common interest: his mode of existence, absolute and independent, can make him regard what he owes to the common cause as a gratuitous contribution, the loss of which will be less onerous to others than its payment is for him; and envisaging the artificial person, in which the state consists, as an abstract being, on the grounds that it is not a man, he would thus enjoy the rights of a citizen while declining to fulfil the duties of a subject, an example of injustice which, if it were to spread, would bring the ruin of the body politic.

In order therefore that the social pact should not be an empty formula, it contains an implicit obligation which alone can give force to the others, that if anyone refuses to obey the general will he will be compelled to do so by the whole body; which means nothing else than that he will be forced to be free;* for such is the condition which, giving each citizen to his country, guarantees that he will not depend on any person.* This condition is the device that ensures the operation of the political machine; it alone legitimizes civil obligations, which without it would be absurd and tyrannical, and subject to the most terrible abuses.

Chapter viii

The Civil State*

THIS passage from the state of nature to the civil state produces in man a very remarkable change, replacing instinct by justice in his behaviour, and conferring on his actions the moral quality that they had lacked before. It is only now, as the voice of duty succeeds to physical impulse and right to appetite, that man, who had previously thought of nothing but himself, is compelled to act on other principles, and to consult his reason before he attends to his inclinations. Although, in the civil state, he deprives himself of a number of advantages which he has by nature, the others that he acquires are so great, so greatly are his faculties exercised and improved, his ideas amplified, his feelings ennobled, and his entire soul raised so much higher, that if the abuses that occur in his new condition did not frequently reduce him to a state lower than the one he has just left, he ought constantly to bless the happy moment when he was taken from it for ever, and which made of him, not a limited and stupid animal, but an intelligent being and a man.

Let us convert the balance of gains and losses into terms that are easy to compare. What man loses by the social contract is his natural freedom and an unlimited right to anything by which he is tempted and can obtain; what he gains is civil freedom and the right of property over everything that he possesses.

In order not to be misled over the compensating advantages, we must clearly distinguish natural freedom, which is limited only by the strength of the individual, from civil freedom, which is limited by the general will; and possession, which is merely the effect of force or the right of the first occupant, from property, which can be founded only on positive entitlement.

To the acquisition of moral status could be added, on the basis of what has just been said, the acquisition of moral liberty, this being the only thing that makes man truly the master of himself; for to be driven by our appetites alone is slavery, while to obey a law that we have imposed on ourselves is freedom.

But I have already said more than enough on this point, and the philosophical sense of the word *freedom* is not my subject here.

Chapter ix

Property *

EACH member of the community, at the moment of its formation, gives himself to it as he then is, together with all his resources, of which the goods he possesses are part. It is not that, by this act, possessions change their nature as the possessor changes, so as to become property in the hands of the sovereign. But, just as the resources of the state are incomparably greater than those of one individual, so too public possession is, in fact, stronger and more irrevocable, although—at least for foreigners—it is no more legitimate. For the state, as regards its members, is master of all their property through the social contract, which in the state acts as the basis of all rights; but as regards other powers it is master only by the right of the first occupant, which passes to it from private individuals.

The right of the first occupant is more real than the right of the strongest, but does not become a true right until the right of property has been established. Every man has naturally a right to everything that is necessary to him; but by the positive legal act which makes him the owner of certain goods he is excluded from all the rest. He has his share, and must keep to it; he no longer has any rights over the community's goods. Here we have the reason why the right of first occupancy, which in the state of nature is so fragile, is respected by all in the civil state. Under this right, it is not so much property belonging to others, but rather property not belonging to us, that we respect.

In general, the following conditions are required in order to justify the right of first occupancy for a given piece of land. First, the land must as yet be uninhabited; secondly, no more must be occupied than is needed for subsistence; and in the third place, possession must be taken not by empty ceremonies, but by work and cultivation, the only mark of ownership which ought, in default of juridical title, to be respected by others.

For if we grant that the needs of the first occupier, and the work he does, create a right, have we not extended this right as far as it can go? How can it not be limited? Does putting one's foot on a piece of land suffice as a claim to ownership? If we have enough strength to keep other men out of it for a while, does that suffice to deprive them of their right ever to return? If a man, or a nation, lays hold of huge territories and denies them to the whole human race, what else is it but an act of usurpation deserving punishment, since it takes from the rest of mankind the dwelling-place and the sustenance which nature gives them in common? When, in the name of the kingdom of Castile, Nuñez Balboa* took possession, on the sea-shore, of the southern seas and the whole of southern America, did that suffice to dispossess all the inhabitants and to keep out all the world's rulers? If things stand thus, there was little purpose in his adding to the ceremonies he performed: all his Most Catholic Majesty had to do was to stay in his cabinet and take possession, all at once, of the whole universe; provided that he then removed from his empire everything already in the possession of other rulers.

It is easy to understand how adjacent pieces of land belonging to individuals become, when combined, public territory, and how the right of sovereignty over subjects is extended to the terrain that they occupy, so covering both things and persons. This places the possessors of property in a further degree of dependence, so that even their resources become guarantors of their fidelity—an advantage which does not appear to have been fully appreciated by ancient monarchs, who by calling themselves kings of the Persians, of the Scythians, or of the Macedonians, seem to have considered themselves as commanders of men rather than masters of countries. Today's monarchs more cleverly call themselves kings of France, of Spain, of England, etc.; they well know that by keeping hold of their territories they will keep their hold on the inhabitants.

The remarkable thing about this transfer of ownership is that when the community receives the possessions of individuals it does not in any way despoil them, but instead ensures that their ownership is legitimate, changing usurpation into genuine right, and enjoyment of use into property. Those having possession being thenceforward considered as persons entrusted with public property, and their rights being respected by all members of the state and maintained against foreigners with all its power, their act of ceding ownership to the state has benefited not only the public but, even more, themselves, and they have as it were acquired everything they have given—a paradox which is easily explained if we distinguish between the rights that the sovereign and the owner have over the same piece of property, as we shall see in due course.*

It can also happen that men begin to form a community before having any property, and that later, as they take possession of land enough for all, they enjoy its use in common or share it between themselves, either in equal proportions, or according to those decided by the sovereign. In whatever manner the acquisition of ownership is carried out, the right that each individual has over his property is always subordinate to the right that the community has over everyone; otherwise, the social bond would be lacking in firmness and the exercise of sovereignty would lack true power.

I end this chapter, and this book, by a remark upon which the entire social system should be based: it is that, instead of destroying natural equality, the fundamental contract substitutes moral and legal equality for whatever degree of physical inequality nature has put among men; they may be unequal in strength or intelligence, but all become equal through agreed convention and by right.[1]

---

[1] Under a bad government, this equality is only apparent and illusory: it serves only to keep the poor wretched and preserve the usurpations of the rich. Laws in reality are always useful to those with possessions and detrimental to those who have nothing: whence it follows that the social state is advantageous to men only if all have a certain amount, and none too much.

BOOK II

Chapter i

*That Sovereignty Cannot Be Transferred**

THE first and most important consequence of the principles laid down hitherto is that only the general will can direct the powers of the state in accordance with the purpose for which it was instituted, which is the common good; for if the establishment of societies was made necessary because individual interests were in opposition, it was made possible because those interests concur. The social bond is formed by what these interests have in common; if there were no point at which every interest met, no society could exist. And it is solely on the basis of this common interest that society must be governed.

I therefore assert that sovereignty, being only the exercise of the general will,* can never be transferred, and that the sovereign, which cannot be other than a collective entity, cannot be represented except by itself;* power can be delegated, but the will cannot.

For although it is not impossible that an individual's will* may in some matter be in agreement with the general will, it is certainly not possible for the agreement to be firm and durable; since the tendency of an individual will is by nature towards making preferences, while that of the general will is towards equality. It is even less possible for any person to guarantee the agreement, even if it were to be permanent, for it would not be due to policy, but chance. What the sovereign can say is: 'What I want at present is what this or that individual wants, or at least what he says he wants'; but it cannot say: 'Tomorrow I shall still want what that individual wants', because it is absurd that the will should bind itself for the future, and it is beyond any will to consent to something contrary to the good of the being whose will it is. If therefore the people simply promises to obey, it dissolves itself by this very act, and loses its character as a people. From the moment that there is a master, sovereign authority ceases, and the body politic is thenceforward destroyed.

This is not to say that a chief's orders cannot pass for acts of the general will, so long as the sovereign authority, while free to reject them, refrains from doing so. In such a case the universal silence implies that the people has consented. I shall explain this at greater length.

Chapter ii

That Sovereignty Cannot Be Divided

SOVEREIGNTY is indivisible for the same reason that it is untransferable: a will is either general, or it is not; it is the will of the body of the people, or of a part only. In the first case, this will, once declared, is an act of sovereignty and has legal authority. In the second, it is only a particular act of will, or an administrative decision; at most it is a decree.

Our political theorists,* however, being unable to divide sovereignty in principle, have divided it according to its object: they separate power from will, legislature from executive, the right to raise taxes from the right to administer justice or declare war, and internal administration from the capacity to negotiate with foreign countries. Sometimes all the separate parts are mixed up, sometimes they are distinguished. The sovereign is made into a fantastic patchwork; it is as if they had made a man composed of more than one body, one having eyes, another arms, another feet, and nothing else. In Japan, it is said, magicians dismember a child before the audience's eyes, and then, throwing all its limbs one after another into the air, they bring it down alive again, all in one piece. Of the same kind, more or less, are the conjuring tricks done by our theorists; they have chopped up the body social by a sleight of hand worthy of a fairground showman, and you cannot tell how they reassemble the pieces.

The cause of their error is that they have no correct idea of the sovereign, and take manifestations of its authority to be parts of it. Thus the acts of declaring war and making peace, for instance, have been regarded as acts of sovereignty, which is wrong, because neither of these acts is in any way a law, but only an application of law, a particular decision determining that the law should take effect, as we shall see clearly when the idea associated with the word *law** is defined.

If the theorists' other distinctions were examined in the same way, it would be found that whenever we believe sovereignty to be divided we are in error, and that the rights that are taken to be parts of the sovereign authority are all subordinate to it, supreme acts of will always being presupposed, and only the power to execute them being bestowed by these rights.

This lack of exactitude has caused an incalculable degree of obscurity in our authors' judgements on political theory when, following the principles they have laid down, they have tried to decide on the respective rights of kings and peoples. Anyone can see, in the third and fourth chapters of Grotius's Book I, how this learned man and his translator Barbeyrac* become confused and entangle themselves in their own sophistries, for fear of going too far or not far enough for what they had in mind, and of offending those interests to which they wished to be conciliatory. Grotius, dissatisfied with his own country, having sought refuge in France and wishing to win favour with Louis XIII, to whom he dedicated his book, spares nothing in order to despoil the people of all their rights and to make them over to the king, which he does with the greatest skill. Barbeyrac too, who dedicated his translation to the King of England, George I, would certainly have liked to do the same. But unfortunately the expulsion of James II, which he calls an abdication, forced him to be reticent, to distort and misrepresent, in order not to portray William as a usurper. If these two writers had adopted true principles, all their difficulties would have been removed, and they would have been consistent throughout; but they would have been telling unwelcome truths and winning favour only with the people. Truth does not lead to success, and the people does not appoint ambassadors or professors or give state salaries.

Chapter iii

Whether the General Will Can Err

IT follows from what precedes that the general will is always in the right,* and always tends to the public welfare; but it does not follow that decisions made by the people have equal rightness. One always desires one's own good, but one does not always see what it is; the people can never be corrupted, but it can often be led into error, and it is only in this case that it seems to desire the bad.

There is often a difference between the will of everyone and the general will; the latter is concerned only with the common interest, while the former is concerned with private interests, and is the sum total of individual wants: but if you take away from these desires their excesses and insufficiencies, the common element remaining from the different desires is the general will.[1]

If, when properly informed, the people were to come to its decisions without any communication between its members, the general will would always emerge from the large number of small differences, and the decision would always be good. But when there are intrigues, and partial associations arise at the expense of the greater one, the will of each of these associations becomes general in relation to its members and particular in relation to the state: it can then be said that the number of voters is no longer the same as the number of men, but only the same as the number of associations. The differences become fewer and give a less general result. Eventually, when one of the associations is big enough to triumph over all the others, the outcome is no longer the sum total of small

---

[1] 'Every interest', says the Marquis d'Argenson, 'has a different basis. Two individual interests agree when having a basis different from that of a third.' He could have added that agreement between all interests is formed through their common basis, in contrast to the interest of each person. If there were no differing interests, we should scarcely be aware of the common interest, which would never meet any obstacle; everything would run by itself, and there would no longer be any skill in politics.

differences, but a single difference; then there is no longer any general will, and the opinion that prevails is only a particular opinion.

It is therefore important, if the general will is to be properly ascertained, that there should be no partial society within the state, and that each citizen should decide according to his own opinion;[1] this sublime institution was due uniquely to Lycurgus.* If there are partial associations, their number should be increased and inequalities between them prevented, as was done by Solon, Numa, and Servius.* These are the only effective precautions if the general will is always to be enlightened and the people is not to fall into error.

Chapter iv

The Limits of Sovereign Power

IF the state or City is solely a collective person which exists through the union of its members, and if its fundamental concern is its own conservation, it must have a coercive force of universal scope, in order to move and control each part in the manner most advantageous to the whole. Just as nature gives each man absolute power over all his limbs, the social pact gives the body politic absolute power over its members; and as I have said, it is this same power, directed by the general will, that bears the name of sovereignty.

But besides the public self we have to consider the private persons of whom it consists, and whose life and freedom are independent of it by nature. The question is how to distinguish clearly between the respective rights of sovereign and citizen,[2]

---

[1] 'In truth,' says Machiavelli, 'some divisions within states are harmful, and some are helpful. Those are harmful which are accompanied by parties and factions; helpful, those which subsist without organized parties or factions. The founder of a republic, being unable to prevent dissension within the state, must at least prevent the existence of faction.' (*History of Florence*, Bk. VII.)*

[2] The attentive reader will not, I beg, be too hasty in accusing me of contradicting myself here. I have been unable to avoid it in the terms I use, given the poverty of the language;* but wait.

and between the duties that citizens have to perform as subjects, and the natural rights which they enjoy as men.

It is agreed that what each person transfers, in accordance with the social pact, as regards his power, his goods, and his freedom, amounts at most to the portion of these things that it is important for the community to use;* but it must also be agreed that the sovereign authority alone judges the degree of importance that is involved.

A citizen owes the state all the services that he can offer it whenever the sovereign asks for them; but the sovereign for its part cannot impose on its subjects any burden which is useless to the community: it cannot even want to impose it; for under the law of reason, as under the law of nature, nothing can be done without a cause.

The undertakings that unite us to the body of society are binding only because they are mutual, and their nature is such that in fulfilling them our efforts for others are efforts on our own behalf also. Why is it that the general will is always in the right, and why is the happiness of each the constant wish of all, unless it is because there is no one who does not apply the word *each* to himself, and is not thinking of himself when he votes for all? And this proves that equality as of right, and the notion of justice to which it gives rise, derive from the preference that each gives to himself, and consequently from the nature of man; that the general will, in order to be truly general, must be so not only in essence but also in respect of its object;* that it must issue from everyone in order that it should apply to everyone; and that it loses its natural rightfulness when it is directed towards some specific, individual object, since in this case we are making a judgement about something foreign to us, and have no true principle of equity to guide us.

For whenever a particular action or right is in question, relating to a point that has not been decided by prior general agreement, the matter becomes contentious.* It is like a case at law, in which the individuals concerned are on one side and the public on the other; but here I can see no law to be followed, nor a judge to decide. In such circumstances it would be ridiculous to want to refer to an explicit decision made by the general will: it would be simply the claim submitted by one side in the lawsuit. For the other side, therefore, it would be only the wish of a particular external body, inclined on this occasion to injustice and subject to error. Thus, in the same way as a particular will cannot represent the general will, so too, if what it is concerned with is particular, the general will changes its nature. Inasmuch as it is general, it cannot pronounce on a man or an act. When the Athenian people, for example, chose and dismissed its chiefs, or decreed honours for one man and punishment for another, and through a multitude of particular decrees exercised indiscriminately all the functions of a government, it did not then have a general will in the proper sense of the term; it was not acting as the sovereign authority, but as the government. This will seem contrary to the usual view; but I must be given time to put mine.*

From this it will be understood that the factor which makes the will general is not so much the number of persons voting, but rather the common interest that unites them, for under this system everyone necessarily submits to the conditions that he imposes on the others; self-interest and justice are in marvellous harmony, bestowing on communal decisions an impression of equity which is notably absent from any discussion on a particular matter, because of the lack of a common interest to unify and integrate the judge's criterion with that of the interested party.

By whichever method we go back to our principle, we always arrive at the same conclusion, namely, that the social pact establishes so great a degree of equality between citizens that they all commit themselves to the same conditions and ought all to enjoy the same rights. Thus by the nature of the pact every act of sovereignty, that is to say every authentic act of the general will, creates an obligation or a benefit for all the citizens equally, so that the sovereign authority has jurisdiction* exclusively over the body of the nation, without giving special treatment to any of its members. What then is an act of sovereignty, properly speaking? It is not an agreement made between superior and inferior, but an agreement between the body and each of its members. The agreement is legitimate, because it is based on the social contract; it is equitable, because it applies to all; beneficial, because its object can only be the general good; and firmly based, because it is guaranteed by communal strength and the supreme power. As long as subjects of the state submit only to such conventions as this, they are not obeying anyone except their own will; and to ask the extent of the respective rights of subjects and citizens is to ask how far the citizens' obligations extend towards themselves, each one towards all, and all towards each one.

We therefore see that the sovereign power, absolute as it is, sacred and inviolable as it is, does not and cannot go beyond the limits of general agreements, and that any man can make full use of that share of his goods and liberty that is left him by these agreements. Consequently the sovereign authority never has the right to place a heavier burden on one subject than on another, because the matter would then become a particular decision, and be outside the sovereign's jurisdiction.

If these distinctions are accepted, nothing is truly renounced by private individuals under the social contract; but instead their situation becomes preferable, in reality, as a result of the contract, to what it was before.* Instead of abandoning anything they have simply made a beneficial transfer, exchanging an uncertain and precarious mode of existence for a better and more secure one, natural independence for liberty, the power of hurting others for their own safety, and reliance on their own strength, which others might overcome, for a position of right that social unity makes invincible. Even their lives, which they have surrendered to the state, are continually protected by it, and when risking life in its defence what are they doing but paying back what it has given them? All have to fight for their country in case of need, it is true; but also, no one ever has to fight for himself. Is it not an advantage to face, for the sake of security, some part of the dangers that we should have to face for ourselves if that security were removed?

Chapter v

The Right of Life and Death

I⊤ has been asked how it is that private individuals, lacking the right to dispose of their own lives, can transfer to the sovereign a right that they do not have.* The question seems difficult only because it is badly put. Every man has the right to risk his own life in order to preserve it. Has it ever been argued that a man is guilty of suicide if, in order to escape from fire, he jumps out of the window? Has such a crime ever been so much as imputed to a man who, knowing the risk as he boards the ship, perishes in a storm at sea?

The purpose of the social treaty is the preservation of the contracting parties. He who wills an end wills the means to that end: and the means in this case necessarily involves some risk, and even some loss. He who wills that his life may be preserved at the expense of others must also, when necessary, give his life for their sake. But the citizen ceases to be the judge of occasions on which the law requires him to risk danger; and when the ruler* has said: 'It is in the state's interest that you should die', he must die, because it is only on this condition that he has hitherto lived in safety, his life being no longer only a benefit due to nature, but a conditional gift of the state.

The death penalty for criminals may be considered from broadly the same point of view: it is to avoid being the victim of murder that we consent to die if we become murderers. According to this pact, our aim is, of course, not to give up our lives, but to preserve them; it is not to be supposed that any of the contracting parties has it in mind to get himself hanged.

Moreover, every wrongdoer, in attacking the rights of society by his crimes, becomes a rebel and a traitor to his country. By violating its laws he ceases to belong to it, and is even making war on it. The preservation of the state becomes incompatible with his own; one of the two must perish; and when a criminal is put to death, it is as an enemy rather than as a citizen.* His trial and the sentence are the proofs and the declaration that he has broken the social treaty and is consequently no longer a member of the state. But since he has acknowledged his membership, if only by his place of residence, he must be removed from it, by exile inasmuch as he has infringed the contract, or by death inasmuch as he is a public enemy. An enemy of this kind is not an abstract entity personified, but a man, and in such a case the right of war is to kill the vanquished.

It will be said, however, that the condemnation of a criminal is a particular act. Agreed: that is why it is not the sovereign's function to condemn him, but a right that it can delegate even though it is not able to exercise it. My arguments being interdependent, I cannot explain them all simultaneously.

It should be added that frequent use of the death penalty is always a sign that the government is feeble or lazy. There is nobody so wicked that he cannot be made useful in some respect. The right to inflict death, even in order to make an example, applies only to a man whose life cannot be preserved without danger.

As regards the right of pardon, or of exempting a criminal from the penalty decreed by law to which the judge has sentenced him, it is the prerogative solely of an authority superior to judge and law, that is, the sovereign. Even so, its rights in this matter are none too clear,* and should be used very seldom. In a well-governed state there are few punishments, not because pardons are often granted but because there are few criminals; when the state is in decline, the multiplicity of crimes ensures impunity. In Rome, under the Republic, neither the Senate nor the consuls ever attempted to grant pardons; nor did the people, though it sometimes revoked its own sentences. Frequency of pardon implies that crime will soon need it no longer, and anyone can see where that leads. But I can feel that my heart is protesting and restraining my pen: let us leave these questions to be debated by the just man who has never sinned, and never had to be pardoned himself.

Chapter vi

*The Law**

BY the social pact we have given existence and life to the body politic; we must now, by legislation, give it the ability to will and move. For the act by which this body is originally formed and unified does nothing to determine what it must do so as to preserve itself.

That which is good, and in conformity with order, is such by the nature of things, independently of human convention. All justice comes from God, he alone is its source; and if we knew how to attain it at so great a height, we should need neither government nor laws. Undoubtedly, absolute justice exists, emanating from reason alone; but in order for it to be accepted among men, it has to be reciprocal. To consider things in human terms, the laws of justice, if lacking any natural sanction, are without effect among men. They merely benefit the wicked and harm the just when the just man observes them towards everyone while no one observes them towards him. Conventions and laws are necessary, therefore, in order to combine rights with duties, and to enable justice to fulfil its object. In the state of nature, in which everything is common property, I owe nothing to others, having promised them nothing; the only things that I recognize as belonging to others are those that are no use to me. It is not the same in the civil state, where all rights are defined by law.

What then, finally, is a law? As long as we are content to define the word in metaphysical terms alone,* we shall go on failing to understand what we are arguing about, and even when we have defined a law of nature we shall be no closer to knowing what a law of the state is.

I have already said* that the general will cannot relate to a particular object. For any particular object of will is either inside the state, or outside. If it is outside the state, a will foreign to it is not general with respect to it; and if it is a thing inside the state, it forms part of it, and in that case, the relationship created between the whole and its part is such that they are two separate things, one being the part and the other the whole minus that part. But a whole lacking a part is not a whole, and as long as this relationship subsists there is no longer a whole, but two unequal parts; whence it follows also that the will of the one is no longer general with respect to the other.

But when the whole people makes a ruling for the whole people it is concerned with itself alone, and the relationship, if created, is between the whole object from one point of view and the whole object from another, the whole remaining undivided. Then the matter on which the ruling is made is general, as is the will that makes it. It is this act that I call a law.

When I say that the objects of laws are always general, I mean that the law considers the subjects of the state as a collectivity and actions in the abstract, but never a man as an individual, nor any particular action. Thus the law can rule that privileges will exist, but it cannot bestow them on any person by name; the law can create different classes of citizen, or even define the qualifications for membership of these classes, but it cannot name this man or that man as members; it can establish a monarchical government and hereditary succession, but cannot elect a king or name a royal family. In a word, no function relating to an individual object belongs to the legislative power.*

It is at once clear, from this principle, that we must no longer ask who has the right to make the laws, since they are acts of the general will; nor whether the ruler is above the law, since he is a member of the state; nor whether the law can be unjust, since no one can be unjust towards himself; nor how it is possible to be free and subject to the laws, since they are nothing but the record of our acts of will.

We can see also, since the law combines universality in its object with universality of will, that anything ordained by a man on his own account, whatever his position, is not a law. Even what the sovereign ordains concerning a particular object is not a law, but a decree; nor is it an act of sovereignty, but of administration.

Consequently I call *republic* any state ruled by laws,* whatever the form of its administration: for it is only thus that the public interest governs, and that all things public count for something. All legitimate governments are republican:[1] I shall explain what is meant by *government* later.

Laws properly speaking are no more than a society's conditions of association. The people, being subject to the laws, must create them; it is the associates who have the right to determine the conditions of society. But how are they to determine them? By sudden inspiration bringing common agreement? Has the body politic some organ by which to articulate its wishes? Who will give it the foresight it needs to produce acts of will and publicize them in advance, or how, in time of need, will it make them known? How can the blind multitude, often ignorant of what it wants, because it seldom knows what is good for it, accomplish by itself so large and difficult an enterprise as a system of legislation? The people, of itself, always wants the good, but does not, of itself, always see it. The general will is always in the right, but the judgement guiding it is not always enlightened. The general will needs to be shown things as they are, and sometimes as they ought to appear, to be taught which path is the right one for it to follow, to be preserved from the seductiveness of particular wills, to have comparisons of times and places made for it, and be told of those remote and hidden dangers which counterbalance the attractions of visible, present advantages. Individuals can see the good and reject it; the public desires the good and cannot see it. All equally need guides. The one side must be obliged to shape their wills to their reason, the other must be taught the knowledge of what it wants. It is then that, from public enlightenment, comes the union of understanding and will in the social body; the parts are then in precise concordance, which results in the greater strength of the whole. This is why it is necessary to have a legislator.

---

[1] By this word I do not refer only to aristocracies and democracies, but in general to any government directed by law, which is the general will. In order to be legitimate it is not necessary that the government should be indistinguishable from the sovereign, but that it should be the minister of the sovereign: then even a monarchy is a republic. This will be clarified in Book III.

Chapter vii

The Legislator

IN order to discover which rules of society suit nations best, a mind of a superior kind would be required, able to see all human emotions, while feeling none; without relationship to our nature, but knowing it to its depths; enjoying its own happiness independently of us, but prepared to be concerned with ours; a mind, in sum, which while preparing distant glory for itself in the fullness of time, could carry out its work in one century and enjoy its achievement in another.[1] It is gods that are needed to give laws to men.

The argument put by Caligula* as regards fact was put by Plato as regards right, in discussing the political leader or man of state, whom he seeks to define in his *Statesman*.* But if it is true that a great ruler is rare, what of a great legislator? The one has only to follow a pattern, the other must devise it; the legislator is the inventor of the machine, the ruler is the mechanic who sets it up and makes it work. 'When societies are born', says Montesquieu,* 'it is the leaders of republics who create their institutions, and afterwards it is the institutions that produce the leaders of the state.'

The man who dares to undertake the establishment of a people has to feel himself capable of changing, so to speak, the nature of man; of transforming each individual, who in himself is a perfect, isolated whole, into a part of a larger whole from which the individual, as it were, receives his life and being; of altering man's constitution in order to strengthen it; of substituting a morally dependent existence for the physically independent existence that we have all received from nature. In a word, he must deprive man of his own strength so as to give him strength from outside, which he cannot use without the help of others. The more completely these natural strengths are

---

[1] A nation becomes famous only when its legislation is on the decline. It is not known during how many centuries Lycurgus's institutions ensured happiness for the Spartans before the rest of Greece took note of them.

destroyed and reduced to nothing, the more powerful and durable are those which replace them, and the firmer and more perfect, too, the society that is constituted: so that, when each citizen is nothing and can do nothing except through others, and when the strength given by the whole is equal or superior to the natural strength of all the individuals together, it may be said that legislation has reached the nearest point to perfection that it can.

Within the state, the legislator is a man extraordinary in every respect. If he is so by genius, he is no less so by function. His office is not a public office, and it is not sovereignty. The function of constituting the republic does not form part of its constitution, but is specific and superior, having nothing in common with human authority; if he who has control of men ought not to control the laws, then he who controls the laws ought not to control men: otherwise his laws would minister to his passions, often doing no more than perpetuate his unjust actions; and he would never be able to prevent his interests as an individual from impairing the sanctity of the work.

When Lycurgus gave laws to his country, he began by abdicating the throne. In most Greek towns, it was the custom to entrust the establishment of their laws to foreigners. The modern Italian republics have often imitated this habit; the republic of Geneva did the same and did well.[1] At Rome's finest period, the city witnessed in its midst the rebirth of all the crimes of tyranny, and came close to destruction, because legislative authority and sovereign power had been combined in the same persons.*

Yet even the decemvirs never arrogated to themselves the right to enact laws on their authority alone. 'None of our proposals', they told the people, 'can become law without your consent. Romans, you must yourselves authorize the laws that will ensure your happiness.'

---

[1] Those who regard Calvin* only as a theologian fail to recognize the extent of his genius. The wisdom of our edicts, to the drafting of which he contributed much, does him as much honour as the *Institutes*. Whatever changes time may bring in our religion, the memory of so great a man will always be blessed among us, so long as love of country and love of liberty are not extinct.

He who frames the laws, therefore, has not, or should not have, any rights of making law; the people cannot, even if it wished to, divest itself of these incommunicable rights, because, according to the fundamental pact, only the general will can be binding on individuals, and it can never be certain that something willed by a particular person is in conformity with the general will until it has been submitted to the free vote of the people. I have already said this, but it is worth repeating.*

We find in the business of legislation, then, two things that seem incompatible: an enterprise seemingly beyond human ability, and nothing, by way of authority, with which to carry it out.

There is another difficulty that deserves notice. Wise men who try to address the common people not in its own language, but in theirs, cannot make themselves understood. But there are innumerable ideas which cannot be translated into the language of the people. Projects of too great generality and concerns that are too remote are equally beyond its reach: each individual, disapproving of any plan for government except the one that suits his own particular interest, has difficulty in perceiving the advantages he must gain from the deprivations that are continually imposed on him by good laws. In order that a people in the process of formation should be capable of appreciating the principles of sound policy and follow the fundamental rules of reasons of state,* it would be necessary for the effect to become the cause; the spirit of community, which should be the result of the constitution, would have to have guided the constitution itself; before the existence of laws, men would have to be what the laws have made them. Thus the legislator is unable to employ either force or argument, and has to have recourse to another order of authority, which can compel without violence and win assent without arguing.

That is why the founders of nations have been forced in every period to resort to divine authority and attribute their own wisdom to the gods,* in order that their peoples, who are subject both to the laws of the state and those of nature, should recognize the same power in the creator of man and in the creator of society, obeying freely and submitting meekly to the enforcement of public felicity.

It is the decisions of this higher reason, beyond the scope of average men, that the legislator ascribes to the Immortals, so

that those who cannot be moved by human prudence will be
led by divine authority.[1] But it does not lie in every man to
make the gods speak, nor to be believed when he proclaims
himself to be their spokesman. The great soul of the legislator
is the true miracle by which his mission is proved. Any man
can write on tablets of stone, or pay for an oracle, or pretend
to be in secret communication with some divinity, or train a
bird to speak in his ear, or find other crude methods of
deceiving the people. A man who knows no more than this may
even, perhaps, be able to gather together a band of demented
followers; but he will never found an empire, and his wild work
will soon perish with him. The bond formed by empty marvels
is ephemeral; only wisdom makes it endure. The Jewish law
that still subsists, and the law of the child of Ishmael,* which
has governed half the world for ten centuries, demonstrate even
today the greatness of the men who decreed them; and while
arrogant philosophers or blind partisanship* see them merely
as fortunate impostors, the true statesman is awed, seeing what
they have established, by that greatness and power of mind
which presides over lasting creations.

From all this, we should not conclude like Warburton that
politics and religion have for us the same objective,* but that
when nations are formed the one serves as instrument to the
other.

Chapter viii

The People

IN the same way as an architect, before constructing a great
building, studies and probes the soil to see whether it will bear
the weight, the wise creator of institutions will not begin by

---

[1] 'And in truth', says Machiavelli, 'there was never an outstanding legislator,
among any people, who did not resort to God, for otherwise his laws would not
have been accepted. There are many advantages known to the prudent man,
which have in themselves no self-evident reasons making it possible to convince
others of them.' *Discourses on Livy*, Bk. I, ch. xi.

drafting laws good in themselves, but will first consider whether the people for whom they are intended is capable of receiving them. This is why Plato refused to give laws to the Arcadians and Cyrenians, since he knew that these two nations were rich and could not tolerate equality; and why in Crete there were good laws and bad men, because Minos had imposed discipline on a people corrupted by vice.*

A multitude of nations have dazzled the earth, but could never have borne good laws, and even for those that could do so it was possible only for the briefest period of their existence. Peoples,* like men, are amenable only when they are young; in old age they become incorrigible. Once customs are established and prejudices ingrained, it is a dangerous and futile enterprise to try to reform them; the people cannot bear to have the disease treated, even in order to destroy it, like those stupid and fearful patients who tremble at the sight of the physician.

Nonetheless, just as some illnesses shake up men's minds and deprive them of the memory of the past, sometimes there are periods of violence during the lifetimes of states, when revolutions have the same effect on nations as certain medical crises on individuals, and revulsion against the past acts like a loss of memory; the state is then, in the flames of civil war, reborn from its ashes, so to speak, and, escaping from the embrace of death, recovers its youthful strength. This happened to Sparta in the time of Lycurgus; to Rome after the Tarquins; and in our own times to Holland and Switzerland after their tyrants were expelled.*

But such events are rare and exceptional, and the reason for the exception always lies in the way in which a particular state is constituted. Nor can the same thing happen twice to one nation, for as long as it is merely uncivilized it can gain its freedom, but it can no longer do so when the springs of social action are worn out. Civil strife can then destroy it, but a revolution cannot revive it; as soon as its chains are broken, it falls into fragments and no longer exists: thereafter it needs a master, not a liberator. There is a maxim that free peoples must remember: Liberty can be acquired, but never regained.

There is a time of maturity in nations as in men,* for which it is necessary to wait before imposing laws on them; but the maturity of a nation is not always easy to recognize, and if action is taken prematurely it will fail. Certain nations can be disciplined when they are born, others cannot even after ten centuries. The Russians will never have a true political order, because they were given one too early. The genius of Peter the Great was for imitation; he did not have true creative genius, of the kind that makes something out of nothing.* Some of the things he did were good, but the majority were misplaced. He realized that his nation was barbarous, but not that it was not yet ready for political organization; he attempted to civilize it when all that was needed was to train it for war. He wanted to produce Germans and Englishmen immediately, when he should have begun by producing Russians: by persuading his subjects that they were something different from their real selves, he prevented them from ever becoming what they could have been. In the same way a French tutor trains his pupil to shine while he is still a child, and to be a nonentity ever afterwards. The Russian Empire will attempt to subjugate Europe and will be subjugated itself. The Tartars, its subjects or its neighbours, will become its masters and ours; it seems to me inevitable that such a revolution will occur. All the kings of Europe are working together that it may happen the sooner.

Chapter ix

The Same Continued

JUST as nature has put limits to the size of a well-formed man, and outside these limits produces only dwarfs or giants, so too, when it is a question of the best constitution for a state, there are limits to the size that it can have, in order that it should neither be too large to be well governed, nor too small to continue to exist on its own. In every political body there is a maximum strength which it cannot exceed, and which it often loses by becoming larger. The further the social bond is stretched, the weaker it gets; and in general a small state is proportionately stronger than a large one.*

There are innumerable reasons for this principle. In the first place, administration is more difficult over large distances, just as a weight becomes heavier at the end of a longer bar, and it also becomes more onerous as the hierarchy of divisions increases; each town, to start with, has its administration, paid for by the inhabitants; each district too has its own, also paid for by the inhabitants; then each province; then the greater administrative areas, satrapies or vice-royalties, the cost of which increases from one level to the next, but still at the expense of the unhappy inhabitants; finally comes the supreme administration that crushes everything underneath.* All these added burdens are a continual drain on the subjects' resources: far from having a better administration at the different levels, they are less well governed than if there were only one above them. There are scarcely any reserves left for emergencies, and when it is necessary to resort to them the state is always on the brink of ruin.

Nor is this all. Not only is the government less swift and vigorous in seeing that the laws are observed, in preventing exactions, redressing abuses, and forestalling the attempts at sedition that can arise in distant places, but the people has less affection for its leaders, whom it never sees, for its country, which it regards as the whole world, and for its fellow-citizens, most of whom are strangers. The same laws cannot be appropriate for all the various provinces, which have different customs and are situated in different climates; while a diversity of law can only engender conflict and confusion among peoples who, having the same leaders and in continual communication, move from one area to another and marry there, never knowing, as they become subject to other customary laws,* whether their heritage is really theirs. Talents are hidden, virtues ignored, and vice goes unpunished among all the multitude of men, unknown to each other, who are gathered together in one place because it is the seat of the supreme administration. The rulers, overburdened by the amount of business, see nothing for themselves, and their clerks govern the state. Finally, the measures necessary in order to maintain the central authority, which so many of its distant representatives try to evade or deceive, absorb all the energies of the public officers; what remains for the welfare of the people is insufficient, and there is scarcely enough for defence in case of need; in this way, a body too large for its own constitution declines and perishes, collapsing under its own weight.

On the other hand, the state must provide itself with a sound base so as to have some solidity, and withstand both the shocks that will inevitably come its way, and the efforts that it will be obliged to make in order not to succumb: for all peoples have a kind of centrifugal force by which they act upon each other constantly, tending to increase their size at the expense of their neighbours, like the vortices of Descartes.* Thus the weak are in danger of being soon swallowed up; and virtually the only way for any one of them to maintain itself is to place itself in a kind of equilibrium with the rest, making the pressure more or less the same everywhere.

It will be apparent from this that there are reasons for expansion and reasons for contraction; and it is not the least of the political thinker's talents to find, in considering both, the proportion best suited to the preservation of the state. In general it can be said that the reasons for expansion, being external and relative, ought to be subordinated to the reasons for contraction, which are internal and absolute. A healthy and robust constitution is the first thing to look for; and more reliance should be put on the vigour born from good government than from the resources furnished by a great area of land.

I should add that there have been certain states organized in such a way that the need to make conquests entered into their very constitution; in order to maintain themselves they were constantly forced to expand. They may perhaps have congratulated themselves on this happy necessity, in which, however, they could have seen that the time when their greatness reached its limit would inevitably be the time of their fall.*

Chapter x

The Same Continued

A POLITICAL body can be measured in two ways: either by the extent of its territory, or by its population; and the most suitable size for the state depends on the proper relationship between these two measures. It is men that make a state, and it is the land that feeds men: the relationship, then, is that the land should be sufficient to provide sustenance for its inhabitants, and that there should be as many inhabitants as the land can feed. The maximum strength of a given population lies in this ratio; for if there is too much land, it is burdensome to guard, it will not be fully cultivated, and some of its produce will be superfluous; it will be a direct cause of defensive war. If there is not enough land, the state depends, in order to make up the deficiency, on the goodwill of its neighbours, which is a direct cause of offensive war. Any nation which, through its position, has no alternatives except trade and war is intrinsically weak; it depends on its neighbours, it depends on events; its existence is always uncertain and brief. Either it makes conquests and changes its situation, or it is conquered and annihilated. It can preserve its freedom only through being very small or very large.

It is impossible to give a fixed numerical ratio for the area of territory and the number of inhabitants that adequately support each other, not only because of the variables that are found in the qualities of the land, its degree of fertility, the nature of its crops, and the effect of the climate, but also because of those that are observable in the temperament of those who live on it, some consuming little in a fertile land, others much on difficult soil. Attention must also be paid to the greater or lesser fertility of the women, to features of the country that may be more or less favourable to population, and to the increase in population that the legislator can hope to encourage by his institutions; so that he should not base his judgements on what he sees, but what he foresees, and should take less account of the present state of the population than of the figure which it will naturally reach. And lastly there are innumerable occasions on which accidents of terrain require or permit the acquisition of more or less land than might seem necessary. Thus the territory will extend further in mountain-ous country, where the natural products, namely those of woodland and pasture, require less work, where experience tells us that the women are more fertile than in the plain, and where a large area of sloping ground is contained in a small horizontal space, the only area that must be counted where vegetation is concerned. On the other hand, the territory can be reduced in coastal regions, even when rock and sand render them almost sterile, for the reasons that fishing can in large part replace the products of the land; that the population needs to be denser in order to repel pirates; and in addition that it is easier, through colonization, to relieve the land of a surplus of inhabitants.

To these conditions for constituting a nation another needs to be added, which does not make up for the deficiency of any, but without which all are useless: it is that the nation should enjoy prosperity and peace; for the time when a state is in the process of being organized, like the time when a batallion is being formed, is when as a unit it is least capable of resisting and easiest to destroy. More resistance would be put up at a time of complete disorder than when things are in a ferment, and everyone is absorbed by questions of rank, not by danger. Should a war, or famine, or revolt occur at a critical period of this kind, the state would inevitably be overthrown.

This does not mean that governments are not frequently set up during such storms; but then it is the governments them-selves that destroy the state. Usurpers always foment or choose times of trouble in order to play on public anxiety and so gain acceptance for harmful laws that the people would never adopt with cooler heads. The time chosen for constituting the nation is one of the clearest marks by which to distinguish the act of a legislator from that of a tyrant.

What kind of people, then, is best suited for legislation? One which, already united by some bond due either to its origins or its interests or to an agreement, has as yet not truly submitted to the yoke of law; one whose customs and superstitions are not deeply embedded; one that has no fear of being overrun by a

sudden invasion; that without taking part in its neighbours'
quarrels is able to resist each of them on its own, or to repulse
one with the help of another; one where each member is
known to all, and where there is no necessity to inflict on any
man a burden heavier than a man can carry; one that can do
without other nations and which every other nation can do
without;¹ one that is neither rich nor poor, but capable of
maintaining itself; finally, one that combines the solidity of an
old nation with the malleability of a new one. What makes the
work of legislation onerous is not the necessity of creating so
much as the necessity of destroying; and what makes success so
uncommon is the impossibility of finding the simplicity of
nature together with the needs of a society. It is true that all
these conditions are not often met with in combination; which
is why few states are well constituted.

There is still one country in Europe that is fit for legislation:
the island of Corsica. The valour and constancy shown by the
worthy Corsicans in regaining and defending their freedom
fully entitle them to be shown by some wise man how to
preserve it.* I have a presentiment that this small island will
one day be the amazement of Europe.

Chapter xi

The Various Systems of Legislation

IF we seek to define precisely the greatest good of all, the
necessary goal of every system of legislation, we shall find that
the main objectives are limited to two only: *liberty* and *equality*;
liberty, because any form of particular subordination* means

---

¹ If there were two neighbouring peoples, one of which could not manage
without the other, the situation would be very hard for the first and very
dangerous for the second. In such a position, any wise nation will quickly attempt
to release the other from dependence. The republic of Tlaxcala, an enclave in
the Empire of Mexico, preferred to do without salt rather than buy it from the
Mexicans, or even be given it *gratis*. Wisely, the Tlaxcalans saw the trap
concealed behind this generous offer. They kept their freedom; and the little state
enclosed in the great empire was eventually the instrument of its destruction.*

that the body of the state loses some degree of strength; and equality because liberty cannot subsist without it.

I have already explained civil liberty;* as for equality, the word must not be taken to mean that the degrees of power and wealth should be exactly the same, but that, as regards personal power, it should not be so great as to make violence possible, and should be exercised only in accordance with social position and the law; and as regards wealth, that no citizen should be rich enough to be able to buy another, and none so poor that he has to sell himself:[1] and this depends on those of high position exercising restraint concerning property and influence, and on the common people restraining their greed and envy.

Equality, it is said, is a theorists' vision, which cannot exist in practice. But if an abuse is inevitable, does it follow that it should not at least be controlled? It is precisely because the force of things always tends to destroy equality that the force of law should tend always to conserve it.

But these general aims for any good scheme of legislation must be modified in every country by the relationships that arise both from its geographical situation and from the character of the inhabitants, and it is on the basis of these relationships that a particular system of laws must be devised for each people, a system which may not, perhaps, be the best in itself, but will be the best for the state for which it is intended. For example, suppose that the soil is hard to work and barren, or the country too cramped for its inhabitants—encourage crafts and industry, the products of which can be exchanged for the commodities that you lack. If on the contrary you live in rich plains and on fertile slopes, or if, on good land, you lack people, devote yourself wholly to agriculture, which causes the population to multiply, and expel crafts and industry, since all they would do is to depopulate the country entirely, by crowding together the country's few inhabitants in a small

[1] If you wish to give the state cohesion, bring the limits of wealth and poverty as close together as possible: do not allow either extreme opulence or destitution.* The two are inseparable by nature, and both are equally damaging to the common good; one produces the instruments of tyranny, and the other produces the tyrants. It is always between them that public liberty is traded, one buying and the other selling.

number of locations.[1] Do you have a long shoreline, easily approached?—cover the sea with ships, apply yourself to trade and navigation, and your existence will be brilliant and short. Do the waves around your coasts beat on almost inaccessible rocks?—then remain primitive and make fish your diet; your life will be more peaceful, perhaps better, and certainly happier. In a word, besides the principles that apply to every nation, there is in each people some cause why they should be applied in a particular manner, making its legislation suitable for it alone. Thus the Hebrews in ancient times, and the Arabs recently, have made religion their primary concern; the Athenians, culture; Carthage and Tyre, trade; Rhodes, its navy; Sparta, war; and Rome virtue. The author of *The Spirit of Laws* has given a multitude of examples showing the skill with which a legislator directs a system of law towards each of these aims.*

The constitution of a state is made truly solid and lasting if the fitness of things is so carefully observed that natural relationships and the laws meet at the same points, the latter doing no more, as it were, than confirm, accompany and rectify the former. But if the legislator mistakes his purpose and follows some principle other than the one arising from the natural situation; if the former should tend towards servitude and the latter to freedom; one to wealth, the other to populousness; one to peace, the other to conquest: then we shall see the laws growing gradually weaker, the constitution will deteriorate, and the state will suffer constant disturbances, until it has been either destroyed or reformed, and nature, which is invincible, has reasserted its power.

---

[1] Any branch of foreign trade, according to M. d'Argenson, brings only false advantages to the nation as a whole; it may enrich a few individuals, or even a few towns, but the nation in general gains nothing from it and the people does not benefit.

Chapter xii

The Categories of Law

In ordering the whole, or giving the republic the best possible form, there are various relationships to consider; first is the relationship of the whole to itself, or of the sovereign authority to the state. It is a composite of the relations between the intermediate terms, as we shall see later.*

The laws regulating this relationship are known as political law. They are also called fundamental law, and not without reason, provided that they are wise; for if in each state there is only one way to order it well, the people that has found it should hold on to it; but if the established order is bad, why should the laws preventing it from being good be regarded as fundamental? Besides, however the case may stand, a people is always free to change its laws, even the best of them;* for if it chooses to do itself harm, who has the right to stop it?

The second relationship is that between the members of the state themselves, or between them and the whole body, and this relationship should be, in the first case, as slight as possible, and in the second as close as possible; in order that each citizen should be perfectly independent of all the others, and extremely dependent on the state; and this is always achieved by the same means, since only the strength of the community can create freedom for its members. This second relation gives rise to civil law.*

A third kind of relation between men and law may be considered, namely, that between disobedience and punishment. This gives occasion for the establishment of criminal laws, which at bottom are not so much a particular category of law as the sanction of all others.

In addition to these three categories of law there is a fourth, which is the most important of all; it is not graven in marble or bronze, but in citizens' hearts; in it lies the true constitution of the state; its strength augments day by day; when other laws decay or become extinct it revives or replaces them, it maintains in the nation the spirit of its constitution, and imperceptibly changes the force of authority into the force of habit. I refer to moral standards, to custom, and above all to public opinion: a part of law that is unknown to our political theorists,* although success in every other part depends on it; an aspect with which a great legislator concerns himself secretly, while seeming to limit himself to specific ordinances. These are only the ribs of the arch, while morals, which are longer in the making, finally become its unshakable keystone.

Of these categories only political law, which establishes the form of government, relates to my subject.*

BOOK III

BEFORE discussing the various forms of government, let me try to define the exact sense of the word, which has not yet been very fully explained.

Chapter i

Government in General

I SHOULD warn my readers that this chapter must be read without haste, and that I am ignorant of the art of making myself clear to those who do not wish to concentrate.

Every free act has two causes, which cooperate in order to produce it. The one, which is moral,* is the will that decides on the act, and the other, which is physical, is the force that carries it out. When I walk towards a thing, it is necessary in the first place that I should want to go towards it, and in the second that my feet should take me there. If a paralysed man wants to run, and if an able-bodied man does not want to, both will stay where they are. The body politic has the same causes of action, and in it we likewise discern force and will, the former under the name of *executive power* and the latter under that of *legislative power*. Nothing is done, or should be done, unless they are in accordance.

We have seen that legislative power belongs to the people, and can belong to it alone.* It is easy to see, on the other hand, following the principles established above, that executive power cannot belong to the generality of the citizens in their legislative or sovereign capacity, because this power consists only in particular decisions, which fall outside the domain of law, and in consequence outside that of the sovereign, every act of which can only be a law.

Public force must therefore have its own agent, to unify it and give it effect following the directions of the general will, to provide the means of communication between state and sovereign, and to fulfil in the political entity the function that is performed in a man by the union of body and soul. This is the reason, in a state, for government, which has been inappropriately confused with the sovereign, of which it is only the minister.

What, then, is government? It is an intermediate body set up between subjects and sovereign to ensure their mutual correspondence, and is entrusted with the execution of laws and with the maintenance of liberty, both social and political.

The members of this body are called *officers* or *kings*,* that is to say *governors*, and the body as a whole has the name of *ruler*.[1]* Hence those who maintain that the act by which a people submits to the authority of chiefs is not a contract* are perfectly correct. Government taken absolutely is only a function or employment, in which the agents of the sovereign exercise in its name the power which it has deposited with them, and which it may limit, modify, or take back when it pleases, the transfer of its rights in these respects being incompatible with the nature of the social body and contrary to the purpose of association.

What I call *government*, then, or supreme administration, is the legitimate exercise of the executive power, and I call *ruler* or principal officer* the man or body of men entrusted with this administration.

It is in government that are located those intermediate forces the relationship between which constitutes the relationship of all to all, or of sovereign to state. The latter may be expressed as the relationship which obtains between the two outside terms of a geometric proportion, the middle term being the government.* The government receives commands from the sovereign and gives them to the people, and for the state to be properly in balance it is necessary, when all the appropriate adjustments have been made, that equivalence should be maintained between the power of the government, or of the middle term multiplied by itself, and the power of the citizens, or of the

---

[1] Thus in Venice the College of Senators is given the name of Most Serene Ruler, even when the Doge is not present.

product of their power as sovereign on one side, multiplied by their power as subjects on the other.

Further, it is impossible to alter any of the three terms without immediately destroying the proportion. If the sovereign insists on governing, or the officers of government insist on making laws, or the subjects refuse to obey, control is replaced by disorder, will and force no longer act in harmony, and the state disintegrates, falling into despotism or anarchy. Lastly, since any three-term proportion can have only one middle term, so too in a state only one good government is possible; but since innumerable eventualities can alter relationships within a nation, different forms of government may not only suit different nations, but may suit the same nation at different times.

In order to try to illustrate the various relationships which may exist between the extremes, I shall take as an example the figures for population, as being the easiest to express as a proportion.

Let us suppose that the state is composed of ten thousand citizens. The sovereign can be thought of only collectively, as a single entity. Yet each particular person, in his capacity as subject, is considered as an individual. Thus the relationship of sovereign to subject is as ten thousand to one. In other words, each member of the state has only one ten-thousandth share of the sovereign authority, although he is entirely subject to it. If the population consists of a hundred thousand men, the position of the subject stays unaltered, each submitting equally to the whole authority of the laws, while the power of his vote is reduced to one hundred-thousandth, and his influence over the creation of law is ten times less. The subject remaining a single unit, then, the relationship between the sovereign and himself grows wider in proportion to the number of citizens. Whence it follows that the larger the state becomes, the more liberty decreases.

When I say that the relationship grows wider, I mean that it moves further away from equivalence. Thus the proportion in mathematical terminology is greater, but in ordinary language the relationship becomes less;* in the former case the relationship is considered quantitatively, and is measured by the division of the last term by the first, while in the latter it is considered according to the nature of the things involved, and is measured by the degree of resemblance.

Accordingly, the smaller the relationship between the wills of individuals and the general will, that is, between moral standards and the law, the greater the force of restraint should be. If, therefore, the government is to be a good one, it must be proportionately stronger according as the size of the population increases.

From another point of view, since any increase in the size of a state gives those who are entrusted with public authority greater temptation, and greater opportunities, to abuse their power, it follows that the greater the strength possessed by the government for the restraint of the people, the greater should be the strength that is possessed by the sovereign in its turn, in order to restrain the government. I am not speaking here of strength in absolute terms, but of the relative strength of the various elements in the state.

The existence of this double relationship means that the concept of a proportion connecting sovereign, ruler, and people is not arbitrary, but a necessary consequence of the nature of political society. Further, since one of the outside terms of the proportion, namely the people considered as subject, is fixed, and represented by a single unit, it also means that whenever the ratio of the outside terms increases or diminishes, the ratio of each to the middle term increases or diminishes similarly, with the result that the middle term alters. This shows that there is no uniquely valid form of government, but that there may be as many governments of different natures as there are states of different sizes.

If it were to be said, turning my theory to ridicule, that in order to find the middle term of the proportion all that is required, in my view, is to take the square root of the population figure, I should reply that I take this number only as an example, and that the relationships which I am discussing cannot be measured solely in terms of numbers of men, but more generally by the quantity of action, which is generated by a multitude of causes; and besides, that although I have borrowed from the terminology of mathematics, in order to express myself in fewer words, I am nonetheless aware that mathematical precision is out of place in the measurement of moral behaviour.

A government is the same on a small scale as the body politic containing it is on a larger scale: a moral agent* endowed with certain faculties, being active like the sovereign and passive like the state, and subsuming, when analysed, other similar relationships. Whence is derived in consequence a new proportional relation, and within this another, as we rise through the ranks of government, until we arrive at a middle term that is not susceptible to further analysis, that is, at a single leader or supreme ruler, who may be represented as unity, at the centre of this progression, situated between the series of fractions and that of whole numbers.

Without becoming involved with this multiplicity of terms, let us be content to consider the government as a new body within the state, distinct from, and intermediate between, people and sovereign. There is an essential distinction between these bodies: the state exists of itself, while the government exists only through the sovereign. Thus the dominant will of the ruling body is only, or should only be, the general will or the law, its power is only the public power concentrated in it, and as soon as it has the desire to do some absolute and independent act of its own, the cohesiveness of the whole begins to be weakened. If at last it were to happen that the ruling body's particular will were more vigorous than the sovereign's, and if, to obey this particular will, it resorted to the public power deposited with it, so that there were to be two sovereigns, so to speak, one by right and the other in fact, then social union would at once disappear, and political society would disintegrate.

However, in order that the body composing the government should have its own existence, a genuine life of its own, making it distinct from the body of the state, in order that all its members may act in concert and fulfil the purpose for which it is established, it needs to possess an individual self, a common sensibility among its members, its own will and force tending to self-conservation. It is a condition of this single mode of existence that there should be assemblies, councils, the power

to deliberate and decide, rights, titles, and privileges belonging
exclusively to the ruler, which will bring the greater honour to
the position of ruling officer in proportion as his post is more
burdensome. Difficulties arise in settling how, within the whole,
this subordinate whole should be ordered, so as to ensure that
it does not weaken the general constitution in strengthening its
own, that it always distinguishes between its own power, meant
for its conservation, and the public power meant for the
conservation of the state, and in a word that it is always ready
to sacrifice the government to the people, and not the people
to the government.

However, although the government is an artificial body, and
created by another artificial body, living as it were a borrowed
and subordinate life, that does not prevent it from acting with
greater or less energy and speed, or from enjoying, so to speak,
more or less robust health. Finally, without completely neglecting the purpose for which it was established, it may diverge
from it more or less, according to the way in which it is
organized.

It is from all these differences that arise the diverse relations
into which the government enters necessarily with the body of
the state, according to the contingent and specific relationships
which affect the state itself. For it can often happen that
intrinsically the best government becomes the most defective, if
its relationships are not modified in accordance with the
deficiencies of the political body to which it belongs.

Chapter ii

The Constituent Principle of
the Various Forms of Government

In order to explain the general cause of these differences, a
distinction must now be made between ruler and government,
in the same way as I distinguished previously between state and
sovereign.

The body of government officers can consist of a larger or
smaller number of members. We have stated* that the relation-

ship of the sovereign authority to the subjects is a ratio that grows wider in proportion as the population is larger, and we can say the same about the government in relation to its members, the parallel being evident.

Further, the total strength of the government, always being the same as the state's, does not vary. From this it follows that the more strength it expends on its own members, the less remains to act on the people as a whole.

Consequently, the larger the number of officers of government, the weaker the government is. Since this principle is fundamental, let us attempt to elucidate it.

In the person of an officer of government, we can discern three essentially different wills: first, the will pertaining to the individual, which tends only to his particular advantage; secondly, the will common to the members of the government, which relates solely to the advantage of the ruling body, and which can be called a corporate will, being general in respect of the government and particular in respect of the state, the government being a part of the state; and in the third place, the will of the people or the sovereign will, which is general both as regards the state considered as a whole, and as regards the government considered as part of the whole.

Under an ideal legislation, the individual or particular will should count for nothing, the corporate will pertaining to the government for very little, and consequently the general or sovereign will should always dominate, and be the rule that uniquely determines the others.

In the natural way of things, however, these different kinds of will become more vigorous in proportion as they are more concentrated. Thus the general will is always weakest, the corporate will has second place, and the particular will comes first of all; so that, in the government, each person is primarily himself, then a member of government, and then a citizen—an order of priorities which is the exact contrary of the one demanded by the social order.

Let us suppose that all government is in the hands of a single man: then we have the individual's will and the corporate will perfectly combined, and the second is at the highest degree of concentration possible. Since it is on the degree of will that the use of force depends, and since the government's power does not vary, it follows that the most vigorous form of government is government by one person.

To get the contrary case, let us unite government and legislative authority; let the sovereign be ruler, and all the citizens be so many members of government. Then the corporate will is indistinguishable from the general will, and its degree of vigour will also be the same, leaving the strength of individual wills undiminished. In this case the activity or relative power of the government, which still has the same power absolutely speaking, is at a minimum.

These relationships are indisputable, and other considerations will also serve to confirm them. It is clear, for instance, that each officer of government is more active within it than the citizen is within the community as a whole, and consequently that a particular will has much more influence in acts of government than in acts of sovereignty; for a member of government is almost always responsible for some governmental function, whereas a citizen, taken singly, has no separate function within the sovereign. Moreover, the further the state expands, the more its real power increases, although power does not increase in proportion to extent; but when the state remains the same size, there is no point in increasing the size of the government, since it does not thereby acquire any greater real power, its power being that of the state and remaining a constant value. In this case the government's relative strength or activity diminishes and it cannot increase its real or absolute strength.

It is certain, moreover, that business is dealt with less expeditiously as the number of people responsible for it increases: that relying too much on prudence means relying too little on chance, that opportunities are not taken, and that the fruits of decision are often lost in the process of deciding.

What I have just demonstrated is that government becomes less effective in proportion as the officers of government multiply, and I have demonstrated previously* that the greater the population is, the more the force of containment ought to be increased. Whence it follows that the ratio between the government and its members should be the inverse of that between the sovereign and its subjects: that is to say, that the more the state expands, the more the government should contract, so that the number of those governing is reduced as the population rises.

I should add that I am speaking here only of the government's relative strength, not of its rightfulness*: for in the opposite case, the greater the number of officers of government, the closer their corporate will approaches to the general will; whereas, when a single person governs, that same corporate will is no more than a particular will, as I have said. Thus a loss on one side can be a gain on the other, and the legislator's skill consists in knowing how to define the point where the government's strength and will, still in reciprocal proportion, are combined in the most advantageous ratio for the state.

Chapter iii

The Classification of Governments *

THE reasons for distinguishing governments into various kinds or forms according to the number of members composing them have been given in the preceding chapter; it remains to see in this how the various governments are created.

In the first place, the sovereign can entrust the responsibility of government to all the people or to the greater part of the people, so that more citizens will be members of the government than are simply individual citizens. The name given to this form of government is *democracy*.*

Or it can restrict government to a small number, so that more will be simply citizens than are members of the government; and this form bears the name of *aristocracy*.

Finally it can concentrate the whole of government in the hands of a single officer, from whom all the others take their power. This third form is the commonest, and is called *monarchy*, or royal government.

It should be observed that all these forms, or at least the first two, can occur in varying degrees, and within quite wide limits;

for democracy can comprise the entire people, or no more than half. Aristocracy in turn can cover anything from half of the people down to the smallest possible number. Even royalty is capable of being shared to some extent. Sparta, under its constitution, always had two kings, and in the Roman Empire up to eight emperors at once were known, without it being possible to say that the empire was divided. Thus there comes a point at which each form of government is indistinguishable from the next, which shows that in reality, though there are only three denominations of government, it is capable of having as many different forms as the state has citizens.

Not only this, but since it is possible for the same government to be split up, in certain respects, into further divisions, one arranged in one way and another in another, the three forms in combination can produce a multitude of mixed forms, and each one can be multiplied by all the simple forms.

At all times there has been much debate about the best form of government, without regard to the fact that each of them is the best in certain cases, and the worst in others.

If in the different states the number of officers of the supreme government must be in inverse ratio to the number of citizens, it follows that in general the democratic form of government will suit small states, the aristocratic form states of moderate size, and the monarchic form large states. This rule is derived directly from the principle above; but how are we to assess the multitude of circumstances which may create exceptions?

Chapter iv

Democracy

THE person who makes a law knows better than anyone else how it ought to be executed and interpreted. It would therefore seem that the best constitution would be one in which the executive power is united with the legislative; but it is just this that makes such a government deficient in certain respects, because things that ought to be distinct are not, and the ruling body and sovereign, being personally the same, produce nothing more, so to speak, than a government which is without government.

It is not good that the person who makes laws should execute them, nor that the body of the people should turn its attention from general considerations towards particular matters. Nothing is more dangerous than the influence of private interests in public affairs, and the abuse of law by the government is a lesser evil than the corruption of the legislative body, to which particular considerations inevitably lead. The substance of the state will be changed, with no possibility of reform. If a people were never to misuse government it would never misuse independence; a people that always governed well would not need to be governed.

If the term is taken in its strict sense, true democracy has never existed and never will. It is against the natural order that the majority should govern and the minority be governed. It is impossible to imagine the people permanently in session in order to deal with public affairs, and it is easy to see that it could not set up commissions for the purpose without the form of administration being altered.

I believe furthermore that we can state as a principle that, when the functions of government are divided between a number of bodies, the greatest authority passes sooner or later to those with the fewest members, if only because their facility in transacting business naturally brings matters before them.

Besides, what an unusual combination of circumstances is presupposed for this government to exist! First, a very small state, such that the people can be assembled without difficulty, and it is easy for every citizen to know all the others; secondly, great simplicity of manners, in order to avoid a great quantity of business and tiresome discussions; further, a considerable degree of equality in rank and fortune, without which equality in rights and power cannot last long; and finally, little or no luxury, for luxury either derives from wealth or makes it necessary; it corrupts both rich and poor at once, one through possession, the other through covetousness; it puts the country on sale to vanity and soft living; it deprives the state of all its citizens, making each of them subject to the other, and all of them to public opinion.

This is why a famous author made virtue the principle of republics,* for these circumstances cannot all be present without virtue; but not having made the necessary distinctions, despite his genius, he often lacks precision and sometimes clarity, and did not see that, the sovereign authority being the same everywhere, the same principle should apply in every properly constituted state, though in greater or less degree, it is true, according to the form of its government.

It should be added that no government is so liable to civil war and internal disturbance than the democratic or popular type, for none has so strong and continual a tendency for its form to change, and none calls for so much vigilance and courage if its form is to be maintained. Under this constitution, more than any other, the citizen must arm himself with strength and constancy, and repeat every day in the depths of his heart the observation made by a virtuous lord palatine[1] in the Polish Diet: 'I prefer freedom with all its dangers to tranquillity with servitude'.*

If there were a nation of gods it would be governed democratically. So perfect a government is not suitable for men.

Chapter v

Aristocracy

HERE we have two very distinct corporate moral agents, namely the government and the sovereign; and in consequence two general wills, one relating to all the citizens, the other only to the members of the administration. Hence, although this government can regulate its internal organization as it wishes, it can never speak to the people unless it is in the name of the sovereign, which means in the name of the people themselves; a point that must never be forgotten.

The first societies were governed aristocratically. The heads of families debated public affairs among themselves, and the

[1] The Count Palatine of Posen, the father of the present King of Poland and Duke of Lorraine.*

young yielded without difficulty to the authority of experience. Hence come the words *priest, elders, senate, gerontes.** The savages of North America are still governed in this way today, and are governed very well.

But, as the inequalities of society become more important than natural inequalities, wealth or power[1] came to be preferred to age, and aristocracy became elective. Finally, along with property, power was transmitted from father to son, which by creating patrician families made the government hereditary, and senators were seen who were twenty years old.

Aristocracy is therefore of three kinds: natural, elective, and hereditary. The first is only suited to simple societies; the third is the worst of all forms of government.* The second is the best; it is aristocracy in the true sense of the word.*

It has the advantage not only that it separates the two powers,* but that its members are selected; for with popular government all citizens are members of it by birth; but membership of aristocratic government is limited to a few, and is obtained by election:[2] by which means integrity, intelligence, experience, and all the other reasons for preference and public esteem, are so many additional guarantees of wise government.

Furthermore, assemblies of government are more easily arranged, its business is better debated and transacted with greater order and diligence, and respected senators will uphold the state's reputation abroad better than an unknown or despised populace.

In a word, the best and most natural order of things is that the wisest should govern the multitude, so long as it is certain that they will govern it for its advantage and not for theirs. The means of action ought not to be needlessly increased, nor twenty thousand men made to do a task that a hundred

[1] It is clear that the word *optimates*, in antiquity, did not mean the best, but the most powerful.*

[2] It is imperative that the manner of electing members of the government should be regulated by law; for if it is left to the wishes of the ruler, a hereditary aristocracy will be the inevitable result, as has happened in the republics of Venice and Berne. In Venice the state has long been non-existent; but in Berne it has been preserved by the extreme wisdom of the Senate: which makes it a very honourable but very dangerous exception.

selected men can do better. But it must be noted that corporate interest here begins to follow less closely the rule of the general will in directing public power, and that by another inevitable process some part of the executive power is no longer available to the law.*

As regards the particular suitability of aristocracy, the state should not be so small, nor its people so simple and upright, that the execution of laws immediately follows the public will, as in a good democracy. Nor should the nation be so large that, those governing it being far distant from each other, each can set himself up as sovereign in his area, and begin by making himself independent in order to end up as master.

But if aristocracy requires slightly fewer virtues than democratic government it also requires some of its own, for instance that the rich should use their wealth moderately and the poor be content with their lot; for it would seem that strict equality would be out of place; even in Sparta it was not maintained.

Moreover, if this government entails some financial inequalities, it is certainly in order that the administration of public business should generally be entrusted to those who can most easily devote all their time to it, and not, as Aristotle claims, in order that the preference should always fall on the wealthy.* On the contrary, it is important that the opposite choice should sometimes teach the people that a man's worth can include more important causes of preference than money.

Chapter vi

Monarchy*

HITHERTO we have considered the ruling body as a collective artificial person, made a unity by force of law, and entrusted within the state with executive power.* We have now to consider this power when it is entirely in the hands of a natural person, a real man, so that he alone has the right to exercise it according to the laws. He is called a monarch or king.

Reversing the position under other administrations, where a collective being is seen as* an individual, here an individual is seen as a collective being, so that the artificial unity constituting the ruling body is at the same time a physical unity, in which all the faculties that the law takes such trouble to combine in the other types of government are associated naturally.

Thus the will of the people, the will of the ruler, the public strength of the state, the private strength of the government, all respond to a single impulse, all the energy of the mechanism is under single control, everything serves the same purpose; there are no opposing forces that nullify each other, and under no other constitution that can be imagined does less effort produce greater action. Archimedes, calmly sitting on the shore and drawing a great ship over the water,* is for me the image of a skilful monarch, governing his huge territories from his study, and making everything move while seeming to be immobile.

But if there is no other government that has so much vigour, there is also none in which a particular will has so much influence and so easily dominates the others: everything serves the same purpose, it is true; but that purpose is not public felicity, and the very strength of the administration constantly operates to the detriment of the state.

Kings want absolute rule, and the cry reaches them from afar that the best way to get it is to make their people love them. It is a fine maxim, and even, in some respects, very true. Unfortunately, among courtiers it will always be derided. The power that comes from the love of the people is certainly the strongest; but it is precarious and conditional; it will never satisfy a ruler. The best of kings want the power to do harm if they wish, without ceasing to be masters. The preacher of political sermons can tell them as often as he likes that, since their strength lies in the strength of their people, their own best interest is that the people should multiply, prosper, and be feared; kings know very well that this is not true. Their personal interest is primarily that the people should be weak and wretched, and that it should never be capable of resistance. I admit that, supposing that his subjects were always perfectly submissive, the ruler's interest might then supposedly be that the people should be powerful, so that their power, being his, would make him formidable to his neighbours; but since this interest is only secondary and subordinate, and the two

suppositions I have made are incompatible, it is natural that
rulers should always give preference to the maxim which is of
most immediate use to them. It was strongly argued by Samuel
addressing the Hebrews; it was demonstrated with the utmost
clarity by Machiavelli,* who, while he pretended to give
instruction to kings, gave valuable lessons to their peoples.
Machiavelli's *Prince* is a book for republicans.[1]

We have established* by abstract reasoning that monarchy is
suitable only for large states, and if we examine it in itself we
shall find the same thing. The more numerous those responsible for government, the less the numerical difference between
ruling body and subjects, and the more nearly equal their
relationship becomes, so that in a democracy the relationship
is unity, or true equivalence. This relationship widens according as the government contracts in numbers, and is at its
maximum when the government is in one man's hands. The
distance between ruler and people is then too great, and the
state loses cohesion. In order that it should be restored,
intermediate orders are therefore necessary:* and in order that
they should be filled, royal princes, great lords, a nobility. None
of this, however, is suitable for a small state, which is ruined by
all these graded ranks.

But if it is difficult for a large state to be well governed, it is
much more so for it to be well governed by a single man, and
everyone knows what happens when a king chooses others to
act in his place.*

An intrinsic and unavoidable defect in monarchical government, which will always make it inferior to a republic,* is that
in a democratic government those who are put into high office
by public vote are almost always enlightened, capable men,
who perform their duties with honour; whereas in a monarchy

---

[1] Machiavelli was a man of integrity and a good citizen; but as a servant of the
Medici family he was forced, while his country was oppressed, to disguise his love
of liberty. Simply by the choice of his execrable hero he revealed his secret
purpose; and the difference between the maxims in his book on the Prince and
those in his *Discourses on Livy* and *History of Florence* demonstrates that he was a
politician of great profundity, whose readers have hitherto been either superficial
or corrupt. The Vatican has strictly banned his book: that was only to be
expected; it is the Vatican that he most obviously describes.

the ones who succeed are petty incompetents, petty scoundrels, petty intriguers, whose trivial talents, those that bring great success at a court, serve only to show the public their owners' ineptitude as soon as they gain office. In making its choices the public errs much less than a king; and it is almost as uncommon to find a minister of genuine ability under a monarchy as a fool at the head of a republican government. As a result, when by some happy chance one of those men who are born for government takes charge of administration in a monarchy almost ruined by a collection of smart jacks-in-office, his resourcefulness is a matter of astonishment, and marks a new epoch in the country's history.*

For a monarchical state to be well governed, its size or extent would need to be calculated so as to suit the abilities of the person governing. It is easier to conquer than to administer. If you had the world at the end of a long enough lever, you could move it with your finger; but to support the world on your shoulders you would need to be Hercules. For a state of any size, the ruler is almost always too small. When the contrary happens, and the state is too small for its ruler, which is very rare, it is still not well governed, because its leader, his mighty projects constantly in mind, forgets the interests of his people, and renders them no less unhappy by misusing his superfluous talents than does an incompetent leader through his lack of capacity. It would be desirable if, so to speak, the kingdom expanded or shrank with each reign, according to the abilities of the new monarch; whereas under a senate, with its more stable range of talent, the state can have fixed limits and the administration will be carried on equally well.

The most evident drawback of government by a single person is the absence of the successive replacements which, in the two other forms, ensure uninterrupted continuity. A king dies, another is required; his selection leaves a dangerous interval; troubles can develop, and unless the citizens show a degree of disinterestedness and integrity that this form of government hardly encourages, plots and corruption play their part. It is rare for someone to whom the state has sold itself not to sell it again in his turn, extorting money from the weak in compensation for the payments he made to the powerful. All things are for sale, sooner or later, under a government of this kind, and the peace enjoyed under such a king is worse than the disorder of an interregnum.

What remedies have been devised for these ills? The crown has been made hereditary within particular families; and an order of succession has been drawn up which eliminates any dispute when a king dies: which means that, the inconveniences of a regency having been substituted for those of an election, the risks of being ruled by children, monsters or imbeciles have been preferred to the necessity of debating the choice of a good king.* What has been lost to sight is that, given the risks in the contrary possibility, the odds are against a favourable outcome. The young Dionysius made a very shrewd remark when his father said, reproaching him for a shameful action: 'Was it I who set you that example?' Said his son: 'Ah! but your father wasn't a king.'*

All things combine to prevent the man who is brought up to command others from possessing justice and reason. Much trouble is taken, so it is said, to teach young princes the art of ruling, but it does not appear that they derive any advantage from their education. It would be better to begin by teaching them the art of obeying. The great kings most celebrated in history were not brought up to rule; it is a form of knowledge that is known least well by those who have studied it most, and which is better acquired by obedience than by giving orders. 'For the quickest and best way of deciding between good things and bad is to ask what you would have wanted and would not have wanted if someone else had been ruler.'*

One consequence of this discontinuity is the inconstancy of royal government, which first follows one plan, then another, according to the king's character, or the character of those who rule for him, and cannot long maintain stability of purpose or consistency in policy: its changeableness makes the state veer from principle to principle and from project to project, something that does not occur with other forms of government, where the ruler remains the same. Moreover, it is noticeable that in general, if greater cunning is to be found at court, there is more wisdom in a senate, and that republics achieve their purposes through steadier and more coherent policies; by contrast, every change of minister under a monarch produces an upheaval in the state, since the principle that is common to all ministers, and to almost all kings, is to do the opposite from their predecessors in everything.

The same lack of continuity is the key to refuting a sophism well known to apologists for royalty: it consists not only in comparing the government of a country to that of a household, and the ruler to the head of a family, an error that I have already disproved,* but also in generously giving their officer of government every virtue that he might need, and forever assuming that a king is what he ought to be: on this assumption, royal government is evidently preferable to any other, since it is undoubtedly the strongest, so that, in order to be also the best, the only thing lacking is a governmental will more in conformity with the general will.

But if, as Plato says,[1] it is so rare to find a man who is a king by nature, how often will nature and chance combine to put one on the throne? And if the education given to royalty necessarily corrupts its recipients, what is to be expected from a succession of men brought up to reign? To confuse royal government with government by a good king, therefore, is deliberate self-deception. In order to see what royal government is in itself, it has to be studied in the persons of kings who are without ability or ill-disposed; for either that is what they are on reaching the throne, or else what they become once there.

These problems have not been overlooked by the theorists, but they have not troubled them. The remedy, they say, is to obey without dissent: God in his wrath gives us bad kings, and they must be endured as a punishment from Heaven.* This is certainly an edifying way to talk, but it may be thought more suitable for the pulpit than for a book on politics. What would we think of a doctor who promised miracles, and whose only treatment was to exhort the sick to patience? Everyone knows that when we have a bad government we must put up with it; the question is how to find a good one.

[1] In his *Statesman*.

Chapter vii

Mixed Forms of Government

STRICTLY speaking, no simple form of government exists. A single leader must have subordinate officers; a government of the people must have a leader. Thus in the distribution of executive power there is always a gradation, going from the larger number to the smaller, the variation being that sometimes the larger number depends on the smaller, and sometimes the smaller on the larger.

On occasion the distribution is equal, either when the component parts are mutually dependent, as with the English constitution, or when the authority of each part is independent, but incomplete, as in Poland.* This last form is bad, because there is no unity in the government, and the state lacks cohesion.

Which is better, a simple or a mixed form of government? The question is much debated among theorists, and calls for the same answer as I gave above when discussing governments in general.*

Simple government is best in itself, precisely because it is simple. But when the dependence of the executive power on the legislative is not great enough, that is to say when the relative dominance of ruler over sovereign is greater than that of the people over the ruler, the disproportion must be remedied by making a division in government; for when it is divided each of the parts has no less authority over the subjects, while the division between them makes them together less powerful with respect to the sovereign.

The same disadvantage can also be avoided by creating intermediate officers, whose only purpose, the government remaining undivided, is to maintain the balance between the two powers and preserve their respective rights. The government is then not mixed, but modified.*

Similar means can be used as a remedy for the contrary failing: when the government is too weak, commissions* can be established in order to reinforce it; this is what is done in all democracies. In the previous case the government was divided in order to weaken it, and in this one in order to strengthen it; for the maximum amounts both of strength and weakness are to be found in the simple governments, and average amounts in the mixed forms.

Chapter viii

That Not All Forms of Government Are Suitable for Every Country

FREEDOM is not a product of every climate, and is not within the reach of every people. The more we reflect on this principle, laid down by Montesquieu,* the truer we feel it to be. The more objections we make, the more openings we give for new arguments to confirm it.

Under every government throughout the world the public person consumes, but does not produce. Where then does the substance it consumes come from? From the work of the members of the public. The subsistence of the public person is provided from the surplus produced by individuals. Whence it follows that civil society can maintain itself only so long as the product of men's work is in excess of their needs.

However, the surplus is not the same in every country in the world. In some it is considerable, in others moderate, in some there is none, while others have a deficit. The relationship depends on the fertility of the climate, on the kind of work demanded by the soil, on the nature of its produce, on the strength of the inhabitants, on the greater or lesser amounts they themselves need to consume, and on several other similar relationships which compose it.

Moreover, not all governments are of the same nature; they are more or less voracious; and the differences between them are based on another principle, namely, that contributions made by the public are the more burdensome the further they are removed from their source. The burden must not be measured by the amount of tax imposed, but by the distance it travels before it returns to the people who paid it. When the redistribution is rapid and well organized, it does not matter whether the payments are large or small; the people is always rich and the finances healthy. By contrast, when the amounts given in tax, however small they may be, do not return to those who pay, the constant giving soon impoverishes them; the state is never rich and the people always destitute.

From this it follows that tax contributions become the more burdensome as the distance between people and government increases. Thus in a democracy the burden on the people is least; in an aristocracy, it is greater; and it is heaviest in a monarchy. Monarchy is only suitable, therefore, to very prosperous nations; aristocracy to states whose wealth and extent are both moderate; and democracy to states that are small and poor.

The more one reflects on this point, indeed, the greater the difference it seems to make between free states and monarchies.* In the former, everything is made to serve the common interest; in the latter, public and private resources are in a relation of reciprocity, one becoming greater as the other diminishes. At the extreme, despotism reduces its subjects to poverty in order to govern them, instead of governing them in the aim of making them happy.

In each climate, then, there are natural causes making it possible to determine which form of government is called for by the influence of the climate, and even to say what kind of people should live there. Barren and difficult land, where the produce is not worth the labour, should remain uncultivated and uninhabited, or populated only by savages; places where men's labour barely produces the necessities of life, and no more, should be inhabited by barbarian tribes: any political organization would be impossible; places in which the surplus of produce over need is adequate are suitable to free peoples; those in which the land is abundant and fertile ought to have a monarchical government, in order that the subjects' additional surplus should be spent on the luxuries of royalty; for it is better that the excess should be absorbed by the government than dissipated by private citizens. There are exceptions, I know; but the exceptions themselves confirm the rule, in that sooner or later they produce upheavals which restore things to the natural order.

General laws should always be distinguished from particular causes which can affect their operation. Even if all the southern regions were to be covered by republics, and all the north by despotic states, it would nonetheless be true that, because of the effects of the climate, despotism suits hot countries, barbarism cold ones, and good political organization the regions in between. I realize however that, even if the principle is granted, there may be argument over the manner of its application: it may be said that some cold countries are very fertile, and some southern countries very unproductive. But this will only be an objection for those who fail to examine the matter in all its aspects. Among them, as I have already said, questions of the work required, physical strength, the consumption of food, etc., must also be considered.

Suppose two regions equal in extent, one having a yield of five units and the other of ten. If the inhabitants of the first consume four units, and those of the second nine, the surplus in the first case will be a fifth of the yield, and in the second a tenth. The surpluses being in inverse ratio to the yields, the region producing five units will give a surplus double that of the region producing ten.

But we are not concerned with a yield that is double another, and I do not believe that anyone would dare to say, in general, that the fertility of cold countries is even the equal of that of hot countries. However, let us assume that they are equal; we can, if we wish, put England on a level with Sicily, and Poland with Egypt. Further south we have Africa and India, and further north there is nothing. Given equality in the products, what difference is there as regards ease of cultivation? In Sicily you have only to scratch the surface of the earth; with what effort is it ploughed in England! So in places where more labour is needed to give the same yield, the surplus must necessarily be smaller.

Besides, you must take into account that the same number of men consume much less in hot countries. The climate there requires men to be frugal in order to stay healthy: Europeans who insist on living in the same way as at home all perish of dysentery or over-eating. 'In comparison with the Asians,' says Chardin,* 'we are wolves; carnivorous beasts. Some authorities ascribe the abstemiousness of the Persians to the fact that their country is less well cultivated; my own belief, on the contrary, is that it is less abundant in produce because the inhabitants need less.' He continues: 'If their frugality were the result of scarcity, it would only be the poor who eat sparingly, not everyone in general; and in each province people would eat more or less according to the region's fertility, whereas the same frugality is found throughout the kingdom. They pride themselves greatly on their way of life, saying that you have only to look at them to see how much better a complexion they have than the Christians. And in fact the Persians have an even complexion; their skin is good, fine and smooth; whereas the complexion of their subjects, the Armenians, who live in European style, is coarse and blotchy, and their bodies large and heavy.'

The closer one approaches the equator, the less the peoples eat. They have hardly any meat; their ordinary diet is rice, maize, couscous, millet, or cassava. In India live millions of men whose food costs less than a penny a day. Even in Europe, we can see noticeable differences in appetite between northern and southern peoples. One meal for a German will keep a Spaniard alive for a week. In countries where men are greedier, the form that luxury takes is also consumption: in England it consists in a table laden with meat; in Italy you are treated to sugar and flowers.

Again, there are corresponding differences as regards luxury in dress. In climates where changes of season are abrupt and extreme, clothes are better and simpler; where clothes are only for display, the aim is ostentation rather than usefulness. In Naples, you can see men walking on the Posilippo every day dressed in gold-braided coats but without stockings. It is the same with buildings: the only concern is grandeur when there is nothing to fear from bad weather. In Paris or London, people want to be housed warmly and comfortably; in Madrid, they have superb drawing-rooms, but the windows cannot be closed, and the bedrooms are rat-holes.

Foodstuffs are much more substantial and succulent in hot countries, a third difference that is bound to affect the second. Why do the Italians eat so many vegetables? Because they are good and nourishing and taste excellent. In France, where they get nothing but water, they are not at all nourishing, and are held in low esteem at table; but they occupy no less ground, and are at least as much trouble to cultivate. It is a fact of experience that Barbary wheat, inferior in other respects to the French varieties, gives much more flour, and that French wheat in turn gives more than in the north. From this it may be inferred that a similar progression may be generally observed as one goes from the equator to the pole. Is it not therefore a tangible disadvantage that equal amounts of produce give less by way of nourishment?

To all these different considerations I can add another which is derived from them and strengthens them: it is that hot countries need fewer inhabitants than cold countries, but can feed more; which produces a double surplus, again favouring despotism. If the same number of inhabitants occupy a larger surface area, rebellion becomes more difficult, because of the impossibility of taking concerted action quickly and secretly, and the ease with which the government can always discover plans and cut communications. But the greater the density of the population, the harder it is for a government to encroach on the sovereign authority: leaders can reach decisions in their houses as safely as the king in council, and a crowd can assemble as quickly in the streets as troops in their barracks. The advantage of a tyrannical government from this point of view, therefore, is that of acting over great distances. Its strength increases the further it extends, like that of a lever, helped by the points of support with which it provides itself.[1] The strength of the people, by contrast, is effective only when

[1] This does not contradict what I have said above (Book II, Ch. ix) about the disadvantages of large states; for there it was a question of the government's authority over its members, and here the question is its strength with regard to its subjects. Its officers in distant posts provide it with support to act from afar on its people, but it has no points of support for action directly on the officers. Thus the length of the lever makes it weak in one case, and strong in the other.

it is concentrated: it is dissipated and lost when spread out, like the force of gunpowder, which ignites only in the mass, and not when it is scattered on the ground. The least populous countries are consequently best suited to tyranny: wild beasts rule only in deserts.

Chapter ix

The Signs of Good Government

WHEN therefore it is asked unconditionally which is the best government, the question is both unspecific and insoluble; or, if you prefer, it has as many correct answers as there are possible ways of combining the relative and absolute circumstances of nations.

But if it were to be asked by what sign we can tell whether a given people is governed well or badly, things would be different; the question would be one of fact, and could be resolved.

However, no solution has been found, because everyone wants to answer in his own way. Subjects extol public order, citizens* the freedom of the individual; one prefers the security of property, and another security of the person; one asserts that the most rigorous government is the best, another argues for the mildest; this one wants crimes punished, that one wants them prevented; one likes to be feared by neighbouring nations, another prefers to be ignored; one is happy about the circulation of money, another insists that the people should have bread. Even if these points, and others like them, could be settled, should we be any further forward? Since degrees of value are not precisely measurable, how, supposing that agreement were reached concerning which sign to rely on, could we agree on its evaluation?

For myself, I am constantly surprised that the obvious sign goes unacknowledged, or that people have the bad faith not to agree about it. What is the purpose of political association? The security and prosperity of the associates.* And what is the most reliable sign that they are secure and prosperous? The population and the birth rate. There is no need to look any further for this much-debated sign. All other things being equal, the government under which, without recourse to extraneous means, with no naturalization or colonies, the citizens most flourish and multiply is indubitably the best. The one under which the population diminishes and wastes away is the worst. The matter is now for mathematicians to decide: let them count, measure, and compare.[1]

---

[1] The same principle should apply in judging which centuries in history have the best claim as regards the well-being of the human race. Those during which the arts and letters have been seen to flourish have been too much admired,* without any realization of the secret purpose behind their cultivation or any consideration of their dire consequences: 'And being unused to it they called it "refinement", though it was part of their enslavement.'* Can we never see, beneath the precepts laid down in books, the crude self-interest that motivates their writers? No, whatever they say, when a country's population declines in spite of its prestige, it is untrue that everything is going well, and it is not sufficient that a poet should have an income of a hundred thousand francs for his century to be the best of all.* Less emphasis should be put on the apparent calm and peacefulness enjoyed by a leading class and more on the well-being of whole peoples, especially in the most populous states. Hailstones damage a few cantons, but seldom cause a shortage of food. Uprisings and civil war make the leading citizens very scared, but are not a real misfortune for the people, who may even have some respite while the dispute about who is to oppress them is going on. It is their permanent situation that creates genuine prosperity or wretchedness for them: the time when everything is crushed beneath tyranny is also when everything declines; when their chiefs destroy them at leisure, and 'having brought desolation call it peace'.* But when the kingdom of France shook with the squabbles of the great, and the Coadjutor of Paris took a dagger in his pocket when going to the Parlement, the French people were not prevented from leading a happy and populous life, in decent circumstances and in freedom.* In ancient times Greece prospered at the height of the most savage wars; blood flowed in rivers, but the whole country was filled with people. According to Machiavelli: 'It seemed that in the middle of murders, proscriptions, and civil wars our republic was growing more powerful because of them; its citizens' virtue, their integrity and independence, did more to strengthen the state than their quarrels did to weaken it.'* A degree of disruption invigorates the soul, and it is not so much peace as freedom that makes the race thrive in a true sense.*

Chapter x

The Abuse of Government and
Its Tendency to Degenerate

JUST as a particular will constantly acts against the general will, so too the government exerts itself continually against the sovereign. The greater its efforts, the more the constitution deteriorates; and since there is no other corporate will to resist the ruling will, it must sooner or later come about that the ruler will dominate the sovereign authority and break the social contract. This is an inherent and unavoidable defect which, as soon as the body politic is born, tends ceaselessly to its destruction, in the same way as old age and death eventually destroy the human body.

Generally speaking there are two ways in which government degenerates: either when it contracts in size, or when the state is dissolved.

A government contracts when it passes from the hands of a larger number into those of a smaller: that is to say, from democracy to aristocracy, and from aristocracy to royalty. That is its natural tendency.[1] If it were to return from the smaller

---

[1] The gradual formation* and expansion of Venice in its lagoons provides a notable example of this evolution; and it is truly remarkable that, after more than twelve hundred years, the Venetians seem only to have reached the second stage, which began with the *Serrar di consiglio* in 1198.* As for their former dukes, an object of reproach for the Venetians, it has been proved, whatever the *Squittinio della libertà veneta** may say, that they were not sovereigns.

An objection that is bound to be made is that the Roman Republic, so it will be said, followed exactly the opposite course, passing from monarchy to aristocracy and from aristocracy to democracy.* I am very far from sharing this view.

The government first established by Romulus was mixed, and it promptly degenerated into despotism. The state perished before its time for special reasons, as a new-born child can die before reaching maturity. The real date of the birth of the Republic was the expulsion of the Tarquins. But the Republic did not immediately acquire a fixed form, because in failing to abolish the patriciate the Romans had left half the job undone. The result was that a hereditary aristocracy, which is the worst of the legitimate kinds of administra-

number to the larger, it could be said to expand: but this reverse movement is impossible.

For in fact a government never changes form unless the mainspring of its power wears out, leaving it too weak to preserve its own form. Then, if by expanding it were to grow slacker still, its power would diminish to nothing, and its life would be even shorter. The spring must therefore be wound up and tightened before it loses power: otherwise the state that depends on it will fall into ruins.

The case of the dissolution of the state can occur in one of two ways.

First, when the ruling body no longer administers the state in accordance with the laws, and usurps sovereign authority. The change that then takes place deserves notice: it is that the state, not the government, contracts in size; I mean that the greater state is dissolved, and that within it another is created, consisting only of the members of the government, which in relation to the rest of the people is no more than its master and tyrant. So that, as soon as the government usurps sovereignty, the social pact is broken; and every ordinary citizen, restored

tion, remained in conflict with a democracy, and the form of government stayed uncertain and ambiguous, to be fixed (as Machiavelli has shown)* only with the establishment of the tribunate; only then did a true government and a genuine democracy come into being. In reality the people was then not only sovereign, but also judge and minister of government; the Senate was no more than a subordinate body with the function of moderating or concentrating the government; and the consuls themselves, though they were patricians, and first ministers, and generals with absolute power when at war, were in Rome only the people's presidents.

Thenceforward it could be seen that the government, following its natural tendency, had a strong inclination to aristocracy. The patriciate ceased to exist almost of its own accord, and aristocracy was no longer confined to the patricians as in Venice or Genoa, but belonged to the senatorial body, which included both patricians and plebeians, and even to the tribunate when it began to usurp active powers: for words do not affect realities; and when the people has chiefs who govern for it, whatever name the chiefs bear, the government is still an aristocracy.

The abuse of aristocracy engendered the civil wars and the Triumvirate. Sulla, Julius Caesar and Augustus became, in the event, real monarchs; and finally, under the despotism of Tiberius, the state was dissolved. Roman history, therefore, does not contradict my principle, but confirms it.

by right to his natural liberty, is forced, but not obliged, to obey.*

The same case also occurs when members of the government separately usurp the power that they ought only to exercise as a body: which is no less an infringement of the laws, and produces even greater disorder. There is then, as it were, the same number of rulers as there are members of the government; and the state, being no less divided than the government, perishes or changes its form.

When the state is dissolved, a wrongful government of any type is given the general name of *anarchy**. To distinguish: democracy degenerates into *ochlocracy*, aristocracy into *oligarchy*; I might add that monarchy degenerates into *tyranny*; but the word is ambiguous and requires explanation.*

In the ordinary sense, a tyrant is a king who governs with violence, and without regard for justice and law. In the exact sense, a tyrant is a private individual who takes royal power for himself without having any right to it. This is the way in which the Greeks understood the word *tyrant*; they bestowed it on good and bad rulers alike if their authority was not legitimate.[1] Thus the words *tyrant* and *usurper* are exact synonyms.

In order to give different things different names, I shall call the man who usurps royal power a tyrant, and the man who usurps the sovereign power a despot. The tyrant is one who sets himself up against the law in order to govern according to law; the despot, one who puts himself even above the law. So the tyrant need not be a despot, but the despot is always a tyrant.

---

[1] 'For all those are considered and called tyrants who have perpetual power in a state that formerly had liberty' (Cornelius Nepos, in his life of Miltiades, ch. viii).—It is true that Aristotle (*Nicomachean Ethics*, Book VIII, ch. x) distinguishes between the tyrant and the king, in that the first governs for his own benefit and the second only for the benefit of his subjects; but apart from the fact that all the Greek writers generally took the word *tyrant* in another sense, as is clear above all from Xenophon's *Hieron*, it would follow from Aristotle's distinction that, since the world began, not a single king has ever been known.

Chapter xi

The Death of the Body Politic

Such is the natural and inevitable propensity even of the best constituted governments.* If Sparta and Rome have perished, what state can hope to last for ever? If we want the constitution that we have established to endure, let us not seek, therefore, to make it eternal. In order to succeed, we must not attempt the impossible, nor flatter ourselves into thinking that the works of men can be given a degree of solidity that is denied to human things.

The political body, like the human, begins to die as soon as it is born, and carries within it the causes of its own destruction. But the one and the other can be more or less robustly constituted, so as to be preserved for a longer or shorter time. Man's constitution is a product of nature; the state's is the result of artifice. It is not within men's power to extend their lives, but they are able to extend the life of the state for the longest time possible by endowing it with the best constitution that it can have. The best constituted state will come to its end, but later than others, provided that no unforeseen accident destroys it prematurely.

The principle of political life lies in the sovereign authority. The legislative power is the heart of the state, the executive power is the mind, which makes every part move. The mind may be unable to function yet the individual can still be alive. A man can be mindless and live, but as soon as the heart ceases to work the animal is dead.

It is not by its laws that the state subsists, but by the legislative power. Today, yesterday's law cannot compel: but tacit consent to it is assumed on the basis of silence, and the sovereign is deemed constantly to reaffirm every law that it refrains from abrogating while able to do so.* Anything that it has once declared to be its will remains its will, unless it is revoked.

Why then are ancient laws the object of so much respect? Precisely because they are ancient. We have to accept that only the excellence of what was willed long ago could have preserved them for such a time: if the sovereign had not acknowledged that they were constantly of benefit, it would have revoked them on innumerable occasions. That is why the laws in every well-constituted state, far from growing weaker, perpetually acquire new vigour; their age is in their favour, and makes them more venerable each day; by contrast, wherever the laws are weakened by age, it is a proof that the legislative power has gone, and that the state is without life.

Chapter xii

How Sovereign Authority Is Maintained

THE sovereign's only strength being its legislative powers, it acts only by its laws; and laws being nothing but the authentic decisions of the general will, the sovereign is unable to act unless the people is assembled. Assembled?—it will be said that I am having visions. It may be a vision today, but it was not two thousand years ago. Have men changed their nature?

In moral matters the limits of the possible are less narrow than we think: it is our weaknesses, our vices, and our prejudices that reduce them. Low minds do not believe in great men; worthless slaves smile in mockery at the word *liberty*.

Let us consider what can be done on the basis of what has been done. To say nothing of the republics of ancient Greece, the Roman Republic, it seems to me, was a great state, and the city of Rome a great city. The final census taken in Rome counted four hundred thousand citizens bearing arms, and the final enumeration of the Empire more than four million citizens, without counting subject peoples, foreigners, women, children, or slaves.*

What unimaginable difficulties there might seem to have been in holding frequent assemblies of the huge population of the capital and the surrounding area! Yet few weeks passed without an assembly of the Roman people, and often there were several. It exercised not only the rights of sovereignty, but a part of the rights of government. It transacted some business, it judged some lawsuits, and all the people, in public meeting-places, were almost as often members of the government as they were citizens.

If we were to go back to the history of nations at their beginnings, we should find that most of the ancient governments, even the monarchies, such as those of the Macedonians and Franks, held councils of this kind. However that may be, this indisputable fact alone answers every difficulty: to infer that something is possible if it has happened seems to me a logical argument.

Chapter xiii

The Same Continued

It is not sufficient for the people to have assembled once in order to settle the constitution of the state by giving its sanction to a body of law; nor is it enough for it to have established a government for perpetuity, nor to have arranged, once for all, the election of its officers of government. Apart from the extraordinary assemblies that may be required in unforeseen circumstances, there must be others, fixed at regular intervals, which nothing can abolish or postpone, so that on the appointed day the people are called together legitimately by the law alone, without the need for any other formal means of convocation.

But except for these assemblies fixed legally according to date, every assembly of the people which has not been called by the government officials appointed for the purpose, or which does not follow the prescribed form, must be regarded as unlawful and its proceedings as void, because the order for an assembly should itself emanate from the law.

As to how often legitimate assemblies should be held, it depends on so many considerations that no precise rule can be given. It can only be said, in general, that the greater the strength of the government, the more frequently the sovereign should make itself visible.*

These provisions, I will be told, may be suitable for a single town: but what if the state includes several? Will the sovereign authority be divided, or should it rather be concentrated in one town, and the others made subject to it?

My reply is that neither should be done. In the first place, sovereign authority is undifferentiated and unique, and cannot be divided without being destroyed. In the second place, neither a town nor a nation can legitimately be subject to another, because the essence of the body politic consists in the union of liberty with obedience, and the words *subject* and *sovereign* are precisely complementary, the concepts being united in the word *citizen*.

I also reply that it is always wrong for a number of towns to be combined into a single state, and that anyone attempting such a combination should be under no illusions that its inherent disadvantages can be avoided. Greater states and their defects should not be made into an objection to the views of one who wants only small states.—But how can small states be made strong enough to resist the greater?—In the same way as the Greek states once resisted the great Emperor, and as Holland and Switzerland more recently resisted the House of Austria.*

However, if the state cannot be limited to a proper size, one resource remains: it is to refuse to have a capital city, and to move the seat of government from town to town, where the country's Estates* will also be assembled in turn.

Spread the population evenly through your territory, extend the same rights everywhere, and everywhere bring life and abundance: this is the way to make the state as strong and as well governed as possible. Remember that town walls are always built from the ruins of houses that stood in fields. Whenever I see a palace being built in a capital city, I seem to see a whole country reduced to living in hovels.

Chapter xiv

The Same Continued

On the instant that the people is lawfully assembled as the sovereign body, all governmental jurisdiction ceases instantly, the executive power is suspended, and the person of the least citizen is as sacred and inviolable as that of the highest minister, because in the place where the body represented meets, there can be no representative.* Most of the disturbances at the Roman *comitia** arose from ignorance or neglect of this rule. The consuls became only the people's presiding officers; the tribunes, simply speakers;[1] the Senate was nothing at all.

These periodic suspensions of power, when the ruling body recognizes, or ought to recognize, its actual superior, have always been a source of alarm to it; and the assemblies of the people, which are a shield for the body politic and a check on the government, have at all times been dreaded by their leaders: which is why they have always made every effort, through making objections, difficulties, and promises, to discourage the citizens from holding them.* If the people is grasping, faint-hearted, and cowardly, fonder of leisure than of liberty, it will not hold out for long against constant pressure from the government; it is in this way that the sovereign authority is eventually dissipated, as the resistance to it continually increases, and thus most states fall, dying before their time.

But between the sovereign authority and arbitrary government a middle power is sometimes introduced, and of this I must now speak.

[1] In more or less the sense given to this word in the English Parliament. The similarity of function would have caused conflict between consuls and tribunes even had all forms of jurisdiction been suspended.

Chapter xv

Deputies or Representatives

As soon as serving the public is no longer the main concern of the citizens, and they prefer not to give service themselves, but to use their purses, the state is already near to ruin. Is there a battle to be fought?—they pay for troops and stay at home; are public decisions to be made?—they choose deputies and stay at home. Through being lazy and having money, they end up with soldiers to oppress their country and representatives to sell it.

Service done in person is changed into money because people are busy with their trade or craft, greedily self-interested for profit, lovers of comfort and material possessions. They surrender a part of their earnings so as to be at leisure to increase them. Pay out money, and soon you will be in chains. The word *finance* is for slaves, it is unknown in a real state. In a truly free state, the citizens do everything with their own hands, and nothing with money: far from paying in order to be exempted from their duties, they would pay in order to carry them out themselves. I do not share the ordinary view at all: I believe that taxes are more contrary to freedom than the enforced labour of the *corvée*.*

The better a state is constituted, the higher is the priority given, in citizens' minds, to public rather than private business. There is even a reduction in the amount of private business, because, when the total sum of public happiness contributes a larger portion to the happiness of each individual, there remains less for him to gain from his own efforts. In a well-ordered republic, everyone hurries to the assemblies; under a bad government, no one is willing to stir a step in order to be there, because no one is interested in what goes on there, nor believes that the general will will dominate, and finally because domestic affairs monopolize everything. Good laws make for better ones, bad laws bring worse. As soon as anyone says, about the affairs of the state, 'What does it matter to me?', the state must be regarded as lost.

The weakening love of country, the energy spent on private interests, the immense size of the state, conquests, and the abuse of government, have suggested the idea of having deputies or representatives of the people in national assemblies. They are what some countries dare to call the Third Estate.* Thus the private interests of two orders are ranked first and second; the public interest comes third.

Sovereignty cannot be represented, for the same reason that it cannot be transferred; it consists essentially in the general will, and the will cannot be represented; it is itself or it is something else; there is no other possibility. The people's deputies are not its representatives, therefore, nor can they be, but are only its agents; they cannot make definitive decisions. Any law that the people in person has not ratified is void; it is not a law. The people of England believes itself to be free; it is quite wrong: it is free only during the elections of Members of Parliament. Once they are elected, the people is enslaved, it is nothing.* Seeing the use it makes of liberty during its brief moments of possession, it deserves to lose it.

The idea of representation is modern: it came from feudalism, that unjust and absurd form of government which degrades the human race, and under which the name of *man* was dishonourable.* In the ancient republics, and even monarchies, the people never had representatives: the word itself was unknown. It is a most remarkable thing that in Rome, where the tribunes were so sacred, no one ever imagined that they might usurp the functions of the people, and that, even surrounded as they were by so great a multitude, they never once tried to hold a plebiscite on their own authority. Yet the problems sometimes caused by the throngs of people may be gauged by what happened at the time of the Gracchi, when a number of citizens cast their votes from the rooftops.

When right and liberty count above everything, inconvenience is nothing.* The wisdom of the Roman people put a true value on everything: it allowed its lictors to do what the tribunes would not have dared to;* it was not afraid that the lictors would try to represent it.

In order to explain the way in which the tribunes did sometimes represent it, however, it is enough to understand how the government represents the sovereign. Law being no more than the declaration of the general will, it is clear that as regards the legislative power the people cannot be represented; but it can and must be as regards executive power, this power being no more than the application of force to law. This shows that, if a careful analysis were made, it would be found that very few nations have laws. However that may be, it is certain that the tribunes, who had no part in the executive power, were never entitled to represent the Roman people by virtue of their office, but only by usurping the rights of the Senate.

Among the Greeks the people did for itself all that it needed to do: it was constantly in assembly in the town square. The Greeks lived in a mild climate; they were not avaricious; slaves did their work; their great concern was liberty. If these advantages are now lacking, how can the same rights be retained? Because of your harsher climate you have greater needs:[1] during six months of the year meetings cannot be held in the public squares; your indistinct tongues cannot be understood in the open air; you are more interested in profit than in freedom, and are less afraid of servitude than of being poor.

So can liberty be preserved only with the help of slaves? Maybe. The one extreme meets the other. Everything that is not natural has its disadvantages, and civil society more than anything else. There are some unhappy situations in which one's liberty can be kept only at the expense of another's, and the citizen can be perfectly free only if the slave is in complete servitude. Such was the position in Sparta. As for you, the modern nations, you have no slaves, but are enslaved; you are paying for their freedom with yours. It is all very well to boast that this is an improvement; I find it cowardly rather than humane.

I do not mean that it is necessary to have slaves, nor that there is a legitimate right to enslave, since I have proved the contrary:* I am simply giving the reasons why modern peoples that believe themselves free have representatives, and why the

---

[1] In cold countries, to adopt the Orientals' love of comfort and luxury is willingly to accept their servitude; it means being under an even greater necessity of submitting to it.

ancient peoples did not. Be that as it may, the moment that a people provides itself with representatives, it is no longer free; it no longer exists.

All things rightly considered, I cannot see how it is henceforward possible among us for the sovereign to retain the exercise of its rights unless the state is very small. But if it is very small, will it be subjugated? No. I shall show later[1] how the exterior power of a great nation can be combined with the good order and ease of administration found in a small state.

Chapter xvi

That the Institution of a Government
Is Not a Contract

ONCE the legislative power has been properly established, the executive power has to be instituted similarly; for since it operates only by acts concerning particulars, it is not essentially the same as the legislative power, and is naturally separate from it. If it were possible for the sovereign authority as such to have executive power, right and acts* would be indistinguishable, so much so that it would be impossible to tell what was a law and what was not; thus the body politic would be denatured, and would soon be prey to the violence which it was set up in order to resist.

All citizens being equal under the social contract, all may prescribe what all should do, whereas none has the right to require another to perform anything that he does not perform himself. But this right, which is indispensable if the body politic is to be made to move and live, is precisely what the sovereign gives the ruling body when it institutes a government.

Some writers have claimed* that the act of establishing a government is a contract between the people and the chiefs who are appointed by it, by which are stipulated the conditions

---

[1] This is what I had intended to do in the sequel to this work,* when in discussing external relations I would have included federation—a totally new subject, the principles of which have not yet been established.

under which one of the two parties binds itself to command and the other to obey. It will be agreed, I am sure, that this is a strange kind of contract to make! However, let us see whether the claim can be maintained.

First, supreme authority can no more be modified than it can be transferred; to restrict it is to to destroy it. It is absurd and contradictory that the sovereign should appoint a superior; to bind oneself to obey a master is to return to a condition of complete freedom.*

Furthermore, it is self-evident that a contract made between the people and certain individuals would be a particular act;* whence it follows that such a contract can be neither a law nor an act of sovereignty, and would consequently be illegitimate.

It will be seen also that, as between themselves, the contracting parties would be solely under the law of nature, without any guarantee that their mutual undertakings would be observed, which is inimical to civil society in every respect. The party which has force at its disposal always controls what is done, so that you might as well call it a contract if a man were to say to another: 'I will give you all I have, provided that you will return to me as much as you choose'.

As regards the state there is only one contract, that of association, which of itself excludes all others. No public contract can be conceived that would not be a violation of this first one.

Chapter xvii

The Institution of a Government

How then should we conceive the act by which a government is instituted? I note first that this act is complex, that is, it consists in two parts, namely the establishment of the law and the execution of the law.

By the first act, the sovereign lays down that a governing body will be established, taking such and such a form; and this act is clearly a law.

By the second, the people appoints the chiefs to whom the government that has been established will be committed; and their appointment, being a particular act, is not a further law, but a consequence of the first, or a function of government.

The problem is to understand how an act of government can occur before the government exists, and how the people, which can be only the sovereign or the subjects, can in certain circumstances become ruler or officer of government.

Here once again is displayed one of those astonishing features of the political body, enabling it to carry out operations which, in appearance, are contradictory; for what happens in this case is the instantaneous conversion of sovereignty into democracy, so that, without any change being visible, but only because of the new relationship between all and all, the citizens become officers of government, and their acts pass from the general to the particular, from making a law to its execution.*

This change in relationship is not a mere subtlety of theory, to which nothing corresponds in practice; it takes place as a matter of course in the English Parliament, where on certain occasions the Lower Chamber sits as a committee, for the more efficient discussion of business, and thus becomes merely a branch of government instead of a sovereign body, which it had been a moment earlier; so that it can later report to itself, as House of Commons, on what it has just decided in grand committee, and resumes the debate, in one capacity, of matters that it has already settled in another.

It is thus an advantage inherent in democratic government that it may be established in fact by a simple act of the general will. After which the provisional government will either retain its authority, if democracy is the form of government which has been adopted, or else it will set up, in the name of the sovereign, the form that has been prescribed by law; and so everything is in order. Any other manner of instituting the government cannot be legitimate and will be a renunciation of the principles set out above.

Chapter xviii

A Means of Preventing Government from Usurping Power

FROM these clarifications it follows, in confirmation of Chapter xvi, that the act by which a government is instituted is not a contract, but a law; that those to whom the executive power is committed are not the masters of the people, but its officers; that it may, as it pleases, confer office on them and deprive them of it; that for them there is no question of entering into a contract, but of obeying; and that in undertaking the functions laid on them by the state, they are doing no more than fulfil their duties as citizens, without in any way having the right to disagree over conditions.

When therefore it is a hereditary government that is instituted by the people, whether it is within one family in a monarchy, or within one order of citizens in an aristocracy, it is not a commitment that the people makes, but a provisional form that it gives to the administration, until it sees fit to arrange things differently.

It is true that changes of this sort are always dangerous, and that no alterations should be made in an established government, except when its continuance is incompatible with the public good; but this circumspection is a rule of policy, not a principle of right, and the state is no more compelled to leave civil authority with its leaders than military authority with its generals.

It is also true that, when the case arises, one cannot take too much care in observing all the formalities that are required, in order to make the difference between a legitimate and regular act and seditious rioting, or between the will of the whole people and the clamour of a faction. Here if anywhere it is necessary, the exercise of right being potentially harmful,* to permit only what cannot be refused by the law at its strictest; but it is also from this necessity that the ruler derives much assistance in preserving his power in spite of the people, without it being possible to say that he is usurping power; for it is very easy for him, while seeming only to exercise his rights, to extend them, and, under the pretext of public security, to prevent assemblies that are intended to restore the proper order; so that, on the grounds that there is silence when it is he who prevents protest, or that irregularities have occurred which he has instigated, he claims that his leadership has the approval of people who keep quiet out of fear, and he punishes those who dare to speak out. It was in this way that the decemvirs in Rome, who were originally elected for a year, and were then maintained in office for a further year, attempted to hold power in perpetuity by refusing the *comitia* any further permission to assemble;* and it is by this simple method that every government in the world, once it is in command of the public forces, sooner or later usurps sovereign authority.

The periodical assemblies of which I have already spoken* are a means of averting or delaying this evil, especially if they do not require formal convocation; for in that case the ruler cannot prevent them without openly declaring himself an offender against the law and an enemy of the state.

These assemblies, the only purpose of which is the preservation of the social treaty, must always open with two questions, which can never be suppressed and must be voted on separately.

The first is: 'Whether the sovereign sees fit to maintain the present form of government'.

The second: 'Whether the people sees fit to leave the administration of government in the hands of those to whom it is now entrusted'.

In this I am assuming what I believe I have demonstrated:* namely, that there is no fundamental law of the state which cannot be revoked, not even the social pact; for if all the citizens assembled in order to break the pact by common consent, there would be no doubt that it had been broken quite legitimately. Grotius even thinks* that anyone may quit the state of which he is a member, and reclaim his possessions and his natural freedom by leaving the country.[1] And it would be absurd if all the citizens together were unable to carry out an act which each of them could perform separately.

---

[1] On the understanding, of course, that we are not leaving in order to evade our duty and exempt ourselves from serving our country when it has need of us. In that case our departure would be criminal and punishable; it would not be withdrawal but desertion.

BOOK IV

Chapter i

That the General Will Is Indestructible

So long as a number of men gathered together consider themselves as a single body, they have a single will also, which is directed to their common conservation and to the general welfare. All the mechanisms of the state are strong and simple, and its maxims clear and luminous; there is no tangle of contradictory interests; the common good is obvious everywhere, and all that is required to perceive it is good sense. Peace, unity, and equality are the enemies of political subtlety. Simple, upright men are difficult to deceive because of their simplicity: elaborate pretexts and allurements fail to impress them; they are not sophisticated enough to be dupes. When, among the world's most fortunate nation,* groups of peasants are to be seen under an oak tree, deciding on matters of state and governing with unfailing wisdom, how can we not despise the refinements found among other peoples, who gain themselves glory and unhappiness with such ingenuity and such an air of mystery?

The state which is thus governed needs very few laws; and when it becomes necessary to promulgate new ones, the necessity for them is universally understood. The first man to propose them merely puts into words something that all have felt already. There is never any question of vote-catching or speech-making in order to make it a law to do what everyone has already resolved that he will do himself, once he is sure that others will do the same.

What misleads the theorists is that, since all the states they have seen were wrongly constituted from the beginning, they cannot believe in the possibility of maintaining a political system of this kind. They laugh as they think of all the foolish ideas that some clever rascal or eloquent flatterer could put into the heads of the crowd in London or Paris. They are not aware that in Berne the people would have sent Cromwell, with a bell round his neck, to do hard labour, and that the Genevans would have put the Duc de Beaufort in a reformatory.*

But when the social tie begins to loosen, and the state to weaken, when particular interests begin to make themselves felt, and smaller groupings influence the greater one, then the common interest no longer remains unaltered, but is met with opposition, the votes are no longer unanimous, and the general will no longer the will of all;* contradiction and argument arise, and the best opinion is not accepted without dispute.

Finally, when the state is close to ruin and subsists only through empty and deluding forms, when in each man's heart the social bond is broken, when the crudest self-interest insolently adorns itself with the sacred name of the public good, then the general will falls silent; the motives of all are kept secret, their votes are no more the votes of citizens than if the state had never existed, and the decrees that are falsely passed, under the name of laws, have private interests as their only aim.

Does this mean that the general will is annihilated or corrupt? No: it remains constant, unalterable, and pure; but it is subordinated to others which have vanquished it. Each man, while detaching his own interests from the common interest, sees clearly that he cannot separate them entirely; but his share of the wrong done to the public seems nothing to him when compared to the exclusive advantage that he intends to take for himself. Except for this private advantage, he has on his own behalf as strong a desire as anyone else for the public good. Even if he sells his vote for money, he does not extinguish the general will that is in him, but eludes it. The mistake he makes is to change the state of the question, giving an answer foreign to what is asked; so that instead of saying, by his vote: 'It is beneficial to the state', he says: 'It is beneficial to this man, or that party, for such-and-such a view to prevail'. Thus in assemblies the law of public order is not so much that the general will must be maintained, but rather to ensure that it is always consulted, and its response always made clear.

At this point there are many reflections that I could make on the simple right of voting in any act of sovereignty, a right of which the citizens can never be deprived; and on the rights of giving an opinion, proposing, distinguishing, and debating, which governments always take great care to reserve to their members;* but this important subject would require a separate treatise, and I cannot say everything here.

Chapter ii

Voting

It will be seen from the preceding chapter that the manner in which matters of general concern are treated can give a fairly reliable guide to the current state of moral attitudes and the health of the body politic. The greater the degree of concord that prevails in public assemblies, that is to say the more nearly unanimous the decisions are, the more the general interest dominates; but long debates, dissension, and disorder are a sign that particular interests are in the ascendant and the state in decline.

This argument will seem less evident when two or more orders of society constitute the state, as in Rome with the patricians and plebeians, whose disagreements often disrupted the *comitia*, even during the best period of the Republic. But the exception is more apparent than real, for in such cases, because of an inherent defect in the body politic, we have as it were two states in one. What is untrue of the two together is true as regards each separately, for in fact, when the Senate was not involved, the plebiscites of the people* went through calmly and with large majorities, even during the most tempestuous times: when citizens had a single interest, the people had a single will.

Unanimity returns at the other extreme, when the citizens fall into servitude and no longer have either freedom or will. Then, by flattery and fear, voting is changed into acclamation; no longer is there any discussion, but only worship or imprecation. Such was the Senate's degraded way of taking votes under the Emperors; and ridiculous precautions were sometimes taken. Tacitus observes* that, under Otho, the senators would rain down curses on Vitellius, but took care at the same time to make an appalling noise, in order that if Vitellius chanced to become their master, he would not know what each of them had said.

It is these general considerations that give rise to the principles to be followed in regulating methods of counting votes and comparing opinions, according as the general will is more or less easily perceptible and the state more or less in decline.

There is one sole law that by its nature demands unanimous consent: it is the social pact. For civil association is the most completely voluntary of acts; each man having been born free and master of himself, no one, under any pretext at all, may enslave him without his consent. To conclude that the son of a slave is born into slavery is to conclude that he is not born a man.*

If therefore when the social pact is agreed there are those who oppose it, their opposition does not invalidate the contract, but merely prevents it from being applied to them: they are foreigners among citizens. Once the state has been constituted, consent lies in residing in it; to live within its boundaries is to submit to its sovereignty.[1]

Except for this original contract, a majority vote is always binding on all the others; that is a direct consequence of the contract. But the question is how a man can be free and forced to conform to the will of others than himself. How can those who are in opposition be free and subject to laws to which they have not consented?

My reply is that the question is wrongly put. The citizen consents to every law, even those that are passed against his opposition, and even those which punish him when he dares to violate one of them. The constant will of all the citizens of the

[1] The assumption is always that the state in question is free; for apart from anything else, a man's family, his property, necessity, violence, or the lack of asylum, may make him continue to reside in a country against his will, and if so the fact of residence does not of itself entail consent to the contract, nor to any violation of it.

state is the general will: it is through the general will that they are citizens and have freedom.[1] When a law is proposed in the assembly of the people, what they are asked is not precisely whether they accept or reject the proposal, but whether it is or is not in conformity with the general will, which is their will; everyone, by voting, gives his opinion on the question; and counting the votes makes the general will manifest. When an opinion contrary to mine prevails, therefore, it proves only that I had been mistaken, and that the general will was not what I had believed it to be. If my particular will had prevailed, I should have done otherwise than I wished; and then I should not have been free.

This argument, it is true, presupposes that all the characteristics of the general will are present also in majority decisions; when they cease to be, whatever view may be adopted, liberty exists no longer.

Having explained previously how particular wills could replace the general will in the deliberations of the people, I have made sufficiently clear what means to adopt so as to forestall this abuse; I shall return to the subject later.* As regards what proportion of the vote suffices to affirm the general will, I have also laid down the principles by which it may be determined. A difference of one breaks a tie, and one opposing voice destroys unanimity; but between unanimity and a tied vote there are various degrees of inequality, each of which can be taken for the proportion in question, according to the condition and needs of the body politic.

Two maxims can be used to determine these relationships: one is that the more important and serious the issue, the closer the deciding vote should be to unanimity; the other, that the greater the urgency of the matter, the smaller the majority required should be. When a debate has to be concluded immediately, it must suffice to decide by a difference of one

[1] In Genoa the word *Libertas* is to be read at the entrances to prisons and on the chains of galley-slaves. This use of the slogan is telling and well-justified, for in reality it is only malefactors, at every level of society, who prevent the citizen from being free. In a country where every person of that kind was a galley-slave the citizens would enjoy the most perfect freedom.

vote. Of these maxims, the first appears more appropriate for
law-making, and the second for the dispatch of business.
However that may be, it is by using them in combination that
the most suitable proportions for majority decisions are established.

Chapter iii

Elections

WITH regard to the election of rulers and officers of government, which as I have said* is a complex action, there are two
methods of proceeding: namely, by choice and by lot. Each has
been employed in a diversity of republics, and even today a
most elaborate combination of the two can be observed in the
election of the Doge of Venice.

'Choosing by lot', says Montesquieu,* 'is of the nature of
democracy.' Agreed: but why is it so? 'The drawing of lots', he
goes on, 'is a method of selection which causes distress to
nobody; it gives every citizen a reasonable hope of serving his
country.' That is not an argument.

If we reflect that the choice of leaders is a function of the
government, not of the sovereign, we shall understand why
election by lot is more natural to democracy, the administration of a democracy being the better the more infrequently it
acts.

In any true democracy the holding of office is not a benefit,
but an onerous duty, which cannot justly be imposed upon one
citizen rather than another. Only the law can place this duty
on him to whom it falls by lot. For in this case, the same
condition applying to all, and the choice not depending on any
human will, there is no particular reference to destroy the
universality of the law.

In an aristocracy, the ruler chooses the ruler, the government
is maintained of itself, and here selection by vote is appropriate.

The election of the Doge of Venice is a case which, far from
destroying this distinction, confirms it: the combination of
methods is appropriate in a mixed government. For it is an

error to take the government of Venice for a true aristocracy. Although the people play no part in governing, the nobles themselves form the people. The multitude of them living in poverty in St Barnabas* have never come anywhere near to holding a government post; all that their nobility gives them is the empty title of Excellency and the right to attend the Grand Council. The Grand Council being as large as the General Council in Geneva, its illustrious members have privileges no greater than a simple citizen has with us.* There is no doubt that, if we set aside the great disparity between the two republics, the burgesses of Geneva correspond exactly to the Venetian patriciate; our natives and inhabitants, to the town residents and the people in Venice; our countrydwellers to the mainland subjects there.* In sum, however the Venetian republic is viewed, and ignoring its size, its government is no more aristocratic than ours. The only difference is that we do not have a ruler for life, and so do not have the same need for appointment by lot.

There would be few disadvantages to appointment by lot in a true democracy, where everything is equal, not only as regards ability and moral standards, but also political principles and wealth, so that the choice becomes almost a matter of indifference. But I have already said* that there is no such thing as a true democracy.

When elections and drawing lots are both employed, the former should be used to fill posts requiring particular abilities, such as military positions; the latter suits those in which common sense, equity, and integrity are sufficient, as with judicial appointments, because in a well-constituted state such qualities are common to all citizens.

Under a monarchical government there is no place for appointment either by lot or by election. The monarch being by right the one and only ruler and officer of government, the choice of his assistants belongs to him alone. When the Abbé de Saint-Pierre proposed an increase in the number of the councils of the King of France, he did not see that he was proposing to change the form of the government.*

It remains for me to speak of ways of voting and counting the votes in the assemblies of the people; but perhaps the history of the Romans' policies in this respect will provide a more vivid explanation of any principles that I might establish. The intelligent reader will not find it a waste of time to see in some detail how public and private affairs were treated in a council consisting of two hundred thousand men.

Chapter iv

The Roman Comitia*

WE lack any reliable written or other evidence concerning the early days of Rome; it even seems highly probable that most of what has come down to us is mythical,[1] and as a general rule the most informative part of a nation's annals, which is the history of its establishment, is the part most often missing. Every day experience reveals to us how revolutions in empires are caused; but since the formation of peoples no longer takes place, we can hardly do more than make conjectures about how they were formed.

From the customs that we find established, we can at least infer that these customs had some origin. Of the traditions which go back to these origins, we should regard as the most reliable those that are attested by the best authorities and reinforced by the most cogent reasons. Such are the maxims that I have tried to follow in studying how the freest and mightiest people on earth exercised its supreme power.

After the foundation of Rome, the infant republic, that is to say the founder's army, made up of Albans, Sabines and foreigners, was divided into three classes, which on account of the threefold division were given the name *tribus*, or tribes.* Each of the tribes was subdivided into ten *curiae*, and each curia into *decuriae*; at their head were put chiefs called *curiones* and *decuriones*.

---

[1] The name *Rome*, which is supposed to come from Romulus, is Greek, and means 'strength'; the name *Numa* is also Greek, and signifies 'law'.* Is it really likely that that the names borne by the first two kings of this city would have anticipated their achievements so exactly?

From each tribe, in addition, was taken a body of one hundred horsemen or knights, called a *centuria*, from which we see that these divisions, of little use in a municipality, were at first only military. But some instinct for greatness, it seems, led the small town of Rome to provide itself in advance with a political system that was suited to the capital of the world.

A disadvantage soon resulted from this first division: it was that the tribe of Albans (the 'Ramnenses') and that of the Sabines ('Tatienses') remained the same size, while the tribe of foreigners ('Luceres') grew larger all the time,* being constantly increased by new arrivals, which before long made it superior to the two others. The remedy that Servius* devised for this dangerous disproportion was to alter the basis of the division, abolishing the division by race, and replacing it by one based on the districts occupied by each tribe in the town. Instead of three tribes he created four, each of which lived on one of the hills of Rome, from which it took its name.* In this way, while remedying inequality in his own time, he prevented its recurrence in the future; and in order to ensure that the divisions lay not merely between places, but between men, he forebade the inhabitants of one district to move to another, which kept the races distinct.

He also doubled the number of the three former *centuriae* of cavalry, and added twelve others, a simple and shrewd move by which he completed the distinction between the knightly order and that of the people, but without causing dissent among the latter.

To the four urban tribes Servius added fifteen others, called the rustic tribes because they consisted of men living in the country, where the inhabitants were divided among the same number of cantons. Subsequently an equal number of new tribes were created, and eventually the Roman people was divided into thirty-five tribes, a number which remained unaltered until the end of the Republic.

This distinction between town and country tribes produced a result which is of interest because it is the only example of its kind; to it Rome owed both the preservation of its moral standards and the development of its empire. One would have expected that the urban tribes would monopolize power and honour, and soon reduce the rustic tribes to inferiority: quite the opposite happened. The early Romans' enthusiasm for rural life is well known; it was due to their wise legislator,* who associated agricultural and military tasks with liberty, while industry, crafts, intrigue, success, and slavery were relegated, so to speak, to the town.

Thus anyone of any distinction in Rome lived in the country and cultivated his land, and it became customary to look only in the country for the upholders of the Republic.* The rural way of life was followed by the best of the patricians and was held in honour by everyone; the simple, industrious life of a villager was rated higher than the craven idleness of the townsmen of Rome, and a man who in the town might have been no more than a wretched member of the rabble became, through working on the land, a respected citizen. It was for good reasons, says Varro,* that our great ancestors made villages the seedbeds of men whose strength and bravery defended them in time of war and supplied them with food in time of peace. Pliny says explicitly that the rustic tribes were honoured because of the men of whom they consisted; whereas men of no worth, whom it was desired to degrade, were ignominiously transferred into the urban tribes. Appius Claudius, a Sabine who came to Rome and had honours heaped on him, was made a member of a rustic tribe, which later took the name of his family. Moreover, freedmen always went into the urban tribes, never into the country ones; and in all the history of the Republic there is no example of a freedman attaining public office, even if he had become a citizen.

The principle involved was excellent, but it was taken so far that it eventually produced a change in social organization that was certainly a change for the worse.

In the first place, the censors,* having long ago taken over the right of transferring citizens arbitrarily from one tribe to another, gave permission to the majority to join whichever they wished, a measure of no utility whatsoever, which destroyed one of their own principal sanctions. Further, the great and powerful having all joined the country tribes, while the freedmen who had become citizens remained in the town tribes with the populace, the tribes in general were no longer linked to a particular place or territory; they were so completely mixed up that membership of one or another could only be established with the help of registers, with the result that the idea denoted by the word *tribe* no longer had anything to do with property, but became personal, and virtually meaningless.

Another factor was that the urban tribes, being closer at hand when the *comitia* were held, were often superior in number, and sold the state to anyone who stooped to buying the votes of the rabble who composed these tribes.

As for the *curiae*, the founder of the state having created ten of them for each tribe, the entire population of Rome, which at that time was contained within the town walls, was made up of thirty *curiae*, each with its temples, its gods, its officers, priests, and festivals, which were called *compitalia*; they resembled the *paganalia* later held by the rustic tribes.

When Servius made a new division of the people, he decided to leave the curiae alone, it being impossible to distribute the thirty of them equally between his four tribes. The *curiae* remained independent of the tribes and became another kind of division of the inhabitants of Rome; but the *curiae* were of no relevance to either the tribes or the people of whom they were composed, because the tribes had become a purely civil institution, another system having been introduced for raising troops, and the military divisions created by Romulus were found to be superfluous. Thus, although every citizen was made a member of a tribe, it was far from being the same with the *curiae*.

Servius made yet another division, his third, which bore no relation to the two previous ones, and which, because of the consequences it produced, became the most important of all. He distributed the whole Roman people into six classes, distinguished not by location nor by persons, but by property; so that the first classes were filled by the rich, the last by the poor, and the middle ones by those of moderate wealth. The six classes were subdivided into one hundred and ninety-three other sections called *centuriae*; and these sections were so distributed that the first of the classes, on its own, included more than half their number, while there was only one section in the last. It thus came about that the class which contained the least

men had the most *centuriae*, and the last whole class in its
entirety was counted only as one subdivision, even though it
alone contained more than half the inhabitants of Rome.

In order that the people would be less conscious of the effects
of this arrangement, Servius devised a way of giving it a
military look: he inserted two *centuriae* of armourers into the
second class, and two of weapons of war in the fourth; in each
class except the last, he separated the young from the old, that
is, those who were obliged to carry arms from those who were
exempted by law on grounds of age—a distinction which was
more important than the distinction of property in making it
necessary often to carry out a census or enumeration; and
finally, he decided that the assembly of the people should take
place on the Campus Martius, and that everyone who was of
military age should attend with his weapons.

The reason why he did not make the same distinction
between young and old in the last class is that the populace
which composed it was not granted the honour of bearing
weapons on behalf of its country; the possession of a home was
required in order to obtain the right to defend it; and out of
the innumerable squadrons of penniless wretches, now the
ornaments of our royal armies, there can hardly be any who
would not have been expelled with derision from a Roman
cohort when its soldiers were the defenders of liberty.

In the lowest class, however, there was still a distinction
between the proletarians and those who were counted by
heads, called *capite censi*. The former were not reduced to
absolutely nothing, but could at least provide the state with
citizens, and sometimes, in time of urgent necessity, with
soldiers. As for those who had no possessions at all and were
enumerated only by a count of heads, they were regarded as
being entirely without status, and Marius was the first to deign
to enrol them.*

Without deciding here whether this third method of counting
was good or bad in itself, I believe I can affirm that it was
rendered practicable only by the simple way of life of the early
Romans, their disinterestedness, their enthusiasm for agriculture, and their scorn for commerce and the desire of gain.
Where could one find a modern nation among which insatiable

greed, inconstancy, intrigues, the continual changes of place, and the perpetual upheavals in personal fortunes, would allow such an institution to last for twenty years without causing a complete revolution in the state? It should be noted, moreover, that in Rome moral standards and the censorship were stronger than the arrangement by class, and compensated for its deficiencies; a rich man could suffer relegation to the poorer class for having displayed his wealth too openly.

It is easy to understand, after all this, why more than five classes are hardly ever mentioned, although in reality there were six. The sixth provided neither soldiers for the army nor voters for the Campus Martius,[1] and was seldom counted for anything, since it served almost no purpose in the Republic.

Such were the different divisions made among the Roman people. Let us now consider what effect they had on the people's assemblies.* These assemblies, when convoked following the law, were called *comitia*; they were normally held in the forum or at the Campus Martius, and were of different kinds, *comitia curiata, comitia centuriata*, or *comitia tributa*, being ordered according to one or other of the three methods of classification. The *comitia curiata* were instituted by Romulus; the *centuriata* by Servius; and the *tributa* by the tribunes of the people.* No law could be sanctioned, and no one elected to public office, except at the *comitia*; and since there were no citizens who were not enrolled in a *curia*, a *centuria* or a tribe, it followed that no citizen was deprived of the right of voting, and that the Roman people was truly sovereign, in law and in fact.

In order for the *comitia* to be legitimately held, and for their decisions to have legal force, three conditions were required: first, that the body or official which called them had the necessary authority; second, that the assembly was held on one of the days permitted by law; and, third, that the omens were favourable.

The reason for the first regulation needs no explanation, and the second was an administrative matter: thus it was not per-

---

[1] I say the Campus Martius because there the *comitia* were assembled in *centuriae*; under the other two arrangements of the inhabitants, the people assembled at the forum or elsewhere, and in this case the *capite censi* had as much influence and authority as the leading citizens.

mitted to hold the *comitia* on a holiday or market-day, when the country people would be in Rome on business and did not have the time to spend the day in the forum. The third regulation allowed the Senate to keep the people's rebelliousness and pride in check, and put a proper degree of restraint on the fervour of seditious tribunes; but the tribunes discovered more than one way of freeing themselves from these hindrances.

The passing of laws and the election of leaders were not the only matters submitted to the *comitia* for decision; the Roman people having usurped the most important functions of government, it may be said that in its assemblies the destiny of Europe was settled. The different forms taken by their assemblies arose from the diversity of their functions, according to the different kinds of question on which they had to decide.

In order to judge these different forms, it is only necessary to compare them. What Romulus had in mind, when he established the *curiae*, was that the people should act as a check on the Senate and the Senate on the people, while he dominated both alike. Thus by this form he gave to the people all the authority of superior numbers, in order to counteract the authority of power and wealth, which he left with the patricians. However, following the spirit of monarchy, he left the greater advantage with the patricians, because of the influence they had on majority voting through their clients.* The patronage of clients was an admirable institution, a masterpiece of humane policy-making, without which the patriciate, contrary as it was to the spirit of the Republic, could not have survived. To Rome alone is due the honour of setting the world so excellent an example, which gave rise to no abuses and which, nonetheless, has never been followed.

The same form of assembly by *curiae* subsisted under the kings down to Servius, the reign of the last Tarquin not being considered legitimate, and this caused the laws made by the kings to be generally known as *leges curiatae*.

The *curiae* under the Republic, being still restricted to the four urban tribes and consisting only of the common people in Rome, were suited neither to the Senate, which headed the patricians, nor to the tribunes, who, though they were plebeians, led the better-off citizens. Hence they fell into discredit, and were held in such low esteem that their thirty lictors together carried out the duties that should have been done by the *comitia curiata*.

The division by *centuriae* was so favourable to the aristocracy that at first sight it is impossible to understand why the Senate did not invariably triumph in the *comitia* named after them, which elected the consuls, censors and other curule officials.* The fact of the matter was that, out of the one hundred and ninety-three *centuriae* forming the six classes of the whole Roman people, the first class included eighty-eight. Since votes were counted by *centuriae*, the first class alone had more votes than all the others. When all its *centuriae* were in agreement, the remaining votes were not even collected; a decision made by the minority passed for one made by the mass; and we may conclude that, in the *comitia centuriata*, matters were settled by weight of gold rather than by weight of numbers.

But this excessive dominance was mitigated by two factors: first, the tribunes usually, and a large number of plebeians always, were in the first class, that of the rich, and counterbalanced the influence of the patricians.

The second factor was this: that instead of beginning the voting by *centuriae* following the order of precedence, which would have meant always beginning with the first *centuria*, one of them was chosen by lot, and proceeded to the election on its own;[1] after which came the turn of all the other *centuriae*, which were summoned on another day in order of rank. They normally ratified the choice already made. Thus the authority of example was denied to rank and bestowed elsewhere by lot, which follows the principle of democracy.*

A further advantage resulted from this custom: citizens inhabiting the country had the time, between the two elections, to obtain information about the qualifications for office of the candidate provisionally nominated, so as to cast their votes knowledgeably. However, the custom was eventually abolished under the pretext of expediting business, and the two elections took place on the same day.

---

[1] The *centuria* which was chosen by lot was called *praerogativa* because it was the first from which a vote was called; whence comes the term 'prerogative'.

The *comitia tributa* were in reality a council of the Roman people.* They could be convoked only by the tribunes; at them tribunes were elected and held their plebiscites. The Senate not only had no standing at these *comitia*, but did not even have the right to be present; forced as they were to obey laws for which they had not been allowed to vote, the senators were in this respect less free than the lowliest of citizens. This injustice, which was entirely unreasonable, was in itself sufficient to invalidate decrees made by a body from which some of its members were excluded. Even if all the patricians had taken part in the *comitia* in accordance with their rights as citizens, they would then have become simple individuals, and would have had scarcely any influence under a voting system which went by the number of heads, so giving the merest plebeian as much power as the leader of the Senate.

It is evident, then, that the various arrangements for counting votes in so large a population not only brought order into the process, but in addition were not merely a matter of form; each had consequences related to the intentions that favoured its creation.

Without going into further detail, it follows from the preceding explanations that the *comitia tributa* were the most favourable to popular government and the *comitia centuriata* to aristocracy. As regards the *comitia curiata*, at which the majority was composed solely of the Roman rabble, all they were good for was to encourage tyranny and sedition, and they were bound to fall into disrepute, since even mischief-makers avoided a method which disclosed their plans too openly. It is certain that the full majesty of the Roman people was only to be found in the *comitia centuriata*, which were the only complete form of assembly, given that the rustic tribes were absent from the *comitia curiata*, and the Senate and the patricians from the *comitia tributa*.

In early times the method of counting votes among the Romans was as simple as their customs, though less simple than in Sparta. Each man spoke his opinion aloud and a teller wrote it down: the majority of votes in a tribe decided the tribe's opinion; the majority of votes among the tribes decided the nation's; and similarly with the *curiae* and *centuriae*. It was a good custom so long as fair dealing remained the rule among the citizens, and men were ashamed to vote publicly for an unjust policy or an unworthy candidate; but when, the nation growing corrupt, it became possible to buy votes, it was more appropriate for them to be cast secretly, in order that lack of trust should discourage the buying of votes, and that the dishonest should be provided with a means of avoiding treachery.

I know that Cicero disapproved of the change to secret ballots, saying that it was partly to blame for the decay of the Republic;* but although I realize that Cicero's authority on the point has great weight, I cannot share his opinion. I think that the reason why the decline of the state was accelerated is that further changes of the same kind were not made. Just as invalids are not suited by a healthy person's diet, so too we must not try to govern a corrupt people by laws that suit the virtuous. The best proof of this principle is the longevity of the Republic of Venice, which in outward appearance still exists, solely because its laws are only suited to men of bad character.

And so writing tablets were distributed to the citizens, in order that each could record his vote without its being known. New rules were also established for collecting the tablets, counting votes, comparing the results, and so on; which did not prevent suspicion often falling on the trustworthiness of the officers in charge of these functions.[1] Eventually, in order to prevent votes being canvassed and traded, edicts were made, their uselessness being demonstrated by their frequency.

In the end the government was often compelled to resort to extraordinary measures in order to make up for the inadequacy of the laws. Miraculous portents were sometimes invented, but this method, while it might deceive the people, did not deceive its rulers. Sometimes an assembly was convoked without notice, before the candidates had had time to campaign. Sometimes, when it was seen that the people had been won over and was about to make the wrong decision, the whole session was used up with speeches. But ambition eluded every device. The amazing thing is that, despite all the abuses, so vast a people

---

[1] *Custodes, diribitores, rogatores suffragium.**

still managed, thanks to its original statutes, to elect its officers, pass laws, give judgements in lawsuits, and deal with business public and private, with almost as much facility as the Senate could have done.

Chapter v

The Tribunate

WHEN it is not possible to establish an exact proportion between the constituent parts of the state,* or when causes which cannot be removed affect the relationship constantly, a particular kind of government office is created, which is distinct from other bodies and restores the terms of the relationship to their proper positions, and makes a link, or middle term, either between the ruling body and the people, or between the ruling body and the sovereign, or, if necessary, fulfils both functions.

This new body, which I shall call the tribunate, is the preserver of the laws and the legislative power. Sometimes its role is to protect the sovereign body from the government, as with the tribunes of the people in Rome; sometimes to support the government against the people, as the Council of Ten does now in Venice; and sometimes to maintain the balance on both sides, as the ephors did in Sparta.*

The tribunate is not a constituent part of the state, and must not have any share of legislative or executive power; but its own power is thereby increased, because, although it can do nothing, it can prevent everything. Being the defender of the laws, it is more sacred, more revered, than the ruler who carries them out or the sovereign which makes them. This became very clear in Rome, when the haughty patricians, who always regarded the entire people with disdain, were forced to yield to a mere officer of the people, who neither had the right to take auspices nor had any jurisdiction.*

The tribunate, within sensible limits, is a good constitution's strongest support; but if its power is excessive by even the slightest amount it overturns everything: weakness is not in its nature; and provided it exists in some form or other, it is always sufficient for what is necessary.

It degenerates into tyranny when it usurps the sovereign power, which it should only moderate, or when it seeks to administer the laws which it ought only to protect. The enormous power of the ephors presented no danger as long as Sparta retained its moral standards, but accelerated the process of corruption once it had started. The blood of Agis, who was slaughtered by these tyrants, was avenged by his successor: the ephors' crime and its punishment both hastened the destruction of the republic, and after Cleomenes Sparta was nothing.* Rome perished in just the same manner; the excessive power of the tribunes, which they usurped by decree, was finally, with the assistance of laws designed for freedom, used to safeguard the emperors who destroyed it.* As for Venice's Council of Ten, it is a court stained by blood, no less dreaded by the patricians than by the people, which far from protecting the laws from on high, serves only, now that they have been degraded, to strike blows under cover of darkness, to which nobody dares to be witness.*

Like a government, the tribunate grows weaker as its membership increases. When the tribunes of the Roman people, who were originally two in number, then five, wanted to double their number, the Senate let them do so, fully confident that it could play off some of them against the others; and this duly happened.

The best way to prevent so formidable a body from exceeding its powers (and a method that no government has yet thought of using) would be to avoid making it a permanent body, and to establish periods during which it would not operate. Such periods, which should not be so long as to allow abuses to develop, can be decided by the law in such a way that it is easy, if required, to set up an extraordinary commission in order to reduce them.

This method seems to me to have no disadvantages, because the tribunate, as I have said, is not part of the constitution and can be removed without damaging it; and it also seems likely to be effective, because an official in a post recently restored does not start with the powers exercised by his predecessor, but with the powers bestowed on him by law.

Chapter vi

The Office of Dictator*

THE inflexibility of laws, which prevents them from being swayed by events, can in certain cases render them harmful, and this, in a crisis, can cause the ruin of a state. Orderliness and the slowness of procedure need more time than circumstances sometimes allow. There are innumerable possibilities for which the legislator has not provided: an essential part of foresight is the awareness that one cannot foresee everything.

It is wrong therefore to attempt to make political institutions so rigid as to deny oneself the power to put them into abeyance. Even Sparta allowed its laws to lie dormant.

But only the greatest of dangers can outweigh the danger of tampering with the order of the state; only when the nation's security is at stake should the sacred power of the laws be suspended. In such cases, which are rare and easily recognized, the safety of the public is provided for by a specific measure, committing it to the person most worthy of the responsibility. There are two ways in which the commission can be given, depending on the type of danger.

If, to remedy the danger, it is sufficient to increase the activity of the government, then government should be concentrated in one or two persons. Thus the authority of the laws is not affected, but only the mode of their administration. But if the danger is such that the apparatus of law is an obstacle in warding it off, then a supreme chief is appointed, who puts all laws to silence, and suspends, for a while, the authority of the sovereign. In these cases the general will is not in doubt, and it is obvious that the people's principal aim is that the state should not perish. The suspension of legislative authority in this fashion does not abolish it; the officer who keeps it silent is unable to make it speak; in overriding it, he is not able to take its place. He can do everything except make laws.

The first method was employed by the Roman Senate when, following a hallowed form of words, it called on the consuls to provide for the safety of the Republic; the second was put into practice when one of the two consuls appointed a dictator;[1] it was a custom that had passed to Rome from Alba.

In the early years of the Republic it was very common to have recourse to the dictatorship, because the state did not yet have a firm enough foundation for it to maintain itself solely by the strength of its constitution.* The standards of behaviour at the time were such as to render superfluous many of the precautions that would have been necessary at other periods, and there were no fears that a dictator would abuse his authority, nor that he would try to retain it beyond its term. Rather it seemed that so great an honour was a burden to the man to whom it was given, such was his haste to lay it down, as if taking the place of the laws was too difficult and dangerous a position.

This is why it is not the risk that this supreme office of government might have been abused, but that it might have been devalued, which makes me disapprove of its indiscriminate use in the early days; for when it was prodigally applied during elections, or at the dedication of temples, matters purely of form, the danger was that in time of need it would become less formidable, and that a title which was used only at empty ceremonies would come to seem empty itself.

Towards the end of the Republic the Romans became more circumspect, and with no better reasons than before, were just as careful with the dictatorship as they had formerly been extravagant. It was easy to see that their fears were unjustified, and that by then the weakness of the capital acted as its safeguard against the holder of any office of government within its walls; that a dictator could, in certain cases, defend public freedom without ever being able to threaten it; and that the chains that might bind Rome would not be forged in Rome itself, but within its armies. The little resistance that Marius put up against Sulla, and Pompey against Caesar, clearly showed

---

[1] The nomination was made secretly and at night, as if it was shameful to put a man above the laws.

how little could be expected from internal authority when faced by external force.*

This mistake caused the Romans to make great errors. One, for instance, was not to have appointed a dictator during the conspiracy of Catilina;* for since only the interior of the city was involved, or at most one of the Italian provinces, a dictator could easily, with the limitless authority given him by law, have broken up the conspiracy, which was quelled only by a combination of happy accidents that could never have been brought about by human prudence.

Instead, the Senate was content to hand over all its power to the consuls, with the result that Cicero was obliged, in order to take effective action, to exceed the limits of this power in one essential point; and so, if in the first transports of joy his conduct met with approval, in the sequel he was rightly called to account, for shedding the blood of citizens contrary to the law, an accusation which could not have been made against a dictator.* But the Consul's eloquence swept all before it, and he himself, despite being a Roman, preferred his own glory to the good of his native land, seeking not so much the most lawful and reliable way of saving the state, but rather the means of obtaining all the honour from the affair.[1] Hence it was both right to honour him for liberating Rome, and right to punish him for infringing the laws. His recall from exile may have been triumphant, but it was certainly a favour.*

For the rest, it is necessary, whatever the manner of conferring this important responsibility, to restrict its duration to a very short period, which can never be extended. In the crises which lead to the establishment of a dictatorship, it is not long before the state is either destroyed or saved; and once the immediate need has passed the office becomes tyrannical or futile. In Rome, where dictators were appointed for six months, most of them abdicated before time. If the period had been longer, they might have been tempted to extend it further, as did the Decemvirs with their year of office. The dictator had

[1] He could not have been sure of this if he had proposed the appointment of a dictator, since he would not have dared to nominate himself, and could not be certain that his colleague would nominate him.

only enough time to deal with the emergency which caused his election; and not enough to make other plans.

Chapter vii

The Office of Censor *

As the declaration of the general will is made through the law, so the declaration of public judgement is made through the censorship. Public opinion is that kind of law of which the censor is the minister, and which, in the same way as the ruler, he applies to particular cases.

A board of censors, then, is in no way the arbitrator of public opinion, but is simply the mouthpiece for it; as soon as they depart from it, their decisions are empty and ineffectual.

It is of no avail to treat a nation's moral conduct separately from the objects of its esteem; for all these things depend on the same principle, and are necessarily associated. Amongst every nation in the world, it is not nature but opinion which determines the choice of pleasures. Put men's opinions to rights, and their behaviour will improve spontaneously. Men always prize what is beautiful or what they find beautiful; but it is in their judgement of beauty that they err; therefore it is their judgements that have to be guided. In judging behaviour we judge honour, and in judging honour we take public opinion for law.

A nation's opinions are engendered by its constitution. Although the law does not control moral standards, it is legislation that gives them birth: when laws grow weak, standards of behaviour degenerate; but the censors' judgement will not then succeed, if the strength of the laws has failed.

From this it follows that the office of censor may be useful in preserving morality, but never in reintroducing it. Establish a censorship when the laws are in their full vigour; as soon as they lose it, the case is desperate; nothing lawful can remain strong when the laws no longer have their strength.

The censorship maintains standards of conduct by preventing the debasement of public opinion, preserving its integrity by applying it wisely, and sometimes even by giving it a fixed form when it is still doubtful. The custom of having seconds in duels, which was taken to crazy lengths in the kingdom of France, was abolished simply by these words, appearing in a royal edict: 'As for those who are cowardly enough to call on seconds'. This expression of opinion anticipated that of the public and fixed it immediately. Yet when other royal edicts tried to establish that it was also cowardly to fight a duel, which is very true but contrary to the usual opinion,* their judgement was derided by the public, which had already made up its mind on the point.

I have argued elsewhere[1] that, since public opinion cannot be constrained, even the slightest trace of constraint should be absent from the court set up to represent it. It is impossible to praise too highly the skill with which this means of influencing behaviour, which we moderns have entirely lost, was practised among the Romans, or, better still, among the Lacedaemonians.

In Sparta, a man of bad character made a valuable suggestion in council; the ephors took no notice, but had the same suggestion made by a man of virtue. What an honour for him, and what disgrace for the other, without praise or blame being given to either! Some drunkards from Samos[2] defiled the court of the ephors: the next day a public edict gave leave to the Samians to be filthy. A real punishment would have been less severe than a reprieve of this sort. When Sparta has decided on what is and is not honourable, Greece does not appeal against its judgements.

---

[1] In this chapter I merely summarize what I have said at greater length in the *Letter to d'Alembert.*

[2] In fact another island, which the delicacy of our language forbids me to name on this occasion.*

Chapter viii

*The Civil Religion**

ORIGINALLY men had no kings except their gods, and no government except theocracy. Their argument was the same as Caligula's;* and in those days it was correct. Ideas and sentiments must go through a long period of development before men can bring themselves to accept one of their own kind as king, and flatter themselves that they will benefit from it.

Simply from the fact that God was put at the head of every civil society, it followed that there was the same number of gods as of nations. Two nations foreign to each other, and almost always enemies, could not keep the same master for long: two armies opposing each other in battle cannot obey the same leader. Thus the division between nations gave rise to polytheism, and subsequently to theological and political intolerance, which are the same in nature, as I shall explain later.

The fanciful notion which the Greeks had, that they could recognize their own gods in those worshipped by barbarian peoples, came from another idea of theirs, that of considering themselves to be the natural rulers of these peoples. But in our own day it is ridiculous to base a branch of learning* on identities between the gods of different nations—as if Moloch, Saturn and Chronos could be the same god! as if the Phoenician Bel, the Greek Zeus and the Latin Jupiter could be the same! as if there could be anything in common between imaginary beings with different names!

Now if it is asked why under paganism, when each state had its form of worship and its gods, there were no religious wars, my answer is that it was precisely because each state had its own worship as well as its own government, and so made no distinction between its gods and its laws. A political war was theological also; the territories of the gods, so to speak, were determined by national limits. The god of one people had no rights over other peoples. The gods of the pagans were not jealous gods; they shared the empire of the world between them. Even Moses and the Hebrew nation sometimes adopted this view when speaking of the God of Israel. It is true that they counted for nothing the Canaanite gods,* the Canaanites being a nation proscribed and doomed to destruction, whose lands the Israelites would duly occupy; but consider the way in which they spoke of the deities of neighbouring tribes whom they were forbidden to attack: 'Is not the possession of what belongs to Kemosh your god', said Jephtha to the Ammonites, 'justly due to you? By the same right we possess the lands that our victorious God has taken.'[1] Here we have, to my mind, a clear recognition of parity between the rights of Kemosh and those of the God of Israel.

But when the Jews, under the rule of the kings of Babylon, and later under the kings of Syria, obstinately persisted in their refusal to recognize any other God but theirs, it was regarded as a rebellion against their conqueror, and it brought down on them the persecution of which we may read in their history, and of which no other example can be found before Christianity.[2]

Every religion, then, was exclusively tied to the laws of the state which prescribed it; there was no other method of converting a nation except to subjugate it, and conquerors were the only missionaries. The law of the conquered being to change their mode of worship, victory was required before any change could be spoken of. Far from men fighting for their gods, it was their gods, as in Homer, who fought for them; everyone asked his god for victory, and paid for it with a new shrine. The Romans, before capturing a stronghold, called on its gods to abandon it; and when they let the people of Tarentum keep their angry gods, it was in the belief that they had subjected these gods and forced them to do homage.* They allowed those whom they conquered to keep their gods as they let them keep their laws. A wreath for the Capitoline Jupiter was often the only tribute that was enforced.

---

[1] 'Nonne ea quae possidet Chamos deus tuus, tibi jure debentur?' (Judges 11. 24). Such is the Vulgate text. Father Carrières translates: 'Do you not believe that you rightfully possess that which belongs to Kemosh your God?' I do not know the import of the Hebrew text, but I observe that in the Vulgate Jephtha positively admits the right of the god Kemosh, and that the French translator weakens his admission by a 'you believe' which is not in the Latin.*

[2] It is clear beyond any doubt that the Phocian* war, called the 'holy war', was not a war of religion. Its purpose was to punish acts of sacrilege, not to make unbelievers submit.*

Finally, when the gods and worship of the Romans had reached out further with their empire, and when they themselves had often adopted the gods of conquered peoples by granting the right of abode to both, the inhabitants of this huge empire gradually found that they had multitudes of gods and modes of worship, which were almost the same everywhere; and in this way paganism finally became, throughout the known world, the same single religion.

This was the situation when Jesus came to establish a spiritual kingdom on earth: which separated the theological from the political system, putting an end to the unity of the state, and causing the internal divisions which have never ceased to trouble the Christian nations.* But the pagan mind could not grasp the new idea of a kingdom of the other world, and the Christians were always considered really to be rebels, who under the hypocritical pretence of submission were only waiting for the moment when they could gain independence and control, and adroitly usurp the authority which they had pretended to respect while they remained weak. In this lay the cause of their persecution.

It happened as the pagans had feared. Then everything took on a new look; the humble Christians changed their tone, and soon the supposed kingdom of the other world was seen in this one to have become, under a visible ruler, the most violent despotism.*

Nonetheless, since there has always been a civil ruler and civil laws, the consequence of this doubling of powers has been a perpetual conflict of jurisdictions, which has made it impossible for there to be any sound polity in Christian states; and no one has ever been able to say whether obedience was due to monarch or priest.

Several nations, however, even in Europe or its vicinity, have tried to retain or restore the older system, but without success; everywhere the spirit of Christianity has triumphed. Religious worship has always preserved, or restored, its independence from the sovereign, and has had no necessary connection with the body of the state. Muhammad's views were extremely sound, and his political system closely knit;* and while his government kept its original form, under the caliphs who suc-

ceeded him, it was wholly united, and in that respect good. But
the Arabs grew prosperous, cultured, civilized, soft, and feeble,
and were subjugated by barbarians;* the division between the
two powers then revived. Although it is less obvious among the
Muslims than the Christians, it is still present, especially in the
sect of Ali;* and in some states, such as Persia, its effects are
felt continually.

Among us, the Kings of England have put themselves at the
head of the Church; and the Czars have gone to the same
lengths.* But by taking the title they have made themselves less
the masters of the Church than its ministers; they have not so
much acquired the right to change it as the power to maintain
it; within it they are not its legislators, but only its rulers.*
Wherever the clergy forms one body,¹ it is master and lawgiver
on its own ground. In England and Russia, therefore, there are
two powers, two sovereigns, just as in other countries.

Among all the Christian writers, only Hobbes, the philosopher, has clearly perceived both the disease and its remedy,
and dared to suggest the reunion of the two heads of the eagle,*
making everything tend towards political unity, without which
neither state nor government will ever be properly constituted.*
But he must have seen that Christianity's urge to dominate
was incompatible with his system, and that the interest of the
priesthood would always be stronger than the interest of the state.
What made his political theory obnoxious was not so much that
some of it was false and abhorrent, but rather that some was
right and true.²

¹ It should be carefully noted that what binds the clergy into a single body is
not so much formal assemblies, as in France, but the churches' communion.
Communion and excommunication are the clergy's social pact: and thanks to
this pact it will always be master of nations and kings. All the priests in
communion together are fellow-citizens, even if they come from opposite ends of
the earth. The device is a political masterpiece. There was nothing like it among
the pagan priests; and therefore they never formed a body of clergy.
² For what Grotius approves of and what he condemns in Hobbes's *De cive*, see
among other things a letter from him to his brother, 11 April 1643.* It is true
that, inclined as he was to be indulgent, the learned writer appears to pardon
Hobbes the good things in consideration of the bad; but not everyone is so
forgiving.

By examining the historical facts in the perspective I have indicated, I believe that one could easily refute the conflicting opinions held by Bayle and Warburton.* The former argues that no religion is useful to the body politic, while the latter maintains the opposite, that Christianity is its firmest support. Against the first I would show that no state was ever founded without being based on religion; and against the second, that the Christian law is at bottom more harmful than useful in strengthening the constitution of the state. In order to make myself fully understood, it is only necessary to give slightly more precision to the rather vague concepts of religion which concern my subject.

Religion considered in relation to society, which can be either society in general or a particular society,* may also be divided into two kinds, namely the religion of the man and that of the citizen. The one, with no temple, no altar, no ritual, limited to the purely internal worship of the supreme God and to the eternal duties of morality, is the simple and pure religion of the Gospel, true theism,* or what may be called natural divine law.* The other, within the boundaries of a single country, gives it its gods, its own protectors and guardians. This religion has its dogmas, its rites, its visible form of worship, ordained by law; it regards everything, apart from the one nation which follows it, as faithless, alien, and barbarian; for it the duties and rights of man do not extend outside its temples. Such were all the religions of the earliest nations, and to them we may give the name of divine civil or divine positive law.

There is a strange third kind of religion, which gives men two legislations, two countries, and two leaders, subjects them to contradictory duties, and prevents them from being simultaneously true worshippers and good citizens. Such is the religion of the Lamas of Tibet and the religion of the Japanese; such is the Christianity of Rome. This kind may be called the religion of the priest. The kind of law that results is an unsociable mixture which has no name.

Considering the three kinds of religion politically, they all have their faults. The third is so obviously bad that it is a waste of time bothering to prove it. Anything that breaks up the unity

of society is worthless; all institutions that put man in contradiction with himself are worthless.

The second is good in that it combines divine worship with
love of law, and by making the citizens' country the object of
their worship, teaches them that to serve the state is to serve its
guardian deity. It is a kind of theocracy, under which there can
be no other pontiff but the ruler, and no other priests but the
officers of government. In this way dying for one's country is
to achieve martyrdom; to violate a law is to commit an impiety;
and to sentence a guilty man to public execration is to abandon
him to the wrath of the gods: *Sacer estod*, 'May you be accursed'.*

But it is bad in that, founded as it is on error and lies, it
deceives men, making them credulous and superstitious, and
drowns the true worship of the Divinity in empty ceremonial.
It is bad also when it becomes exclusive and tyrannical, making
its people bloodthirsty and intolerant, so that it breathes out
murder and slaughter, and believes that to kill anyone who
denies its gods is a holy action. Such a nation is thus put in a
natural state of war against all others, which is extremely
damaging to its own security.

There remains then the religion of man, or Christianity—not
the Christianity of today, but of the Gospels, which is entirely
different. In this true, sacred, and holy religion men, the
children of the same God, all acknowledge each other as
brothers,* and the society in which they are united is not
dissolved even in death.

But because this religion has no particular relationship with
the body politic, it does not add to the strength of the laws, but
leaves them only the strength they derive from themselves;
so that one of the greatest bonds of particular society remains
ineffectual. And furthermore, so far from giving to the citizens,
in their hearts, an attachment for the state, it detaches them
from the state, as from everything else on earth. I know of
nothing that is more deeply opposed to the social spirit.*

We are told that a people of true Christians would make the
most perfect society that can be imagined.* I can only see one
great difficulty with this supposition: it is that a society of true
Christians would no longer be a society of men.

I say further that this supposed society, with all its perfection, would be neither the strongest nor the most durable of societies; through being perfect it would lack solidity; its very perfection is a fatal defect.

Every man would do his duty; the people would be obedient to the law, its leaders would be moderate and just, its officers loyal and incorruptible, and its soldiers would scorn the fear of death; there would be neither vanity nor luxury. So far so good; but let us look further.

The religion of Christianity is entirely spiritual, and concerned solely with heavenly things; the Christian's country is not of this world. He carries out his duty, it is true, but does so with complete indifference to the success or failure of his efforts. Provided he has nothing to reproach himself with, it is of small importance to him that things are going well or badly here on earth. If the state prospers, he scarcely dares enjoy the public success: he is afraid of taking pride in his nation's glory; if the state declines, he blesses the hand of God as it lies heavy on his people.*

It would be necessary, if this society were to remain peaceful and harmony were to endure, for all the citizens without exception to be equally good Christians; but if by bad fortune there were a single ambitious man among them, or a single hypocrite, a Catiline, for example, or a Cromwell, such a man would undoubtedly get the better of his pious compatriots. Christian charity does not easily allow us to think badly of our neighbour. As soon as he discovers, by some ruse, the art of imposing on them, and acquires some share of public authority, you have a man invested with dignity: and it is God's will that he should be respected; soon you have a man with power: and God's will is that he should be obeyed. Suppose that the depositary of this power abuses it: he is the rod with which God chastises his children. It would be contrary to conscience to expel the usurper, since public disorder would be inevitable; violence would have to be used, blood would be shed, and that kind of thing is hard to reconcile with Christian meekness; after all, what does it matter whether one is a free man or a serf in this valley of woe? The one thing needful is to go to Paradise, and submissiveness is simply another means of achieving it.

Suppose there is war against another country: the citizens march gladly into battle; to none of them does it occur to run away; they do their duty, but without any ardour for victory: they are better at dying than conquering. Whether they are the conquered or the conquerors, what does it matter? Does not Providence know better than they what is good for them? Imagine what an advantage their stoicism would give to a fierce, bold, and impassioned enemy! Set them against one of those nations full of spirit, fired by an ardent love of glory and their country; imagine your Christian republic facing Sparta or Rome: the pious Christians would be beaten, crushed, and destroyed before they knew where they were; or their preservation would be due solely to the scorn that their enemies would feel for them. The oath sworn by Fabius's soldiers was to my mind a fine one: they did not swear to conquer or to die, but to return as conquerors, and they kept their word.* No Christians would ever have sworn such an oath: they would have thought that they were tempting God.

But I am mistaken in saying 'a Christian republic'; the two words are mutually exclusive. Christianity preaches nothing but servitude and dependence. Its spirit so favours tyranny that the tyrant always benefits from it. True Christians are made to be slaves; they know it and are hardly bothered by it; since this short life, in their eyes, is worth too little.

Christian troops are excellent, you say. I deny it; show them to me. For my part, I know of no Christian troops. You will point to the Crusades. Without disputing the valour of the Crusaders, let me observe that, far from being Christians, they were soldiers of the priesthood, citizens of the Church: they were fighting for their spiritual country, which it had somehow turned into a secular country. Properly understood, this was a return to paganism; since the Gospels did not institute a national religion, no holy war is possible for Christians.*

Under the pagan emperors, the Christian soldiers were brave: every Christian author says so, and I believe it: fighting with pagan troops, their honour was at stake. Once the emperors became Christian this rivalry ceased, and when the cross superseded the eagle* all Rome's valour disappeared.

But leaving political considerations aside, let us return to the important question of right, and define the principles involved. The right given to the sovereign over subjects by the social pact does not exceed the limits of public utility, as I have said.[1] Subjects therefore are not accountable to the sovereign for their opinions, except insofar as those opinions are of concern to the community. Now it does concern the state that each citizen should have a religion which makes him cherish his duties; but its dogmas do not concern the state or its members, except to the extent that they relate to morality, and to the duties that a man who professes that religion is obliged to fulfil towards others. Everyone may have whatever additional opinions he wishes, without the sovereign having any jurisdiction over them; for since it has no authority in the other world, the fate of its subjects in the life to come, whatever it may be, is not its affair, provided they are good citizens in this one.

There is therefore a purely civil profession of faith, the articles of which it is the business of the sovereign to determine; not exactly as religious dogmas, but as sentiments of sociability, without which it is impossible to be either a good citizen or a loyal subject.[2] Although it cannot force anyone to believe them, it can banish from the state anyone who does not believe them; he can be banished, not for impiety, but for being unsociable, and for being incapable of cherishing the laws and justice sincerely, or of sacrificing, when necessary, his life for his duty. And if, having publicly accepted these same dogmas, any person conducts himself as if he did not believe them, let him

[1] 'In the republic', says the Marquis d'Argenson, 'everyone is perfectly free to do any act that is not harmful to others.'* That is the precise limit; it would be impossible to define it more exactly.—I have been unable to resist the pleasure of quoting this manuscript work at times, even though it is not publicly known, so as to honour the memory of a man of integrity and renown, who even as a minister continued to be a true citizen at heart, and retained his sound and upright beliefs about the government of his country.

[2] When Caesar spoke in Catiline's defence, he tried to prove the doctrine of the mortality of the soul.* In order to refute him, Cato and Cicero did not waste their time philosophizing; they contented themselves with showing that Caesar's words were those of a bad citizen, and that the doctrine he was putting forward was pernicious to the state. And this, not the question of theology, was the proper question for the Roman Senate to decide.

be punished by death;* he has committed the greatest of crimes: he has lied before the law.

The dogmas of the civil religion must be simple and few, precisely expressed, without explanations or commentary. The existence of the Divinity, powerful, intelligent, beneficent, prescient, and provident, the life to come, the reward of the just and the punishment of the wicked, the holiness of the laws and the social contract; such are the positive dogmas. As for those excluded, I limit them to one: intolerance; it belongs to the religions that we have rejected.

It is a mistake, in my view, to distinguish between civil and theological intolerance. The two are inseparable. It is impossible to live at peace with people whom one believes to be damned: to show them brotherly love would mean hating God, who is punishing them; one has an absolute duty to convert them or to persecute them. Wherever theological intolerance is allowed it necessarily has some civil effect:[1] and as soon as it has, the sovereign is no longer the sovereign, even in the secular domain; from then on the priests are the true masters, and kings no more than their officers.

Now that there is no longer, and cannot be, an exclusive national religion,* all those which tolerate other religions ought

---

[1] Marriage, for instance, is a civil contract and has civil effects, without which, indeed, society could not subsist.* Let us suppose therefore that a body of clergy manages to obtain the exclusive right of ratifying the contract, a right which, in any intolerant religion, it is bound to usurp. In this case, is it not clear that if the clergy makes good use of the authority of the Church, it will nullify the authority of the ruler, who will have no more subjects unless the clergy kindly decides to give him some? Empowered to marry or not to marry a couple, according as they believe or do not believe some particular doctrine, as they accept or reject some particular formula, or as they are more or less loyal to the clergy, is it not clear that, if it holds firm and conducts itself prudently, the clergy alone will have control over legacies, public appointments, the citizens and the state itself, which could not subsist if its members were all illegitimate?—But it will be argued that appeals will be entered, adjournments declared, warrants issued, possessions reclaimed from the Church. And what then?—the clergy, provided it has even the slightest good sense (I do not say courage), will take no notice and continue on its course; it will calmly let the appeals, the adjournments, the warrants, and the repossessions take place, and will end up in control. It is not much of a sacrifice, I think, to give up a part, when you are certain of taking possession of the whole.

to be tolerated, to the extent that their dogmas contain nothing contrary to the duties of the citizen. But anyone who dares to say: 'There is no salvation outside the Church' must be expelled from the state—unless the Church is the state and its pontiff the ruler. Such a dogma is of value only under a theocratic government; under any other it is pernicious. The reason for which Henri IV is said to have embraced the religion of Rome* ought to have made any honourable man leave it, and especially a ruler capable of rational argument.

Chapter ix

Conclusion

HAVING set down the true principles of political right and attempted to lay the basis for the foundation of the state, it remains for me to give it stability in its external relationships. This would involve international law, trade, the law of warfare and conquest, public law, federations, negotiation, treaties, etc.* But all these form a new subject which extends too far for my weak sight; I should always have kept it fixed on things closer to me.

APPENDIX
THE GENERAL SOCIETY OF THE HUMAN RACE

THE second chapter (with Chapter i as introduction) of Book I: First Notions of the Social Body, in the surviving part of an early draft (the 'Geneva manuscript') of the *Social Contract*. Paragraphs within square brackets are crossed out in the manuscript.

Chapter i
The Subject of the Work

SO many famous authors have discussed the maxims of government and the rules of civil right that there is nothing useful to be said on the subject that has not been said already. Perhaps, however, greater agreement would have prevailed, perhaps the best relationships within the social body would have been more clearly established, if at the outset its nature had been better determined. This I have tried to do in what follows. The subject is not, therefore, the administration of the social body but its constitution. I make it live, not act. I describe its motive forces and its components and arrange them in their places. I put the machine in a condition to work; others, wiser than I, will regulate its operation.

Chapter ii
*The General Society of the Human Race**

LET us begin by asking where the necessity for political institutions has its source.

The strength of a man is so exactly in proportion with his natural needs and his original state that, if his state alters and his needs increase, even by the smallest amount, the assistance of his fellows becomes necessary, and when eventually his desires embrace the whole of nature, they can scarcely be satisfied even with the help of humanity in its entirety. In this way the causes that make us wicked also turn us into slaves, subjugating us by corrupting us. Our sense of our own weakness derives not so much from our nature as from our cupidity; our needs bring us together at the same time as our passions divide us, and the more we become enemies to our fellow-men, the more we need them. Such are the first bonds between us in our general society; such are the foundations of that universal benevolence which, if recognized as necessary, seems to smother sentiment,* each one wanting to take his advantage from it without being obliged to cultivate it; for, as regards identity of nature, it is devoid of effect in this situation,* since for men it is as much a cause of strife as of unity, and puts competition and jealousy between them as often as it puts mutual understanding and agreement.

From this new order of things* a multitude of relationships arise, lacking measure, regularity, or solidity, and continually changed and interfered with by men, a hundred of them attempting to destroy them for every one who attempts to stabilize them; and since the relational existence of a man in the state of nature depends on thousands of other relations which are in continual flux, he can never be assured of remaining the same for more than an instant at a time; for him, peace and happiness pass in a flash; nothing is permanent, except for the wretchedness which is the result of all these vicissitudes; even if his sentiments and ideas were able to rise to the level of the love of order and the highest notions of virtue, it would be impossible for him ever to apply his principles reliably, living under conditions that would prevent him from distinguishing both good from evil and the virtuous man from the wicked.

The kind of general society, therefore, that can be engendered by our mutual needs does not offer any effective assistance to a man overtaken by misery and poverty, or rather, all it does is to furnish new strength to the man who already has more than enough, while the weaker man, lost, stifled, and crushed amidst the multitude, can find no refuge in which to shelter, nor any support for his infirmity, and finally perishes a victim of the fallacious union in which he had expected to find happiness.

[If once one becomes convinced that the motives that lead men to form a union among themselves contain nothing which is related to the fact of unification; that far from having in mind the goal of common felicity, from which each may draw his own, the happiness of one man brings the unhappiness of another; if finally one realizes that, instead of all directing their energies towards the common good, men come together only because they all depart from it—then one must also appreciate that, even if such a state could continue, it would be no more than a source of crime and misery for men, each seeing his own interest, following his own inclinations, and attending to his passions only.]

Thus the gentle voice of nature is no longer an infallible guide for us, nor the independence which we received from her a state to be desired; peace and innocence escape us before we have tasted their delights; the happy life of the Golden Age,* which went unrecognized by the brutish men of the earliest times and was lost by their more enlightened successors, is a state that has always been foreign to the human race, either because men did not understand what they had when they were able to enjoy it, or because they lost it when they could have known what it was.

There is yet more. This perfect independence and freedom from rules, even if it were to stay joined to pristine innocence, would still have suffered from an intrinsic defect, an obstacle to the progress of our most excellent faculties, namely the lack of any connection between the parts that constitute the whole. The earth would be covered with men between whom there would be scarcely any communication; we would make contact at a few points but nowhere would we be united; each would remain isolated in the midst of others, each would think only of himself; our understanding would be unable to develop; we should live without feeling, we should die without having lived; the sum of our happiness would be ignorance of our misery; there would neither be goodness in our hearts nor morality in our acts, and we should never have enjoyed the soul's most delicious sensation, which is the love of virtue.

[It is certain that the idea presented to the mind by the words 'the human race' is no more than a collectivity, without any assumption of a real union between the individuals which compose it, but, if it is so wished, let us include such an assumption, and let us conceive the human race as a corporate moral entity endowed both with a sentiment of common existence, which confers individuality on it and unifies it, and with an all-embracing motivation that makes each part act for a general purpose relating to the whole. Let us conceive that this communal sentiment is the sentiment of humanity, and that the law of nature is the active principle of the entire body. Let us then observe the results, as regards man's relations with his fellows, if he is constituted in this way: they will be quite the opposite of what we had supposed; we shall find that the development of society, by arousing personal self-interest, stifles humane feelings in men's hearts, and that notions of the natural law, which should rather be called the law of reason, do not begin to develop until the prior development of the passions makes all its precepts useless. From this it will be seen that a social treaty supposedly dictated by nature is sheer fantasy; because its provisions are always unknown or impossible, and because we are necessarily either ignorant of them, or infringe them.]

[If society in general existed anywhere else but in philosophers' theories, it would be a corporate entity, as I have said, with its own properties, distinct from those of the individual beings of which it consists, in rather the same way as chemical compounds have properties which they do not receive from any of the elements which compose them. There would be a universal language which would be taught to all men by nature, and which would be the first instrument of communication between them; there would be a kind of common *sensorium** which would ensure that all parts were coordinated; the public good, or its opposite, would not merely be the total of individual goods and ills as in a simple aggregation, but would reside in the conjunction between the individuals and would be greater than this total; and public felicity, far from being founded on the happiness of individuals, would be the source of it.]

It is false to say that, in a condition of independence, reason leads us to contribute to the common good through consideration for our own interests. Private interest and the general welfare, far from being combined, exclude each other in the natural order of things, and social laws are a tie which each man will gladly impose on others, but by which he will not be bound himself. 'I realize that I bring fear and anxiety among the human race', says the independent man, whom the wise man throttles; 'but it is necessary either for me to be unhappy, or for me to cause unhappiness to others, and none is dearer to me than I am.'* 'It is in vain,' he might add, 'that I attempt to reconcile my interests with the interests of others; everything you tell me about the benefits of the social law might be true, provided only that, while I observed the law towards others, I could be sure that they would all observe it towards me; but what assurance can you give me? And could I be in a worse situation than to be exposed to all the wrongs that the strong might want to inflict on me, but not to dare to take compensation from the weak? You must either give me a guarantee against any unjust attack on me, or expect me to attack in my turn. It is useless to say that, by renouncing the duties imposed on me by the law of nature, I deprive myself of the rights it gives, or that if I resort to violence, I authorize others to act as violently as they wish towards me. I agree, and the more readily because I am unable to comprehend how, by employing restraint, I could preserve myself from their violence. Furthermore, it will be in my interest to get the strong on my side by giving them a share of the plunder I take from the weak; that will contribute more than justice can to my advantage and my security.' The proof that an intelligent and independent man would argue in this manner is that it is the policy adopted by every self-governing nation which is answerable only to itself for its conduct.

What reliable response can be made to such a speech, unless we are prepared to bring religion to the aid of morality, and bind together human society by the direct intervention of God's will? But the sublime concept of God that wise men have, the gentle laws of fraternity he imposes, the social virtues of pure souls, which are the kind of worship he truly asks from us, will never be within the grasp of the multitude. It will always be given gods as insensate as itself, to whom it will sacrifice some slight advantages in order to allow free passage, in honour of its gods, to its countless horrible and destructive passions. The whole of the earth would be covered in blood, and the human race would soon be annihilated, if philosophy and the law did not restrain the fury of fanaticism, and if the voices of men were not stronger than those of the gods.

For if the notions of the Supreme Being and the law of nature were indeed innate in all men's hearts, it was entirely superfluous for either of them to be taught expressly: we were merely being taught what we already knew; and the way the teaching was done was better calculated to make us forget it. If such notions are not innate, anyone to whom God did not give any knowledge of them is dispensed from knowing them; but as soon as some particular sort of instruction about them is required, each people will have its own ideas of God and natural law, it will be given proofs that they are the only good ones, and they will more often give rise to carnage and murder than to peace and concord.

Let us therefore leave on one side the sacred precepts of the various religions, the abuse of which causes as many crimes as their use can avoid, and let a question that theologians have never discussed without detriment to the human race be handed over to the philosopher for examination.

But he will send me back to the human race itself, which alone has the right to decide, because the only desire it has is for the greater good of all. He will say:* what the individual ought to consult is the general will, in order to find out how far his duties reach as man, citizen, subject, father, and child, and when it is appropriate that he live or die. 'I admit that I can certainly see here a rule for me to follow, but what I cannot yet see,' our independent man will say, 'is a reason for me to submit to this rule. It is not a matter of teaching me what justice consists in; it is a matter of showing me what interest I have in being just.'* And indeed no one will deny that the general will, in each individual, is a pure act of understanding which, while passion is silent, reasons on what a man can demand from his fellow and what his fellow can demand from him. But where is the man who can separate himself from himself in this manner? and if concern for his own conservation is the first of nature's precepts, can he be forced to consider humankind in general in such a way as to impose duties on himself, when he cannot see their connection with his individual constitution? Do not the preceding objections still subsist, and does it not still remain unclear how it is that his personal interest requires his submission to the general will?

Besides, since the art of generalizing ideas in this manner is one of the most difficult and advanced exercises of the human understanding, will the majority of men ever be in a position to deduce principles of conduct from this way of reasoning? Were it necessary to consult the general will on a particular act, on how many occasions would it not happen that a well-intentioned man would err concerning the rule or its applicability, and simply follow his own inclination while believing that he was following the law? What therefore can he do in order to preserve himself from error? Will he follow the interior voice?* But this voice is only formed, so it is said, by habits of judgement and feeling developed within society and according to its laws: it cannot, therefore, assist in establishing them; and it would be necessary further that his heart should be free of any of the passions which, by speaking louder than conscience, drown its timid voice, and make the philosophers maintain that it does not exist. Will he consult the principles of written law, the social actions of all the nations, even the tacit conventions of the enemies of the human race?* The original difficulty still remains; only from the social order already existing among us do we derive the idea of the order that we imagine. We conceive a general society on the model of our particular societies, the establishment of small states makes us think of a larger one, and only after having been citizens do we begin properly to become men. And this shows what we ought to think of those so-called cosmopolitans whose justification for loving their country is their love of the human race, and who boast of their love for all so as to have the right not to love anyone.

What is proved in this respect by rational argument is perfectly confirmed by the facts, and from even the slightest research into classical antiquity it will easily be perceived that sound ideas on natural law and the universal fraternity of all men were quite late in developing, and progressed through society so slowly that it was only Christianity that disseminated them adequately. We find that even in the Code of Justinian* the violence of early times is still authorized in many respects, not only towards declared enemies, but towards anyone not a subject of the Empire; so that the humane attitudes of the Romans extended only to the area over which they were dominant.

In fact it was long believed, as Grotius observes,* that it was permissible to rob, pillage, and mistreat foreigners, and especially barbarians, even to the point of enslaving them. This is why strangers might be asked, without giving offence, whether they were brigands, or pirates, since their calling, far from being a matter of shame, was regarded at that time as being honourable. The first heroes, such as Hercules or Theseus, who made war on brigands, nonetheless exercised brigandage themselves; and among the Greeks the name 'peace treaty' was often given to treaties made between peoples who had not been at war. For a long time the words for foreigner and enemy were synonymous among several ancient nations, even the Latins; 'For among our ancestors', Cicero says, 'a man was called an enemy whom we should call a foreign traveller'.* The error made by Hobbes, therefore, is not so much his assertion of a state of war between independent men in society, but his supposition that this state is natural to the species, and to have made it the cause of the vices by which it was produced.

But although there exists naturally no general society of men; although when they become members of society they become unhappy and immoral; although the laws of justice and equality are as nothing for those who live in the freedom of the state of nature and, at the same time, are subject to the requirements of the social state; far from thinking that there is no virtue or happiness for us, and that Heaven has left us abandoned without resources to suffer the depravation of the species, let us endeavour to find the cure for the disease within the disease itself. By new forms of association let us, if we can, correct the faults in the general form of association. Let our violent debater himself judge the outcome. Let us show him, by perfecting the social art, how to mend the damage done to nature by this art in its beginnings; let us show him all the misery of a state that he believed to be happy, and all the falsity of an argument that he believed to be solid. May he see, in society better constituted, good actions rewarded, bad ones punished, and justice and happiness amicably combined. Let us enlighten his reason with new understanding and warm his heart with new emotions; and may he learn to augment his being and his contentment by sharing them with his fellows. Unless my enthusiasm for the enterprise has blinded me, let us have no doubt that this enemy of the human race, with strength of soul and rightness of mind, will finally abandon both his hatred and his errors, that his reason, which had led him astray, will bring him back to humanity, that instead of his apparent interests he will learn to prefer his interests properly understood; that he will become good, virtuous, and compassionate, and be, in a word, no longer the fierce brigand that he had wished to be, but the strongest upholder of a well-ordered society.

EXPLANATORY NOTES

Political Economy

3 *see the article 'Paterfamilias'*: in French '*Père de famille*', an article which must have been planned but is not to be found in the relevant volume of the *Encyclopédie*. Rousseau's novel *Julie* contains much didactic material on 'domestic economy'; see especially Pts. IV, Letter x, and V, Letters ii–iii.

a private person: the passage consisting of this paragraph and the next four appears in much the same form in the Geneva MS of the *Contract*, I. v.

only on conventions: in the sense of agreements between consenting parties. This is a basic concept for Rousseau; see *Contract*, I. i, end.

by virtue of the laws: after this sentence the 1782 edition adds: 'The father's power over his children is based on their particular advantage and cannot, by its nature, extend as far as the right of life and death; but the sovereign power, the only object of which is the common good, has no limits except those of public utility properly understood. This is a distinction I shall elucidate in due course.' However, there is no further reference to the subject. On capital punishment in the *Contract*, see II. v.

4 *property, which is anterior to it*: because man in the state of nature can assert a right to property; see section III of the article, pp. 25–6.

5 *no right can authorize it*: Rousseau was to say more on the subject of slavery in the *Contract*, I. iv. His reason for mentioning it here was presumably that Aristotle had done so (*Politics*, I iv–vii, on domestic economy).

6 *ten men capable of governing their fellows*: in the 1782 edition, the end of this sentence reads: 'but since the world has been in existence, human wisdom has made very few good officers of government' (*magistrats*).

in his work entitled Patriarcha: Filmer (*c*.1590–1653) published his *Patriarcha, or the Natural Power of Kings* in 1680; it had been written long before. It is the extreme expression in English of the theory of the divine right of kings, to which Rousseau refers in the words 'detestable theory'.

by writing against it: John Locke (1632–1704), whose works on philosophical and political subjects were enormously influential both in England and France during the eighteenth century, devoted the first of his two *Treatises on Civil Government* (1690) to an attack on Filmer. The other writer is the republican Algernon Sidney (1633–83), whose *Discourses concerning Government* were published in 1698.

the error in question: not the divine right of kings, unknown to Aristotle, but the assimilation of king to *paterfamilias*. In Aristotle, see e.g. *Politics*, I. i, vii.

which I call government . . . which I call sovereignty: a basic distinction in Rousseau's political theory; see *Contract*, e.g. I. vii, III. i.

7 *is also a moral being*: in French 'être moral'. On this and related expressions see Introduction, p. xvii, and *Contract*, I. vi, end (on the result of the acceptance of the social contract).

by stealth: according to the Life of Lycurgus by Plutarch (*c*.46– after 120), one of Rousseau's favourite authors, Spartan boys were encouraged as part of their military training to steal food, in order to supplement their deliberately meagre diet. Hobbes (*De cive*, vi. 16) had also commented on the legal aspect.

which the present article does no more than develop: Rousseau here credits Diderot with the invention of the concept of the general will. See Introduction, p. xiv.

own self-interest and code of conduct: this passage is perhaps the clearest account of another of Rousseau's basic concepts, that of 'partial' or 'particular' groups or societies within a society as a whole, a frequent cause of concern to him, as for instance in *Contract*, III. ii. See Introduction, p. xx.

8 *that I have given*: four paragraphs previously, where Rousseau says that separate nations have the same relation to each other as do individuals in the state of nature.

a few clever men: compare the more moderate and abstract discussion in *Contract*, II. iii, 'Whether the General Will Can Err'.

an objection to my argument: Rousseau may have been thinking of the sentence of death passed on Socrates in Athens (399 BC), which would be an example of the fault he has just mentioned, declaring the innocent guilty. His view of the influence of Athenian philosophers (*savants*) and orators had been similar in the first Discourse.

9   *the article 'Right'*: Diderot had written: 'Alas! the beauty of virtue
    is such that its image is respected even by brigands in the depth
    of their caverns.' The meaning is apparently that, between
    themselves, brigands observe rules of behaviour which are
    analogous to the laws of society at large.

    Machiavelli's satires: the reference must be to *The Prince* (1513);
    Machiavelli also wrote a satirical play, *Mandragola*. See *Contract*,
    III. vi, for Rousseau's view of Machiavelli as a true republican,
    not the unscrupulous cynic that he is often thought to be.

    lawful or popular government: in French 'gouvernement légitime ou
    populaire'. The phrase may seem odd; it is explained by the
    principles expounded in the *Contract*, where *lawful* or *legitimate*
    means, roughly, 'according to the fundamental laws laid down
    by the people as sovereign', the object of which can only be the
    general good.

10 *in order to make them free*: the argument behind this passage (which
    appears also in the Geneva MS, I. vii) must be the origin of the
    controversial phrase 'force them to be free' at the end of *Contract*,
    I. vii.

11 *in Plato's opinion*: in the *Laws*, IV (719e to end).

12 *the first duty of a legislator*: the term here has superficially its
    normal meaning, but it is also compatible with the special sense
    given to *legislator* in the *Contract* (II. vii–xi).

13 *the nearest I can find*: no doubt ironically meant; the idea is that
    good examples cannot be found nearer to home than China.
    Rousseau's source has not been traced, which could imply that
    he was inventing an imaginary situation.

    in his district: in French 'département', which like other terms in
    this passage (except for the ostentatiously Chinese 'mandarin')
    are typical of the French situation that Rousseau presumably
    had in mind.

14 *his will as much as his actions*: compare the closing reflections in
    Book II of the *Contract*, on the kind of law that is 'graven . . . in
    citizens' hearts'.

17 *Cato*: 'the Younger' or 'Cato of Utica' (95–46 BC), famous for his
    sense of justice and uncompromising principles. He sided with
    Pompey against Caesar in the civil wars, and at Utica, in North
    Africa, in order to avoid capture by Caesar, committed suicide
    by stabbing himself, having previously read Plato's treatise on
    the immortality of the soul, the *Phaedo*.

combats the Sophists: the Sophists were itinerant professional educators whose subject was, broadly, how to make a success of life. They are often attacked in Plato's Socratic dialogues. Plato relates the events leading to his teacher's death in the *Apology, Crito,* and *Phaedo.*

18 *fundamental conventions*: all this passage is concerned with the concept to which Rousseau was later to give the name 'social contract'.

20 *the right to do so*: Rousseau discusses Cicero's usurpation of this right in the *Contract,* IV. vi.

the Porcian law: of the three laws so named, the one meant here was probably passed under the praetorship of Cato the Elder in 198 BC.

21 *the most tangible causes*: all are directly relevant to France, where, for example, taxes were collected by private individuals, who purchased the right to do so from the government, and many public offices were in effect venal.

22 *a sublime virtue*: for a similar passage on the formation of the citizen, see *Contract,* II. vii.

23 *Public education*: Rousseau is probably following Plato's *Republic* here. The education in *Emile* is not public, but Emile's society is that of monarchical France.

24 *the Cretans, the Lacedaemonians, and the ancient Persians*: this view of education organized and controlled by the state seems also to come from Plato, who in the *Laws,* I. i, mentions Lacedaemonia and Crete. The reference to the Persians or Parsis may come originally from Xenophon.

the reader will easily understand: none the less, the implication is no longer very clear. Rousseau may be alluding to the fact that education in his time was virtually monopolized by religious bodies, and could not have been taken away from them.

to do without it: Roman children under the early Republic, the period Rousseau consistently admires, were educated within the home, the first schools being opened only in the 3rd century BC.

the censor: for Rousseau's general view of this office, see *Contract,* IV. vii.

25 *the administration of property*: see *Contract,* I. ix, for Rousseau's treatment of the theoretical basis of property. In the *Political Economy* he is more clearly influenced by Locke's views (see next

note). His moderation of tone contrasts with the sharp attack on property at the beginning of Part II of the *Discourse on Inequality*, but his arguments are none the less radical.

25 *property is the true foundation of civil society*: also later, on taxation, 'the foundation of the social pact is property' (p. 32 above), which is not the view put forward about its foundation in the *Contract* (I. vi; in I. viii, the right of property is one of the principal gains of existence in the 'civil state'). Here in the *Political Economy* Rousseau is nearer to Locke: 'The chief end therefore, of men's uniting into commonwealths, and putting themselves under government, is the preservation of their property' (Second *Treatise on Civil Government*, ix. 124; also 134, etc.).

26 *as Pufendorf has shown*: Samuel Pufendorf (1632–94) was a German university professor in law and one of the most important writers in the Natural Law tradition. The reference is to his best-known work, *De iure naturae et gentium* (*The Law of Nature and Peoples*) (1672), IV. x. 4.

27 *aerarium or treasury*: the Latin term signified the Roman treasury building, in which the state's supply of precious metals was held.

the public demesne: in French 'le domaine public', for which like other translators I use a special term, 'the public domain' having too wide a meaning here.

the same view as Bodin: Jean Bodin (1530–1596), French writer on political, religious and economic subjects, published his *Six Books of the Republic* in 1576, during the French Wars of Religion. He advocates monarchical government, limited by estates-general. Rousseau's reference here is to Book VI. i.

28 *made by Romulus*: according to legend, the founder of Rome, having acquired the land around the city by conquest, allotted it in equal proportions to religious use, to the nascent state, and to his subjects.

the assembly of the people or the country's estates-general: the difference between the two is that the *ancien régime* institution, dating back to the Middle Ages, of estates-general (or states-general) was an assembly of representatives or deputies, not of the people as a whole. Its members came from the three 'estates' or orders of Church, nobility, and commons (the 'Third Estate'). No estates-general (as opposed to consultative provincial estates) were held in France between 1614 and 1789.

the integrity of Cato, as quaestor: another reference to the exemplary rectitude of the younger Cato.

few enough Galbas: Galba (*c.*3 BC–AD 69) was emperor in 68–9. The anecdote is told about a flute-player (not a singer) by Plutarch in his life of Galba.

30 *on the face of the building*: the inscription means 'It nourishes and enriches'.

Joseph with the Egyptians: Genesis 41, 47. As Pharaoh's minister he put grain in store during years of plenty, then sold it in time of shortage to the Egyptians, taking money, cattle, and eventually the men themselves in payment.

31 *A liking for conquest*: probably directed at the expansionist policies of Louis XIV (1638–1715), which were accompanied by severe authorit-arianism and, in the early eighteenth century, impoverishment.

in order to subjugate the latter: in the eighteenth century European armies were becoming more professionalized, as Rousseau mentions a little later, and he is no doubt warning of the risks involved. He makes a similar observation in the *Considerations on Poland*, xii.

the siege of Veii: this sentence is in the 1782 edition but not in 1755; it appeared first in the Du Villard edition (1758). Veii, an Etruscan city, was a constant enemy to early Rome, and was conquered after a siege in 396 BC.

the war against Jugurtha: among various army reforms made by Gaius Marius (157–86 BC) was the enrolment of professional volunteers as well as the conscripted citizens of whom the army had wholly consisted before. Jugurtha was a king of Numidia, in northern Africa, against whom the Romans fought many campaigns.

33 *has been generally recognized*: by Locke, second *Treatise on Civil Government*, xi. 140, and Bodin, *Republic*, VI. ii.

real, when they are due on things: the term's etymology is relevant: Latin *realis*, from *res* 'thing'.

in The Spirit of Laws: De l'Esprit des lois (1748), the other great eighteenth-century French work, besides the *Contract*, on political theory, but on many other things also, by Charles de Secondat de Montesquieu (1689–1755), a member of the legal aristocracy. It is known especially because of its theory of the limitation of powers (Bk. XI): each of the legislative, executive, and judicial powers in a state, if separated, acts to check the abuse of power by the others and so preserve civil liberty. The reference here is to XIII. xiv.

34 *for the rich and powerful*: the eloquent social protest here may be compared with the more optimistic assessment of the benefits of social life in the *Contract*, I. viii.

35 *if the corvée has to be done, or a militia raised*: the *corvée* was enforced labour, a spell of work imposed by the state on the unprivileged, often taking the form of the construction or repair of roads. Militias were raised by drawing lots, but the duty could be avoided by paying for a replacement.

36 *the social pact between the two classes*: likewise, in a satirical passage in Pt. II of the *Discourse on Inequality*, the rich man suggests to his poorer fellows a specious type of social contract from which he will derive much more benefit than they.

37 *Chardin says . . . the testimony of Herodotus*: the *Voyages en Perse et aux Indes Orientales* (*Travels into Persia and the East Indies*), by Jean Chardin (1643–1713), appearing first in 1686 and often reprinted, were and remain an authority on the East at the time. Herodotus: the *Histories*, Bk. III.

   without increasing in price: the assumptions in this passage are that the price of corn is fixed and that the tax referred to is not a tax on sales, but on the land which produces the corn.

41 *I have said*: the reference is presumably to the passage on p. 33 in which Rousseau takes Bodin as an authority.

   whom Bodin calls imposers: in French *imposteurs*, i.e. those who create imposts, but the word also (and usually) means 'impostors'; Bodin, *Republic*, VI. ii.

The Social Contract

43 *. . . foederis aequas Dicamus leges*: 'Let us propose equitable conditions for a treaty'; from King Latinus's speech in Virgil's *Aeneid*, xi. 321–2.

45 *what is allowed by right*: in French 'ce que le droit permet'. The French *droit* can also mean law in the abstract, whereas English *right* and *law* are separate concepts, which often imposes a choice of not entirely equivalent terms in translating.

   its sovereign body: in French 'membre du souverain'. *Souverain* being usually the equivalent of 'monarch', the sense in which

EXPLANATORY NOTES 183

Rousseau habitually uses the word, to signify the supreme political authority, of whatever persons it is composed, blurs the distinction between monarchical and popular authority. In Geneva, Rousseau had been by right a member of the General Council ('Grand conseil'), also called the Sovereign Council, of 1,200 citizens and burgesses.

Man was born free: in French 'L'homme est né libre', often translated and quoted as 'Man is born free', which would be the equivalent of 'L'homme naît libre'. The past tense implies that natural liberty existed once; the present, that it exists for every man at birth, as in the Declaration of the Rights of Man in 1789, 'Men are born and remain free, and with equal rights'. In I. iv Rousseau writes, about the children of slaves: 'they are born men and free', but IV. ii has: 'each man having been born free'.

46 *only through convention*: the argument here, taken largely from Locke (second *Treatise on Civil Government*, 1690, ch. vi), was directed at the defenders of monarchy, who often assimilated it to paternal power. Rousseau's case is made more fully in the *Discourse on Inequality* and Book I, Ch. v of the Geneva MS of the *Contract*.

for the benefit of the governed: Hugo Grotius or de Groot (1583–1645), the creator in modern times of the Natural Law approach to political theory. Rousseau alludes here to his treatise *De iure belli ac pacis* (*On the Law of War and Peace*) (1625), I. iii. 8.

47 *Hobbes's view also*: Thomas Hobbes of Malmesbury, 1588–1679, perhaps the most formidable of the pro-monarchical predecessors of Rousseau, but despite the hostile comment here he saw absolute monarchy as being beneficial to its subjects, insofar as it protected them against civil war. Rousseau tacitly refers to Hobbes's position in I. iv (third paragraph).

the Emperor Caligula: Caius Caligula, emperor of Rome AD 37–41, notorious for his cruelty and depravity. The opinion ascribed to him here by Philo of Alexandria (?–c. AD 54), which must have been found by Rousseau in a 1668 translation of the *History of the Jews* by Flavius Josephus, was to the effect that those commanding all creatures in the world ought to be considered as being gods rather than men.

Aristotle: the reference is to Aristotle's *Politics*, I. 2.

with whom they have been identified: this alludes to arguments in Filmer's *Patriarcha*.

47 *the M. d'A.*: the Marquis d'Argenson, political writer, minister, and brother of a more successful politician, the Comte d'Argenson; the passage quoted comes from his best-known work, usually known as 'Considérations sur l'ancien gouvernement de la France', written before 1738.

a short treatise by Plutarch: the Greek moralist and biographer Plutarch. The work he refers to is set on Circe's island, where the sorceress had turned some of Odysseus' men into pigs (Homer, *Odyssey*, X).

48 *with apparent irony*: 'The stronger man's arguments are always the best' ('la raison du plus fort est toujours la meilleure') is a proverbial French expression used with irony by La Fontaine in a celebrated fable, *The Wolf and the Lamb* (*Fables*, 1668, I. x), to which Rousseau is probably alluding.

'Obey the powers that be': this summarizes the opening of the thirteenth chapter of St Paul's Epistle to the Romans, which Rousseau quotes directly two lines later. The King James Bible has 'there is no power but of God'. Such authorities were much used in works by apologists of royal power, such as the *Politique tirée des propres paroles de l'Écriture Sainte* (*Politics taken from the very words of Holy Scripture*), 1709, by Louis XIV's bishop, Bossuet.

49 *agreed convention*: in French 'les conventions'; other translations have 'conventions' or 'covenants'. It is the idea of free consent that is essential here.

to transfer: in French the legal term 'aliéner', which with its derivatives occurs often in the *Contract*. I avoid translating by *alienate* because of the more recent meanings that the word has acquired.

subject to a king: in these considerations Rousseau's target is the Natural Law school generally; here the reference is to Grotius's *De iure belli ac pacis*, I. iii, and soon after to both Grotius and Pufendorf, who argued that a man might sell himself in order to get his subsistence. This was denied by Montesquieu (*Spirit of Laws*, XV. ii).

50 *the cave of the Cyclops*: *Odyssey*, IX; Locke used the same example in the first *Treatise on Civil Government*, ch. xix.

the so-called right of slavery: the argument for slavery based on the right of war is made both by Grotius (*De iure belli ac pacis*, III. vii) and Hobbes in the *De cive* (*Of the Citizen*) (1642), ch. viii, which is followed by Pufendorf.

51 *not naturally enemies*: see Part I of the *Discourse on Inequality* for Rousseau's full description of the state of nature, which is in direct opposition to Hobbes's view that men's natural state is 'the war of all against all'.

relationships between things: i.e. between states, as is made clear two paragraphs later.

the Establishments . . . the Peace of God: the former were a compilation of edicts ascribed to Louis IX (1214–1270); the Peace, or Truce, of God refers to Church decrees, repeated at intervals in the tenth and eleventh centuries, proscribing feudal warfare on certain days.

polity: in French 'politie', an archaic word for Rousseau, but one which he often uses in the sense of the political organization of society. He emphasized in a letter to his publisher Rey (23 December 1761) that it was not to be confused with *politique* 'policy'.

The Romans . . . of all: this note was added in 1782.

52 *less to national powers than to their subjects*: I translate literally as regards *less . . . than* (in French: 'moins des avertissements aux puis- sances qu'à leurs sujets'), but it may seem that the context calls for 'notices given to national powers rather than their subjects.'

are based on reason: the arguments also resemble those of Montesquieu, *Spirit of Laws*, X. iii, 'The Right of Conquest'.

53 *give itself to a king*: the reference is to *De iure belli ac pacis*, I. iii. 8, but the arguments in this paragraph are mainly directed against the concept of the 'double contract' in Pufendorf (*De jure naturae et gentium*, VII. ii), which combines a contract of 'association', creating a society, with one of 'submission', accepting a ruler.

54 *there has been unanimity*: Rousseau re-emphasizes this point in IV. ii.

a point in the development of mankind: the supposition recalls the passage from the state of nature to the social state, described in the later sections of Part I of the *Discourse on Inequality*, but in the *Contract* the historical aspect is virtually eliminated.

55 *Each of us . . . part of the whole*: in French 'Chacun de nous met en commun sa personne et toute sa puissance sous la suprême direction de la volonté générale, et nous recevons en corps chaque membre comme partie indivisible du tout.' The last words in the Geneva MS. are 'comme partie inaliénable du

tout', 'as an inalienable part of the whole'. The formulation of
the contract is the first passage in the work in which the term
volonté générale appears.

56   *citizens who make the City*: Rousseau's use of *cité* here seems to be
influenced by the word from which it is derived, Latin *civitas*, the
place inhabited by *cives*; it meant 'state' and later 'township',
implying a degree of local autonomy.

taking the one for the other: broadly, Genevan citizens (*citoyens*) were
eligible for public office in the city and they and burgesses
(*bourgeois*) could be members of the governing councils. Others,
the 'natives' and 'inhabitants' (*natifs, habitants*) had official permission to dwell within the city but few or no political rights.
The categories were based on parentage and place of birth.
Rousseau was a *citoyen* by virtue of being born within the city
walls of a father who was a *citoyen*. The error he complains of in
Jean Bodin (to whom he probably owes the distinction between
town and city that he elaborates here) is found in some but not
all editions of his *Six Books of the Republic*, 1576, I. vi. The long,
celebrated, and controversial article by d'Alembert to which
Rousseau refers in the next sentence appeared in the seventh
volume (1757) of Diderot and d'Alembert's *Encyclopédie*; it was in
answer to it that Rousseau wrote his *Lettre à M. d'Alembert sur les
spectacles* (*Letter to M. d'Alembert on Theatre*), 1758.

57   *the sovereign . . . the state*: this passage contains perhaps the clearest
illustration of what Rousseau means by the key terms *sovereign*
and *state*, both of which, for him, denote the association of
citizens, not a person or body set over them and distinct from
them.

no kind of fundamental law . . . binding on the people as a body: in the
view of the chief legal officer of Geneva, the *Procureur général*,
when arguing that the *Social Contract* should be condemned,
Rousseau implied in this passage that a government could be
removed and changed by its people; the book was therefore
'destructive of every government'.

57   *the sanctity of the contract*: in IV. viii, this is one of the articles of
the civil religion.

58   *any form of guarantee to its subjects*: literally, 'has no need of a
guarantor in its relation to the subjects' ('n'a nul besoin de
garant envers les sujets'), the meaning being clarified by what
follows. The sentence is important because the idea of a guarantee against state power was a central issue in attacks on

Rousseau made by liberals such as Benjamin Constant, in his *Principes de politique* (*Principles of Politics*), 1815.

as we shall see later: see II. iv, especially the last three paragraphs.

forced to be free: on this notorious remark, see the Introduction, p. xxi

will not depend on any person: in French 'le garantit de toute dépendance personnelle', i.e. he is answerable only to the law and the state, not to an individual having power over him, such as a king or nobleman.

59   *The Civil State*: it is interesting to compare what Rousseau says in this chapter with the description of the state of nature in the *Discourse on Inequality*, which has often been claimed to be inconsistent with it.

60   *Property*: more exactly 'real estate' or 'realty', the French *domaine réel* being a legal term. The discussion is more sophisticated than in the *Political Economy* (section III, beginning; see p. 25), where the emphasis is more on the individual owner.

61   *Nuñez Balboa*: Balboa (1475–1517), discoverer of the Pacific Ocean in 1513, is here taken as an example of the Spanish *conquistadores*. In Part II of *Emile* he is unfavourably compared to Emile on the grounds that Emile has a right to land because he has cultivated it.

62   *as we shall see in due course*: in II. iv.

63   *cannot be transferred*: in French 'est inaliénable'; compare *transfer* for 'aliéner' on p. 49, and the note.

being only the exercise of the general will: a different definition of sovereignty is contained in the corresponding chapter (I. v) of the Geneva MS: 'There is therefore in the state a common force which sustains it, a general will which directs this force, and it is the application of the one to the other which constitutes sovereignty'. Rousseau adopts this definition later in the final version (II. iv, end of first paragraph).

cannot be represented except by itself: this is argued at length in III. xv.

an individual's will: as the end of the paragraph makes clear, the 'individual' here is a monarch, the passage being directed against the idea that the general will could be vested in any one person. A few lines later, although the words given to the 'sovereign authority' ('le souverain') are 'I . . . want', the reference must be to the people as sovereign.

64   *Our political theorists*: specialist opinion is divided concerning the
     identity of the thinkers meant here; Rousseau refers later in the
     chapter to the Natural Law school (Grotius etc.), but it seems likely
     that Montesquieu also is under attack, since his famous interpre-
     tation of the English constitution (*Spirit of Laws*, XI. vi) involves
     dividing political power into legislative, executive, and judicial.

65   *the idea associated with the word law*: see II. vi.

     his translator Barbeyrac: the important translation of Grotius's *De
     iure belli ac pacis* by Jean Barbeyrac (1674–1744) appeared in 1724
     under the title *Du droit de la guerre et de la paix*.

66   *is always in the right*: in French 'la volonté générale est toujours
     droite', sometimes translated 'is always right', which is mislead-
     ing, because the English *right* can mean 'correct', but the French
     'droite' lacks this sense. As the immediate sequel shows, Rous-
     seau firmly denies that the general will always correctly knows
     its own good.

67   *Lycurgus*: according to legendary tradition, Lycurgus gave laws to
     Sparta, whose customs were much admired by Rousseau; com-
     pare II. vii, etc.

     Solon, Numa, and Servius: Solon, the historical legislator of Athens
     (640–548 BC), is probably mentioned because of his division of the
     body of citizens into four classes according to wealth; Numa, the
     legendary second king of Rome (seventh century BC), because he
     created numerous associations based on trade (in order, accord-
     ing to Plutarch, whom Rousseau seems to be following here, to
     reduce larger-scale civil conflict); and Servius Tullius, king of
     Rome in the sixth century BC, because he organized the *centuriae*,
     as Rousseau explains in detail later (IV. iv).

     History of Florence, Bk. VII: Rousseau quotes Machiavelli in
     Italian, here and later.

     the poverty of the language: Rousseau seems to mean that, since he
     has just said that the sovereign has absolute power over citizens,
     he might appear to contradict himself by mentioning citizens'
     rights against the sovereign. Men in the social state, apparently,
     have something similar to natural rights, but no word for them
     is available. The idea is conveyed by a statement in the chapter's
     penultimate paragraph: 'any man can make full use of that share
     of his goods and liberty that is left to him by these agreements'.

68   *for the community to use*: compare Locke, to whom Rousseau may
     be referring at the beginning of the paragraph: 'though men

when they enter into society give up the equality, liberty, and executive power they had in the state of nature . . . the power of the society or legislative constituted by them can never be supposed to extend farther than the common good' (second *Treatise on Civil Government*, IX. 131).

not only in essence but also in respect of its object: 'in essence': because its source is everyone generally; 'its object': what it is applied to, also everyone generally.

the matter becomes contentious: in French 'contentieuse', which refers not merely to matters of dispute, but (as Rousseau indicates) specific-ally to those cases between private persons and public authorities which have not been envisaged in any relevant law.

69 *time to put mine*: see the discussion of government in Bk. III.

has jurisdiction: in French 'connaît', which here has its legal sense (cp. English 'take cognizance').

70 *preferable . . . to what it was before*: this passage adds to the description of the advantages of the social state found in I. viii.

71 *a right that they do not have*: the question originates from two passages in Locke's second *Treatise on Civil Government*, one stating that a man 'not having the power of his own life cannot . . . put himself under the absolute arbitrary power of another to take away his life when he pleases' (IV. 23), the other asking why a man 'will give up his empire' [in the state of nature] 'and subject himself to the domination and control of any other power' (IX. 123).

the ruler: in French 'le prince', the first occurrence of the word in the *Contract*; I usually translate as 'ruler' (compare Latin *princeps*) or 'ruling body', although these terms exclude the semantic element of royalty. Rousseau's usage is his own and is explained in III. i.

as an enemy rather than as a citizen: the argument here relies on that previously expounded in I. iv concerning war.

72 *its rights in this matter are none too clear*: because, as the preceding chapter has emphasized, the sovereign can pronounce only on general matters.

73 *The Law*: see section I of the *Political Economy* for a sustained eulogy on the subject (p. 10), found also in the Geneva MS, I. vii.

in metaphysical terms alone: commentators agree that the target of this remark is Montesquieu's famous definition: 'Laws in the broadest sense are the necessary relationships which derive from the nature of things' (*Spirit of Laws*, I. i). However, in the last two chapters of Book II, there seems to be at least some trace of Montesquieu's definition in the importance Rousseau gives to 'relationships'.

73   *I have already said*: see II. iv.

74   *to the legislative power*: this passage well illustrates a distinction that is fundamental in Rousseau's political thought, that between sovereign and government (discussed at the beginning of III. i), which partly corresponds to the standard distinction between legislative and executive.

75   *any state ruled by laws*: cp. the definition at the beginning of section I of the *Political Economy*: 'a lawful or popular government, that is to say a government which has as its object the good of the people' (pp. 9–10).

76   *the argument put by Caligula*: see I. ii.

       his Statesman: the dialogue also known as the *Politicus*.

       says Montesquieu: in his *Considerations on the Greatness of the Romans and their Decadence* (1734), 1748 edition, ch. i.

77   *combined in the same persons*: of the various *decemviri* (councils of ten) in Roman history, Rousseau is referring, here and in what follows, to the decemvirs who in 451 BC were entrusted with absolute power and given the task of drawing up proposed laws, which when they were enacted as statutes by the *comitia centuriata* (see IV. iv) became the 'Twelve Tables'. The crisis he mentions occurred, according to legend, when a father killed his daughter in order to save her from one of the decemvirs; this supposedly brought about a revolution in which the decemvirs were overthrown.

       Calvin: Jean Calvin was born in northern France, moving to Geneva in 1541 at the age of 32. The *Institution of the Christian Religion*, mentioned in Rousseau's note, was first published in 1536.

78   *worth repeating*: see II. i; it is also repeated in III. xv.

       the fundamental rules of reasons of state: in French 'les règles fondamentales de la raison d'Etat'. The last phrase would usually be translated as 'reason of State' and denote political expediency in a bad sense, implying unscrupulousness, but such seems not to be the meaning here.

attribute their own wisdom to the gods: as his remarks in the next paragraph indicate, Rousseau has in mind instances such as Moses, bringing down from Mount Sinai the tablets on which was written the Decalogue, or Numa (mentioned in II. iii), said to have received counsel from the nymph Egeria.

79 *the law of the child of Ishmael*: i.e. the religion of Muhammad.

arrogant philosophers or blind partisanship: an obvious reference to the 'party' of the *philosophes* from whom Rousseau is distancing himself, most of them taking a destructively sceptical view of figures such as Moses or Muhammad.

the same objective: the allusion is not very clear, but what is meant is probably the idea in William Warburton's *The Divine Legation of Moses* (1737–41), well known in its time, that religion deterred wrongdoers by the belief in rewards and punishments after death.

80 *the Arcadians and Cyrenians . . . a people corrupted by vice*: Plato was asked, according to Diogenes Laertius, to legislate for the new town of Megalopolis in Arcadia (not in fact a rich country); the subjects of Minos, the legendary king of Crete, were proverbially given to lying and were said by Aristotle (*Politics*, Bk. II) to favour homosexuality.

Peoples: the 1782 edition reads: 'Most nations'. See the note after next.

their tyrants were expelled: Lycurgus's reforms are supposed to have been made after he returned from Crete to Sparta at a time of great disorder there; the second Tarquin was the last king of Rome, after whose expulsion in 510 BC the republic was formed; the modern tyrants are Philip II of Spain, against whom the United Provinces rebelled in the later sixteenth century, and the Hapsburg rulers of Germany, against whom Swiss independence was gained during the fourteenth century.

in nations as in men: in the 1782 edition the beginning of this paragraph runs: 'Youth is not childhood. Nations, like men, have a time of youth, or perhaps I should say maturity . . . '. The revisions (like that given in the note one above) were no doubt made in order to reduce the inconsistency between the first version of the passage and the statement in the chapter's second paragraph that nations are docile only when young.

81 *something out of nothing*: these remarks were certainly meant as a criticism of the idealized presentation of Peter in the recently

published first part of Voltaire's *History of the Empire of Russia under Peter the Great.*

81 *stronger than a large one*: Rousseau's views resemble Aristotle's (*Politics*, IV. iv), but his decided preference for small states was more certainly influenced by the example of the Greek city states, the early Roman republic, and Geneva. See also III. vi and xv.

82 *everything underneath*: in this passage, despite the suggestion in the term 'satrapies' that the states in question are Oriental, Rousseau was no doubt criticizing the situation in France.

other customary laws: in French 'd'autres coutumes', in the old sense of laws based on custom and codified; in France they varied greatly from region to region.

83 *the vortices of Descartes*: according to Descartes's theory of 'tourbillons' (*Principles of Philosophy* (1644), III. 65 ff.), all matter in the universe had circular motion, on a larger or smaller scale.

the time of their fall: commentators usually relate these reflections to remarks on the Roman Empire made by Machiavelli (*Discourses*, I. vi) and Montesquieu (*Considerations*, ch. ix).

86 *how to preserve it*: the Corsicans had been resisting Genoese rule for some thirty years, and were generally admired for it. In 1764, one of their leaders, Buttafoco, was to write to Rousseau, quoting from this chapter and urging him to draw up a constitution for the island; he responded with the *Project for a constitution for Corsica.*

particular subordination: this is presumably the same as the dependence on persons mentioned in I. vii (p. 58).

the instrument of its destruction: the Tlaxcalans, members of a small, free state within the Aztec empire, had no natural supplies of salt; the difficulties they incurred from its lack were apparently a reason why, having been subdued by the *conquistadores* under Hernando Cortès, they assisted him in his defeat of Montezuma (1519-20).

87 *civil liberty*: see I. viii.

extreme opulence or destitution: apart from Rousseau himself in the *Discourse on Inequality*, both Plato (*Laws*, Bk. V) and Aristotle (*Politics*, VI. x) advise against allowing excess of wealth and poverty.

88 *each of these aims*: see Montesquieu, *Spirit of Laws*, XI. v, for an analogous list, the most interesting point of difference being that for Montesquieu the Romans' aim was expansion.

89 *as we shall see later*: it is the government which, as III. i will explain, is intermediate between sovereign and state (on the abstract relationship between these, see I. vi).

even the best of them: that the sovereign may change its laws is argued in I. vii.

civil law: usually defined as the part of law which regulates the private dealings of citizens among themselves (cf. Montesquieu, *Spirit of Laws*, I. iii: besides political laws, men have laws 'in the relationship which all citizens have amongst themselves, which is civil law'). Rousseau adopts this meaning (which can be seen in the first words of the paragraph now in question), but in accordance with the definition of the social contract in I. vi.

90 *unknown to our political theorists*: Montesquieu however emphasized the importance of custom, for instance in *Spirit of Laws*, Bk. XIX. Rousseau may be referring to theorists of whom he thinks less well, such as Grotius and Pufendorf.

only political law . . . relates to my subject: despite this disclaimer, Rousseau discusses aspects of punishment in I. vi, II. v. and IV. viii, and the influence of custom in IV. vii.

91 *which is moral*: the eighteenth-century French word *moral* used here can correspond approximately to English *psychological* as well as to *moral*, which I retain because the ethical aspect is important in Rousseau's usage of the word.

can belong to it alone: see II. iv and vi.

92 *are called officers or kings*: in French 's'appellent magistrats ou *rois*'. In eighteenth-century French *magistrat* could have the Latinate sense of 'officer of government', but it tended to be applied to legal officials, including judges; Rousseau seems to exclude the legal aspect. To apply the term *kings* to members of a government is unusual, to say the least, and seems also to be based on Latin, the word *rex* (the origin of the French *roi*) meaning a ruler generally as well as a king.

the name of ruler: on *prince*, see the note to the word *ruler* on p. 71.

is not a contract: Rousseau is here arguing against a commonplace of seventeenth- and eighteenth-century contract theory, the concept of a pact of submission, which he criticizes in detail in III. xvi.

ruler or principal officer: in French '*prince* ou magistrat'.

the middle term being the government: a geometric (or continuous) proportion is here a double ratio, e.g. A is to B as B is to C,

A :B ::B : C, with B as the 'middle term'. If the middle term is identical in both single ratios, as in this example, the expression can be called 'a three-term proportion', as Rousseau does later. The difficult eighteenth-century mathematical language in this chapter was elucidated by Marcel Françon in two articles on which editors and translators have since relied: 'Le langage mathématique de J.-J. Rousseau', *Isis*, 40 (1949), 341–4; 'Sur le langage algébrique de Rousseau', *Annales de la société Jean-Jacques Rousseau*, 33 (1953–5), 243–6. See in English the notes in the edition of the *Contrat social* by Ronald Grimsley (Oxford, 1972), 155–7, which give more details than I can give here.

93 *the relationship becomes less*: to take one half and one twentieth as an example: the relation 1 : 20 is, for Rousseau, greater in mathemat-ical terminology than 1 : 2, but in ordinary language there is less of a relationship between 1 and 20 than between 1 and 2.

95 *a moral agent*: in French 'une personne morale', one of the expressions conveying that a corporate entity, such as a government, can in various respects act like an individual, on which see Introduction, p. xvii.

96 *We have stated*: in the preceding chapter; see p. 93.

98 *I have demonstrated previously*: another reference to p. 93.

99 *its rightfulness*: in French 'rectitude', in Rousseau's sense (as shown in the sequel) of conformity to the general will.

The Classification of Governments: a standard element in political theory. Rousseau's division based on numbers resembles that of Aristotle, Machiavelli, and Hobbes rather than Montesquieu, who distinguishes between republic, monarchy, and despotism (*Spirit of Laws*, II. i). For Rousseau a republic is 'any state ruled by laws' (II. vi), the people associated in the state retaining sovereign authority.

is democracy: as is often noted, this form of government by the people (criticized in the next chapter) is not what is usually meant nowadays by *democracy*, which corresponds more closely to the elective aristocracy mentioned by Rousseau in III. v.

102 *made virtue the principle of republics*: Montesquieu (*Spirit of Laws*, III. iii); although both writers make the same point about republics, *republic* for Montesquieu covered only aristocracy and democracy (ibid., I. ii), while for Rousseau it is, in this passage, 'every properly constituted state'.

'*I prefer . . . servitude*': quoted by Rousseau in Latin: 'Malo periculosam libertatem quam quietum servitium'.

the present King of Poland and Duke of Lorraine: Stanislas Lesczynski (1677–1766) was the titular king of Poland from 1704, but ruled only for short periods; in 1738 he became the sovereign duke of Lorraine. Rousseau may have found the quotation in his *Observations on the Government of Poland* (French edn. 1749).

103 *priests, elders, senate, gerontes*: all these terms are etymologically connected with words meaning 'old' (Greek *gerontes*: 'elders', 'chiefs').

the worst of all forms of government: Rousseau's long note to III. x, about Roman political history, says that 'hereditary aristocracy is the worst of the legitimate kinds of administration'. In the *Letters from the Mountains*, VI, summarizing *Contract* III. v, he makes a distinction: 'The best form of government is aristocracy; the worst form of sovereignty is aristocracy'.

aristocracy in the true sense of the word: here Rousseau is alluding to the Greek etymology, *aristoi* 'the best', *-kratia* 'power', 'rule'.

the two powers: the legislative and executive powers, as defined in III. i.

the most powerful: Latin *optimates*, from *optimus* 'best', is the term used by Cicero, etc., for 'the aristocratic party' in Roman politics.

104 *no longer available to the law*: cf. above, III. i, p. 95: 'the dominant will of the ruling body is only, or should only be, the general will or the law, its power is only the public power concentrated in it, and as soon as it has the desire to do some absolute and independent act of its own, the cohesiveness of the whole begins to be weakened'.

fall on the wealthy: however, in the passages of the *Politics* (IV. v–vii) to which Rousseau is presumably referring, Aristotle's assumption is that the rich are preferred in oligarchy, a particular and inferior form of aristocracy, but in true aristocracy merit as well as wealth qualifies for rule.

Monarchy: Rousseau's pronounced dislike of monarchies is expressed with comparative restraint here; it is more overt in his unpublished works, e.g. the *Considerations on the Government of Poland*, ch. 8.

the ruling body . . . executive power: another reminder of the arguments advanced in III. i.

104   *is seen as*: in French 'un être collectif représente un individu . . .
      un individu représente un être collectif', in which the sense of
      représente is obscure, as editors have noted; it cannot however
      mean *represent* in the sense of 'act as representative for'.

105   *drawing a great ship over the water*: Rousseau probably read the
      anecdote in Plutarch's *Life of Marcellus*.

106   *by Samuel . . . by Machiavelli*: 1 Samuel 8: 10–18; as regards Ma-
      chiavelli, the reference is to *The Prince* generally. Rousseau's
      ensuing note argues against taking the conventional view of the
      book as a manual for cunning and unscrupulous rulers.

      We have established: in III. iii, final paragraph.

      intermediate orders are therefore necessary: on this important point
      Rousseau is following Montesquieu (*Spirit of Laws*, II. iv).

      others to act in his place: probably a reference to what, in his
      Judgement on the Abbé de Saint-Pierre's *Polysynody*, Rousseau
      denounces as a 'vizirate', when the vizir or minister serves his
      own interest instead of that of the king or the people.

      inferior to a republic: this seems to be a momentary inconsistency
      in the use of terms, *republic* here meaning some form of democ-
      racy rather than, as is usual in the *Contract*, any state governed
      by laws (II. vi).

107   *a new epoch in the country's history*: this paragraph, added while the
      book was printing, was intended—so Rousseau says in the
      Confessions, Bk. XI—to flatter the Duc de Choiseul and thus
      facilitate the circulation of the book in France, but unfortunately
      produced the contrary effect.

108   *the choice of a good king*: the references to hereditary rule and
      regency in this paragraph make it clear that the main target is
      the French monarchical system (regency of Anne of Austria:
      1643–61; of Philip of Orléans: 1715–1723).

      your father wasn't a king: this anecdote about Dionysius II, ruler of
      Syracuse in the fourth century BC, is in Plutarch's *Sayings of Kings*.

      if someone else had been ruler: Tacitus, *Histories*, I. xvi, quoted by
      Rousseau in the Latin.

109   *that I have already disproved*: see I. iii.

      as a punishment from Heaven: perhaps no specific reference is
      intended here, but the idea is found in both Calvin (*Institution*,
      1560 edn., IV. xx. 24) and Bossuet (*Politics*, VI. ii. 6).

110   *the English constitution . . . Poland*: on England, Rousseau must be
      following the famous analysis of the British constitution in

Montesquieu, *Spirit of Laws*, XI. vi; on Poland, he himself gives an analysis in the *Considerations*, ch. 7.

when discussing governments in general: i.e. the answer will vary according to circumstances (III. iii. end).

not mixed, but modified: the meaning is somewhat clarified by Rousseau's remarks on the Roman tribunate (IV. v, second paragraph).

commissions: in French 'tribunaux', which usually signifies courts of law, but here, presumably, committees assigned particular functions.

111   *laid down by Montesquieu*: in the four books devoted to the subject of climate in *The Spirit of Laws*, see particularly XVII. ii.

112   *between free states and monarchies*: in this paragraph Rousseau seems to have in mind Montesquieu's division of governments into repub-lican, monarchical, and despotic (cp. note to the title of III. iii, p. 99).

114   *Chardin*: Rousseau seems to have found the quotations in the Amsterdam, 1735 edition of his *Voyages en Perse*, 4 vols., Vol. III, 76, 83–4.

116   *subjects . . . citizens*: the former are ruled by a monarch, the latter have some degree of self-rule.

The security and prosperity of the associates: the inclusion of prosperity, as well as security, is an addition to the terms of the problem defined in I. vi, to which the social contract is the solution: 'Find a form of association which will defend and protect . . . the person and property of each associate . . .'.

117   *too much admired*: probably a criticism of the Introduction to Voltaire's *Siècle de Louis XIV* (1751), in which Voltaire states that the 'centuries' of classical Greece and Rome, Renaissance Italy, and France under Louis XIV are the greatest in human history. Rousseau's distrust of civilization goes back to the first Discourse, on the arts and sciences.

of their enslavement: from Tacitus, *Agricola*, xxi, on the Britons' reaction to Roman civilization.

to be the best of all: another unfriendly allusion to Voltaire; known largely as a poet, he was also wealthy, which was very unusual for a writer.

having brought desolation call it peace: Tacitus, *Agricola*, xxx, from a Caledonian chief's speech against the Romans.

117   *in decent circumstances and in freedom*: an anecdote from the French
       civil war, the Fronde (1648–52), recounted in his Memoirs by the
       Cardinal de Retz (1613–79) about himself when assistant to the
       Archbishop of Paris; Rousseau's contention that the country was
       prosperous at the time is untenable.

       'It seemed . . . to weaken it': not a quotation, but a summary of a
       passage in the preface to Machiavelli's *History of Florence* (1520–5).

       The gradual formation: This note (like his note to the preceding
       chapter) was added while the book was in the press; the
       connection it makes between prosperity and liberty suggests that
       he was trying to adapt his argument in this chapter to the firm
       statement in II. xi that the greatest political good lies in liberty
       and equality.

118   *the Serrar di consiglio in* 1198: the Maggior Consiglio (Great
       Council) of 480 members elected by districts, dating from 1171,
       was 'closed' in 1297 (not 1198) by constitutional measures which
       resulted in rule by an oligarchy formed by the city's great
       commercial families.

       the Squittinio della libertà veneta: 'The Squeaking of Venetian
       Liberty', the polemical title of an anonymous pamphlet, 1612,
       arguing that the Holy Roman Emperor had the right to rule
       Venice.

       from aristocracy to democracy: because, in the common view, Rome
       after Romulus, its founder and first king, was a monarchy until
       the expulsion of the Tarquins, then, during what is known as the
       Republican period, an aristocracy governed by the patrician
       class, then (after the lengthy Conflict of the Orders, patricians
       against plebeians) a senatorial democracy, from about the begin-
       ning of the third century BC. Rousseau's critique discounts the
       regal period, and argues that the Republic, having no definite
       form initially, became first a democracy, then a senatorial
       aristocracy, the civil wars in the first century BC making it a
       monarchy under Julius Caesar and the first of the emperors,
       Augustus.

119   *as Machiavelli has shown*: in the *Discourses*, I. iv.

120   *forced, but not obliged, to obey*: i.e. the moral obligation binding
       every citizen who accepts the social contract no longer exists.

       the general name of anarchy: i.e. a government can remain, but
       there is no state in Rousseau's sense of a society controlled by
       the laws made by the people as sovereign.

democracy . . . explanation: the first two terms mean mob rule and rule by the few. The observations on the proper sense of *tyrant* may have been suggested by Machiavelli's analogous comments (*Discourses*, I. ii), in which he says that a monarchy degenerates into a tyranny, but without specifying further.

121   *even the best constituted governments*: cf. Aristotle, *Politics*, V. iv; Montesquieu, *Spirit of Laws*, XI. vi.

while able to do so: possibly based on Hobbes, *Leviathan*, XXVI. iii: 'When long use obtaineth the authority of a law, it is not length of time that maketh the authority, but the will of the sovereign signified by his silence, for silence is sometimes an argument of consent.'

122   *The final census . . . children or slaves*: neither the distinction Rousseau makes between census (*cens*) and enumeration (*dénombrement*), nor the dates to which he refers, is clear. The *Oxford Classical Dictionary*, under 'Population', suggests a figure above 200,000 for the number of males of military age in the third century BC, rising to over 900,000 in the first. The argument may be directed against the Genevans; cf. the note below to p. 125.

123   *should make itself visible*: in *Poland*, ch. vii, Rousseau reiterates this point with regard to the Polish national assembly.

124   *resisted the House of Austria*: i.e. by alliances or confederations (cp. III. xv, end), which do not create 'combinations' of states. The great emperor is the Persian King Xerxes, defeated by the Greek city-states in 480–479 BC; on Holland (as the United Provinces) and the Swiss cantons see the third note to p. 80.

the country's Estates: or estates-general, on which see the note to p. 28.

125   *there can be no representative*: i.e. the government cannot act for the sovereign (the 'body represented' in this passage). On representation generally see the next chapter.

the Roman comitia: on these see IV. iv.

discourage the citizens from holding them: in the *Letters from the Mountains*, VII, in a hostile account of the increase in the Genevan Petit Conseil's power, Rousseau makes the same point about its tactics.

126   *the enforced labour of the corvée*: in French simply 'les corvées', on which see the note to the *Political Economy* p. 35. In the *Constitution for Corsica*, Rousseau admits that it was very unpopular in France, but says that in Switzerland no one complained of it.

127   *the Third Estate*: Rousseau chooses to consider only the repres-
       entatives of the bourgeoisie, or Third Estate (*Tiers Etat*), as
       speaking for the people as a whole.

       it is nothing: this attacks the view of English constitutional
       freedom accepted by many in France, notably Voltaire (e.g. in
       the *Letters Concerning the English Nation*, or *Philosophical Letters*,
       1733–4) and Montesquieu, in a famous chapter (XI. vi) in the
       Spirit of Laws.

       the name of man was dishonourable: Rousseau is alluding to feudal
       'homage' (from *homme*, 'man'), according to which a lord's tenant
       or vassal bound himself to the lord's service.

       inconvenience is nothing: cf. III. xii, end.

       the tribunes would not have dared to: the lictors were attendants and
       escorts for state officials (magistrates); what Rousseau is referring
       to is perhaps that they are known to have acted sometimes as
       executioners.

128   *I have proved the contrary*: see I. ii, iv.

129   *the sequel to this work*: this must be the project mentioned in the
       Prefatory Note. In the summary of the *Social Contract* contained
       in *Émile*, Bk. V, Rousseau speaks of the possibility of leagues or
       confederacies, within which, he says, each state can be autono-
       mous as regards its internal affairs.

       right and acts: i.e. the rightful laws made by the sovereign and the
       actions taken by the executive power or government.

       Some writers have claimed: in the second Discourse Rousseau writes
       of a similar but not identical formula as 'the common opinion'
       which he adopts provisionally ('to consider the establishment of
       the body politic as a true contract between the people and the
       chiefs whom it chooses for itself'); he goes on to imply, in the
       immediate sequel, that the government cannot alter fundamen-
       tal decisions taken by the people.

130   *to return to a condition of complete freedom*: perhaps because the
       obligation comes from oneself and the person obeyed is there-
       fore oneself also; but the remark is somewhat obscure.

       a particular act: see II. vi.

131   *from making a law to its execution*: editors connect this with a
       passage in Hobbes: 'Those who met together with intention to
       erect a city, were almost in the very act of meeting, a democracy'
       (*De cive*, VII).

132 *the exercise of right being potentially harmful*: a free translation of the French *cas odieux* (in 'ne donner au cas odieux que ce qu'on ne peut lui refuser dans toute la rigueur du droit'). The obscure legal phrase (literally 'odious case') is an old term denoting a case in which the exercise of a right, if permitted, would be harmful in some way.

133 *permission to assemble*: another reference to the episode referred to on p. 77.

of which I have already spoken: see III. xiii, xiv. These further remarks, as well as others in the chapter, were considered highly objectionable by the authorities in Geneva and constituted one of the main reasons for the book's condemnation there.

what I believe I have demonstrated: see I. vii.

133 *Grotius even thinks*: in the *De iure belli ac pacis*, II. v. 24; the section includes a comment which makes the same point as Rousseau's note.

134 *the world's most fortunate nation*: those meant are generally assumed to be the people of the rural Swiss cantons.

135 *hard labour . . . a reformatory*: the Bernese form of punishment referred to was called *Schallenwerk*. Beaufort is put with Cromwell as being a leader of rebels in a civil war, the Fronde having been almost contemporaneous with the civil wars in England.

the general will no longer the will of all: the distinction is first made in II. iii (second paragraph). The passage that follows in IV. i, analysing the interaction of particular and general interests, may be compared with the remark in II. iv: 'why is the happiness of each the constant wish of all, unless it is because there is no one who does not apply the word *each* to himself, and is not thinking of himself when he votes for all?'

136 *take great care to reserve to their members*: it is not entirely clear whether Rousseau means to approve of governments on this score, or to criticize them for it; a passage in the *Letters from the Mountains*, VII, suggests the latter, since in it Rousseau is critical of the fact that in Geneva the Petit Conseil (here equivalent to 'government') does not allow the Conseil Général (the 'sovereign') the right to express its opinions or to determine which questions it can discuss.

the plebiscites of the people: in French 'les plébiscites du peuple', a slightly misleading phrase as regards Rome, since the plebeians, who passed plebiscites in their assemblies, were not the whole of the *populus*, 'people', this including the patricians.

137   *Tacitus observes*: in the *Histories*, I. 85. The year in question is AD
      69, when first Otho, then Vitellius, were briefly emperors.

      that he is not born a man: a similar point is made in I. iv.

138   *I have made sufficiently clear . . . I shall return to the subject later*: the
      references back are to various passages in III. x to xviii; and
      forward to IV. iii, iv.

139   *which as I have said*: see III. xvii.

      says Montesquieu: *Spirit of Laws*, II. ii.

140   *The multitude of them living in poverty in St Barnabas*: in French 'une
      multitude de pauvres Barnabotes', Rousseau employing a Vene-
      tian term for those living in a parish known for its poverty.

      has with us: Rousseau is generally considered to have exagger-
      ated the resemblance between the two republics, perhaps be-
      cause he wanted to make a point about the aristocratic nature
      of the Genevan (rather than Venetian) government.

      the mainland subjects there: on the categories of Genevan citizen-
      ship see the note to p. 56. In the present passage Rousseau refers
      also to the *sujets* of Geneva, who lived outside the city and had
      no political rights.

      I have already said: see III. iv, end.

      change the form of the government: the political writings of the Abbé
      de Saint-Pierre (1658–1743) were closely studied by Rousseau,
      who wrote a long abridgement of, and a 'Judgement' on, the
      Discours sur la Polysynodie (1718), to which he refers here in
      defining its main proposal.

141   *comitia*: in French *comices*; there is no corresponding English
      term. Rousseau defines them as assemblies of the Roman people
      convoked by law, and devotes the first long part of the chapter
      to examining the methods of defining the various population
      groups according to which the *comitia* were organized. The
      chapter has been much criticized (like the succeeding chapters
      on Rome) for being no more than historical padding and for its
      second-hand erudition, taken largely from Machiavelli's *Discours-
      es* and an obscure work, *De antiquo jure civium Romanorum* ('On the
      ancient laws of the citizens of Rome', 1560) by another Italian
      author, Carolus Sigonius. Rousseau's aim was no doubt to
      reinforce his abstract arguments about democracy (in a broad
      sense) with a detailed study of the political organization of a
      state that was universally respected. The message, in the con-
      cluding paragraph, seems to be that wisely drafted laws can

ensure the efficient transaction of political affairs by means of public assemblies, even allowing for the defects of 'men as they are' (see the preamble to Bk. I).

tribus, or tribes: again the etymology is probably false, but there may be some connection between *tribus* and *tres*.

'strength' . . . 'law': the etymological meanings viewed sceptically by Rousseau, based on the Greek *rhome* 'strength, might' and *nomos* 'law', are certainly incorrect, but almost nothing is known of the Etruscan language from which the Roman names originate. The names of Romulus and his twin Remus do appear to be subsequent inventions for the mythical founders of Rome, which is part of Rousseau's point.

142   *the tribe of Albans . . . all the time*: I have incorporated the Latin names in the text, Rousseau giving them as footnotes. Tatienses seems to be an error for Titienses, the correct form.

Servius: Servius Tullius, not a legendary but a real figure, ruled as king in the mid-sixth century BC.

from which it took its name: this first increase in the number of 'tribes' was not certainly carried out by Servius; Rousseau is following a traditional account.

143   *their wise legislator*: i.e. Servius.

the upholders of the Republic: i.e. public officials.

says Varro: both this reference, to the poem *De re rustica* ('On Farming'), III. i, by Varro (116–27 BC), and the following one, to the *Natural History*, XVIII. iii, of Pliny the Elder (AD 23 or 24–79), are taken by Rousseau from Sigonius.

the censors: the office of censor, which effectively lasted from the fifth to the first century BC, was originally created for the taking of the census, but came to have moral authority because the two censors had the right to deny citizenship to those guilty of various offences. On Rousseau's view of the office generally see IV. vii.

145   *Marius was the first to deign to enrol them*: cf. the *Political Economy*, p. 31.

146   *what effect they had on the people's assemblies*: this is the point at which, having explained the categorization of the population, Rousseau moves on to the second main part of the chapter, in which he discusses the more obviously political aspects of the arrangements for holding *comitia*.

146   *the tribunes of the people*: the *tribuni plebis*, who numbered ten by
       the mid-fifth century BC, were originally responsible for the
       protection of the plebeians (against the patricians), and had
       important duties and rights as regards the passing of plebiscites
       and the obstruction by veto of measures taken by patrician
       functionaries. See the next chapter for Rousseau's view on the
       value of a tribunate in a modern state.

147   *their clients*: clientship was a personal and customary bond of
       mutual service between poorer and richer citizens ('patrons'), for
       instance between a freedman and his former master. Rousseau's
       eulogy omits to say that the relationship could easily degenerate
       into parasitism. In *Poland*, III, end, he mentions an analogous
       institution.

148   *other curule officials*: the curule magistracies were so called be-
       cause they gave the right to a 'curule seat', a folding ivory chair.

       follows the principle of democracy: see IV. iii.

149   *in reality a council of the Roman people*: this is probably the chapter's
       most important argument, the rest of the paragraph indicating
       how the laws concerning the *comitia tributa* could have been
       modified so as to make them more completely representative of
       the Roman people.

150   *the decay of the Republic*: Cicero's opinion is to be found in his *De
       legibus* ('On Laws'), III. xv, but here Rousseau is probably
       conducting a dialogue rather with Montesquieu (*Spirit of Laws*,
       II. ii), who gives the reference to Cicero, and whose view is that
       open voting was necessary in a democracy and secret ballots in
       an aristocracy.

       Custodes . . . suffragium: *custodes*, 'guardians', are here the officials
       who guarded the urns in which votes were placed; *diribitores*,
       'tellers', those who counted the votes by separating them out;
       rogatores, 'callers', those who among other things marked points
       against candidates' names.

151   *the constituent parts of the state*: in French 'parties constitutives de
       l'État', an obscure phrase which, to judge by what follows in this
       chapter, means government (executive) and sovereign (legisla-
       tive).

       the ephors did in Sparta: the five ephors of ancient Sparta, elected
       annually by the citizens (not a majority of the population), came
       to have administrative dominance, even over the kings, but also
       enforced the famous Spartan discipline among the citizens.

forced to yield . . . any jurisdiction: not a reference to any specific incident, it seems, but to the tribunician veto in general. Other civil officers (censors, praetors, etc.) had the responsibility of taking auspices and definite areas of jurisdiction, but Rousseau is probably exaggerating the extent to which the tribunes were excluded from such functions.

152 *after Cleomenes Sparta was nothing*: in the third century BC Spartan institutions, and power, were in decline. Rousseau's source here, Plutarch, wrote lives of the kings Agis IV, whose attempts at reform were crushed by the ephors, and Cleomenes III, who abolished the ephorate.

the emperors who destroyed it: first Julius Caesar, then Augustus, in the first century BC, took over tribunician authority.

to which nobody dares to be witness: the Council of Ten, which enjoyed a sinister reputation of the kind indicated here, was one of the most important political bodies in Venice until the end of the Republic in 1797. Dating from 1310, and headed by the Doge, its original purpose was to prevent *coups d'état* or other treasonable crime, but over the centuries it extended its executive powers very widely, while remaining responsible for state security.

153 *The Office of Dictator*: the meaning, as becomes clear, is not at bottom the modern one, but is based on Roman custom, also admired by Machiavelli (*Discourses*, I. xxxiv), by whom Rousseau was no doubt influenced in this respect.

154 *the strength of its constitution*: dictatorship in its early form was a regular part of the constitution from the late sixth to the late third century BC; it superseded the powers of the consuls in a crisis, usually military, and lasted for six months at most.

155 *when faced by external force*: Sulla's dictatorship, which like Caesar's resembles those of modern times in being of unlimited duration and including legislative powers, lasted from 81 BC until his death in 78 BC; Marius was a political and military rival. The same relationship existed between Pompey and Caesar, who kept the dictatorship he had obtained in 48 BC until his death in 44 BC.

the conspiracy of Catilina: in 63 BC Catilina, defeated by Cicero as candidate for the consulship, conspired to seize power, but was foiled after being denounced by Cicero in the Senate.

could not have been made against a dictator: Cicero as consul, after the Senate had decided on the death penalty for five associates

of Catilina, had them executed without allowing them the
traditional legal right of appeal to the people.

155 *it was certainly a favour*: Cicero was exiled in 58 BC under a law
passed in that year by an enemy, the tribune Clodius, which
decreed exile for anyone who had had a citizen put to death
without proper trial. In his comments Rousseau disregards the
political reasons for Cicero's banishment (and his return in 57
BC), which are connected with the shifting alliances and enmities
between himself, Clodius, and Pompey.

156 *The Office of Censor*: the meaning here is wider than the modern
sense of control of the media, and is closer to that of moral
control over behaviour, exercised in Geneva and elsewhere by
the religious authorities, a point not mentioned by Rousseau.
Montesquieu (*Considerations*, VIII) had also expressed admiration
for the Roman form of the institution.

157 *contrary to the usual opinion*: Rousseau's views on duels are to be
found in the *Letter to d'Alembert* and *Julie*, Pt. I, Letter 57.

forbids me to name on this occasion: the island of Chio. As pronounced in the eighteenth century, its name would have offered
an obvious play of words on *chier* 'to shit'.

158 *Civil Religion*: on this extremely controversial chapter see Introduction, p. xxi. Although added at a late stage—it was not in the
version of the work sent by Rousseau to his publisher Rey late
in 1760—its central argument, that states should have a civil
religion, is found in a long and well-known letter to Voltaire, the
'Letter on Providence' of 18 August 1756. The Geneva MS
contains an untitled draft of the chapter.

the same as Caligula's: see I. ii.

a branch of learning: i.e. early studies in what is now comparative
religion.

159 *the Canaanite gods*: Rousseau's argument is that Canaan was the
Promised Land and that, in the history of the Israelites' conquest
of it (as recorded in the Books of Judges and Joshua), its gods
were therefore spoken of in a particular manner, not applicable
in the example he then gives.

to do homage: Tarentum, in southern Italy, originally a Greek
settlement, was conquered by the Romans in 282 BC.

not in the Latin: literally translated, the Latin runs: Are not those
things that Kemosh your god possesses owed to you by right?
The *New English Bible* has: 'It is for you to possess whatever

Kemosh your god gives you; and all that the Lord our God gave us as we advanced is ours'; different versions can be found elsewhere. Rousseau's suggestion is that the Catholic translator realized the polytheistic implications in the Latin and sought to tone them down.

Phocian: in French *Phocéen* 'Phocaean', apparently in error, from the town of Phocaea in Asia Minor, instead of *Phocien*, from the town of Phocis, in central Greece, which was the town involved in the war.

not to make unbelievers submit: three Holy or Sacred Wars are usually distinguished in ancient Greek history, from the sixth to the fourth century BC, involving a league of states based on the Apollonian shrine at Delphi. The war referred to here, 355–347 BC, was mainly between Phocis and Thebes. Although the issues were no doubt political as well as religious, Phocis seeking greater independence, the immediate cause was the cultivation by the Phocians of fields said to be sacred to Apollo.

160 *the Christian nations*: Rousseau's firm statement of the opposition between religious and political law, the basis of his controversial views on Christianity in this chapter, were anticipated by Montesquieu in the *Spirit of Laws*, Bk. XXVI (e.g. ch. ii), although Montesquieu's arguments are more cautious. The disruptive effects of religion are also a common theme in the writings of Voltaire and other *philosophes*.

the most violent despotism: the 'visible ruler' is the Pope (as opposed to God); the expression comes from Montesquieu (*Spirit of Laws*, XXIV, vi).

closely knit: the meaning is presumably that the Islamic 'law' applies both in the secular and the religious domain.

161 *subjugated by barbarians*: this seems to refer to the decline of the Caliphate and the defeats at the hands of the early Ottoman emperors in the Middle Ages.

the sect of Ali: now usually known as the Shiite branch of Islam, originating with Muhammad's son-in-law Ali and dominant in Persia.

the Czars have gone to the same lengths: this avoids the affirmation that the Czar is the head of the Russian Orthodox Church, which would not have been correct; Rousseau may be following Voltaire, *History of the Empire of Russia under Peter the Great*, Pt. I (1759), ch. x, on the changes carried out by Peter in 1721: 'If the

Czar did not make himself the head of the Russian Church, as the kings of Great Britain are of the Anglican Church, he became in effect its absolute master.'

161   *only its rulers*: in French 'ses princes'; for the distinction between legislator and ruler see III. i.

the reunion of the two heads of the eagle: the phrase is puzzling. The two-headed eagle, an imperial emblem used by the House of Austria among others, denotes rule over east and west, as in the Roman Empire, but Rousseau's implication is that it denotes authority in both the secular and the religious domain.

properly constituted: Hobbes had stated (*De cive*, xviii, 28, end, to which Rousseau is presumably alluding) that in a Christian state the secular power should have both political and religious control.

a letter . . . April 1643: Barbeyrac's preface to his translation of Grotius's *De iure belli ac pacis* quotes the letter, which says that according to Hobbes individuals should follow the religion approved in their country by the public authorities.

162   *Bayle and Warburton*: Pierre Bayle (1647–1706), French Protestant author of works in favour of tolerance and of a very influential dictionary of ideas (*Dictionnaire historique et critique*, 1697), had argued in an early work, the *Pensées diverses sur la comète* (*Diverse Thoughts on the Comet*, 1683), that as regards morality atheism was better than superstition or idolatry, by which he probably meant Catholicism. Montesquieu refers to this idea in the *Spirit of Laws*, XXIV. ii, by which Rousseau seems here to have been influenced. On Warburton, see note to p. 79, concerning his *Divine Legation of Moses*, ii, 5–6; but the view that Christianity helped to maintain society was of course a cliché in religious writings.

either society in general or a particular society: in French 'la société, qui est ou générale ou particulière'; this is the concept of a 'general society of the human race' which is discussed in the abandoned chapter from the Geneva MS of the *Contract* (see Appendix).

the simple and pure religion of the Gospel, true theism: here Rousseau is making the large claim that what is now usually called deism (a term which then had derogatory overtones lacking in *theism*) was essentially the same as Christianity. A much fuller treatment of the subject is found in *Émile*, IV.

natural divine law: in French 'droit divin naturel'; like the phrase at the end of the paragraph, 'divine civil or divine positive law' ('droit divin civil ou positif'), this appears to be of Rousseau's invention, and was presumably based on *droit divin*, literally 'divine law', as in *roi de droit divin*, 'king by divine right', where the phrase means that the royal right is a law divinely ordained. As for *natural* and *positive*, they convey the difference between laws of nature and those instituted by men.

163   *Sacer estod, 'May you be accursed'*: Rousseau gives only the Latin phrase, literally 'May you be dedicated to the gods', i.e. to be destroyed by them if they see fit. The formula outlawed the person so addressed; anyone killing him was not liable to prosecution.

  all acknowledge each other as brothers: i.e. all Christians without distinction of country, thus weakening the attachment to any one nation-state.

  nothing that is more deeply opposed to the social spirit: this was one of the sentences that aroused particular opposition among readers; Rousseau felt obliged to explain himself both in letters to his friends and in published works (the *Letter to Christophe de Beaumont* and the first of the *Letters from the Mountains*).

  the most perfect society that can be imagined: The reference may be to ch. vi, one of the two chapters on Bayle, in Bk. XXIV of Montesquieu's *Spirit of Laws*, in which he takes issue with the view he attributes to Bayle, that true Christians could not form a viable state, and argues that a Christian people would be stronger than any other state.

164   *as it lies heavy on his people*: Rousseau's views here are close to those expressed by Machiavelli (*Discourses*, II. ii), and may have been influenced by him.

165   *and they kept their word*: as recorded by Livy, *Histories*, II. 45.

  no holy war is possible for Christians: this may seem inconsistent with the early part of the chapter, in which the assumption was that religious wars have been a feature of Christianity as opposed to paganism.

  when the cross superseded the eagle: i.e. when the Roman empire became Christian, conventionally dated to the reign of Constantine the Great (306–337).

166   *'In the republic . . . not harmful to others'*: according to critical editions of Rousseau, this sentence is not to be found in the published text of d'Argenson's *Considérations*, but I am indebted to Professor Patrick Coleman (personal communication) for the

information that he has traced it in the 1765 edition, in the chapter on Holland.

the mortality of the soul: on Catilina's conspiracy see the note to p. 155; Caesar spoke for him in the Senate after Cicero's revelation of the plot.

167   *let him be punished by death*: another extremely controversial passage; it is perhaps comparable to the intolerance shown towards atheism at the time (e.g. in Locke, *A Letter Concerning Toleration*, which is however less extreme); Plato (*Laws*, X) recommends prison for impiety, and the death penalty if the offence is repeated.

an exclusive national religion: apparently a reference to the survival of French Protestantism described in the next note.

Marriage . . . society could not subsist: the true subject here is Protestant marriage in France, a topical issue. France had officially been an exclusively Catholic country since 1685, when the Revocation of the Edict of Nantes ended tolerance for the Calvinist Huguenots, but many had stayed in France, more or less concealing their real religious affiliation. A decree of 1724 had reiterated, among other things, that Protestants should be married only by Catholic priests. The reality of intolerance had been dramatically illustrated late in 1761, when Jean Calas, a Huguenot tradesman, had been accused of the murder, for religious motives, of his son; he was executed in March 1762. When the *Contract* was at the proof stage of publication Rousseau decided to abandon the note, presumably because he felt the subject was too delicate at the time, and wrote to Rey requesting its removal, but copies containing it found their way into circulation, and it was restored in the 1782 edition.

168   *to have embraced the religion of Rome*: in 1593 the future Henri IV, at that time the leader of the Huguenots in the Wars of Religion, abjured Protestantism and so paved the way for his coronation as King of France. The reference is apparently to an anecdote preserved by the historian Hardouin de Péréfixe in his *History of Henry the Great* (1661): Henri is supposed to have been told by a Protestant minister that he could achieve Christian salvation if he were a Catholic, and, remarking that the Catholics denied that he could be saved if he were a Protestant, opted for the prudent course and Catholicism.

international law . . . treaties, etc.: these subjects are presumably those that Rousseau had meant to discuss in the more general work which, in his Prefatory Note, he says he has abandoned.

Appendix

169 *The General Society of the Human Race*: the chapter's original title, deleted in the MS, was 'That There Is No Natural Society Among Men'.

seems to smother sentiment: this passage is apparently an attack on the notion that 'universal benevolence' is a necessary element in human psychology, and would be an adequate basis for men in society to behave well to each other. Rousseau's view seems to be that if we were all automatically benevolent to each other, the sentiment of goodwill would disappear.

170 *as regards identity of nature, it is devoid of effect in this situation*: i.e. the fact that all men are of the same nature is inadequate (like 'universal benevolence') as a basis for cooperation among men living together; the later argument will be that only the social contract provides a proper basis.

this new order of things: when men move from living in isolation to living in some kind of society, but one that is not rightly based. The phrase also occurs in Pt. II of the *Discourse on Inequality*.

the Golden Age: in Graeco-Roman myth, the time when all human needs were satisfied without the necessity for work.

172 *common sensorium*: an ancient phrase, strictly meaning the location of sensation in the brain, but more widely the brain itself.

'I realize that . . . than I am': this sentence combines passages from two sections of Diderot's article 'Natural Right' ('Droit naturel'). The spoken words are those of a man imagined by Diderot; he is 'tormented by passions so violent' (section III) that life is a burden unless he satisfies them, and he is prepared to give his fellows the right to kill him provided he has the same right against them. The 'wise man' (Rousseau's description) who will throttle him is the writer of the article, deciding how to answer the violent man 'before we throttle him' ('avant de l'étouffer', section V).

173 *He will say*: what follows, until 'live or die', is a slightly altered version of remarks in 'Droit naturel'.

'what I cannot yet see . . . what interest I have in being just': this passage is perhaps the clearest indication that Rousseau is taking the arguments of the 'independent man' further than Diderot had in order to show that his position in the *Encyclopédie* article is inadequate.

174   *the interior voice*: i.e. conscience; the word occurs a few lines later.

Will he consult . . . of the human race?: this is taken from 'Droit naturel', paragraph 8: ' "But," you will say, "where is the general law deposited? Where can I consult it? . . . In the principles of every civilized nation's written law; in the social actions of savage and barbarian peoples; in the tacit conventions of the enemies of the human race among themselves." '

the Code of Justinian: a compilation of Roman Imperial constitutions, the major part being those of Diocletian, drawn up under Justinian, emperor from 527 to 565.

as Grotius observes: in his *De iure belli ac pacis*, II. xv. 5.

175   *'For among our ancestors . . . a foreign traveller'*: the remark, quoted in Latin, is from Cicero's *De officiis*, and was no doubt found by Rousseau in the passage from Grotius mentioned in the last note.

INDEX

References are given to the Introduction, text, and Explanatory Notes.

A page-number followed by n. indicates that the index entry is mentioned in the Explanatory Notes for that page, but not in the text.

THOMAS AQUINAS	**Selected Philosophical Writings**
GEORGE BERKELEY	**Principles of Human Knowledge** and **Three Dialogues**
EDMUND BURKE	**A Philosophical Enquiry into the Origin of Our Ideas of the Sublime and Beautiful** **Reflections on the Revolution in France**
THOMAS CARLYLE	**The French Revolution**
CONFUCIUS	**The Analects**
FRIEDRICH ENGELS	**The Condition of the Working Class in England**
JAMES GEORGE FRAZER	**The Golden Bough**
THOMAS HOBBES	**Human Nature** and **De Corpore Politico** **Leviathan**
JOHN HUME	**Dialogues Concerning Natural Religion** and **The Natural History of Religion** **Selected Essays**
THOMAS MALTHUS	**An Essay on the Principle of Population**
KARL MARX	**Capital** **The Communist Manifesto**
J. S. MILL	**On Liberty and Other Essays** **Principles of Economy** and **Chapters on Socialism**
FRIEDRICH NIETZSCHE	**On the Genealogy of Morals** **Twilight of the Idols**
THOMAS PAINE	**Rights of Man, Common Sense, and Other Political Writings**
JEAN-JACQUES ROUSSEAU	**Discourse on Political Economy** and **The Social Contract** **Discourse on the Origin of Inequality**
SIMA QIAN	**Historical Records**
ADAM SMITH	**An Inquiry into the Nature and Causes of the Wealth of Nations**
MARY WOLLSTONECRAFT	**Political Writings**

*The
Oxford
World's
Classics
Website*

www.worldsclassics.co.uk

- Information about new titles
- Explore the full range of Oxford World's Classics
- Links to other literary sites and the main OUP webpage
- Imaginative competitions, with bookish prizes
- Peruse *Compass*, the Oxford World's Classics magazine
- Articles by editors
- Extracts from Introductions
- A forum for discussion and feedback on the series
- Special information for teachers and lecturers

www.worldsclassics.co.uk

American Literature

British and Irish Literature

Children's Literature

Classics and Ancient Literature

Colonial Literature

Eastern Literature

European Literature

History

Medieval Literature

Oxford English Drama

Poetry

Philosophy

Politics

Religion

The Oxford Shakespeare

A complete list of Oxford Paperbacks, including Oxford World's Classics, OPUS, Past Masters, Oxford Authors, Oxford Shakespeare, Oxford Drama, and Oxford Paperback Reference, is available in the UK from the Academic Division Publicity Department, Oxford University Press, Great Clarendon Street, Oxford OX2 6DP.

In the USA, complete lists are available from the Paperbacks Marketing Manager, Oxford University Press, 198 Madison Avenue, New York, NY 10016.

Oxford Paperbacks are available from all good bookshops. In case of difficulty, customers in the UK can order direct from Oxford University Press Bookshop, Freepost, 116 High Street, Oxford OX1 4BR, enclosing full payment. Please add 10 per cent of published price for postage and packing.